グレン・マーカット
シンキング・ドローイング／ワーキング・ドローイング

GLENN

Glenn Murcutt: Thinking Drawing / Working Drawing

First published in Japan on June 15, 2008
Fifth published on December 1, 2023

TOTO Publishing (TOTO LTD.)
TOTO Nogizaka Bldg., 2F
1-24-3 Minami-Aoyama, Minato-ku
Tokyo 107-0062, Japan
[Sales]Telephone: +81-3-3402-7138 Facsimile: +81-3-3402-7187
[Editorial]Telephone: +81-3-3497-1010
URL: https://jp.toto.com/publishing

MURCUTT

Thinking Drawing / Working Drawing

Produced with cooperation of Glenn Murcutt
Authors: Maryam Gusheh, Tom Heneghan, Catherine Lassen, Shoko Seyama
Photos: Anthony Browell
Publisher: Akira Watai
Book Designer: Tetsuya Ohta
Printing Director: Noboru Takayanagi
Printer: Tokyo Inshokan Printing Co., LTD

ISBN978-4-88706-294-8

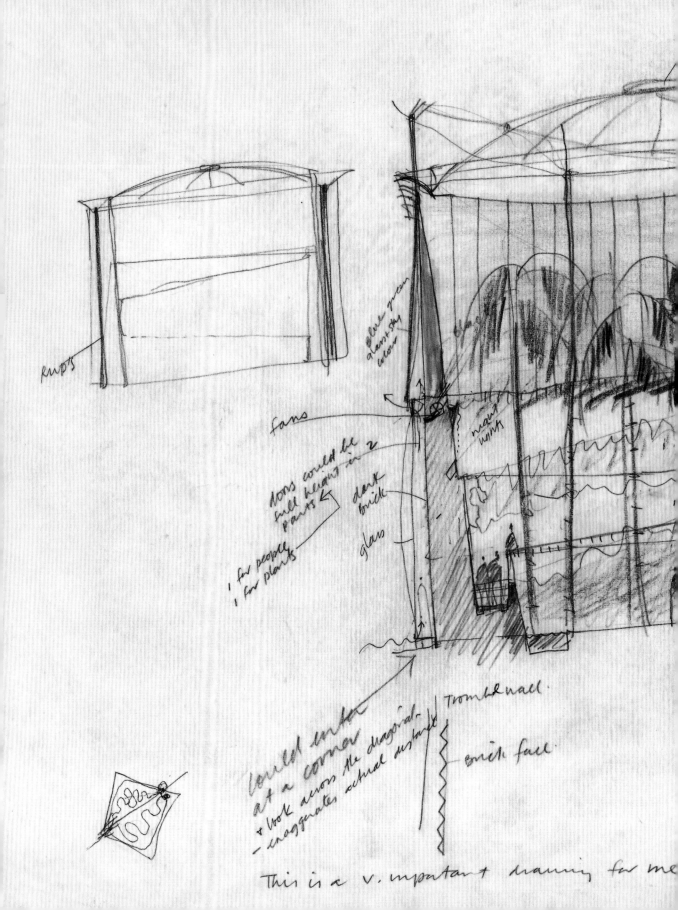

RWPS

glue-green
giant-sky
colour

fans

doors could be
full height in 2
parts

1 for people
1 for plants

dark
brick

glass

giant
whorls

could enter
at a corner –
+ look across the diagonal –
– exaggerates actual distance

trombe wall.

brick face.

This is a v. important drawing for me

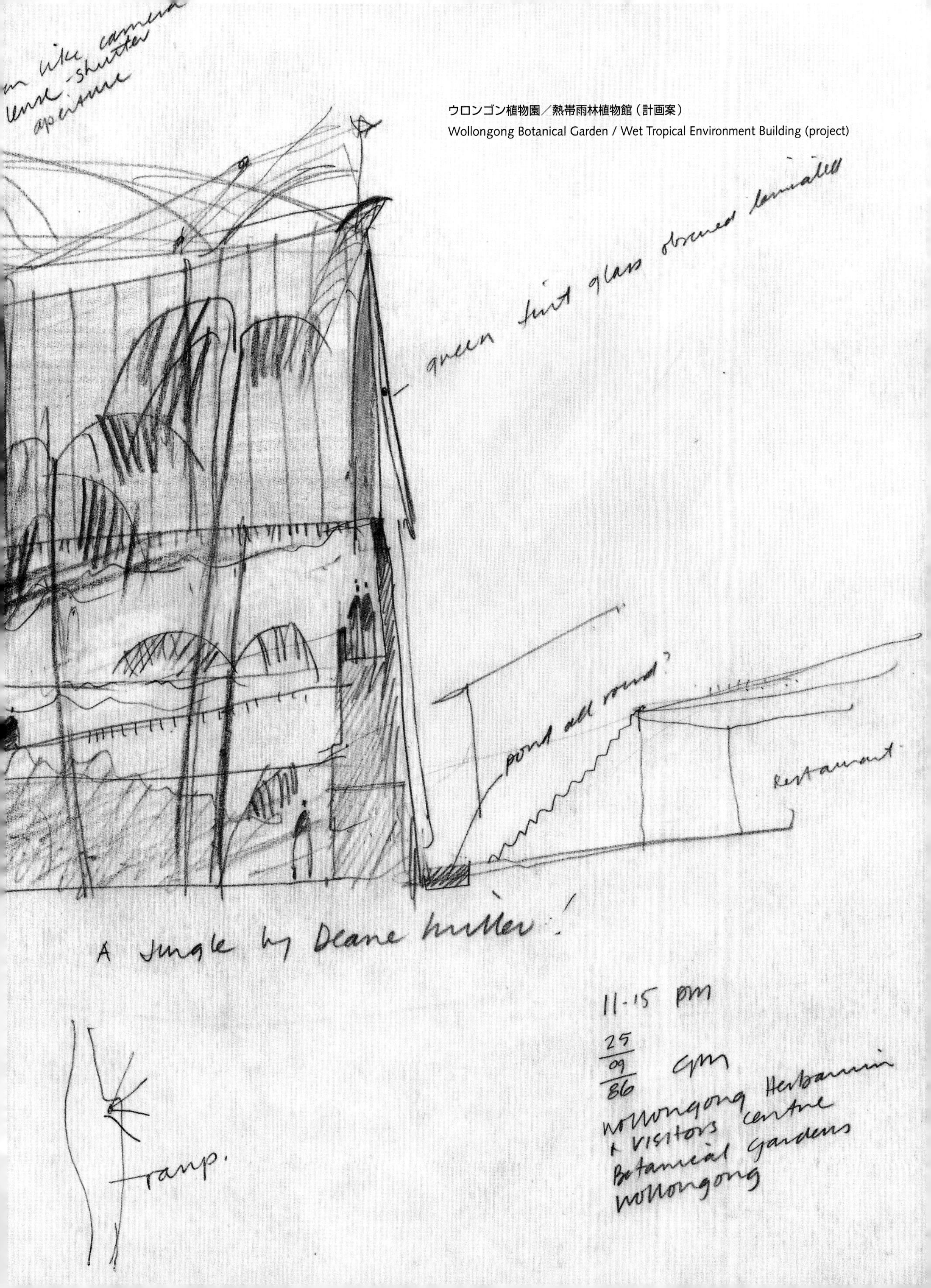

ウロンゴン植物園／熱帯雨林植物館（計画案）
Wollongong Botanical Garden / Wet Tropical Environment Building (project)

m like camera
lens -shutter
aperture

green tint glass obscured laminated

pond all round?

restaurant

A Jungle by Deane Miller!

11·15 pm

25
09
86

gm

Wollongong Herbarium
& Visitors centre
Botanical Gardens
Wollongong

ramp.

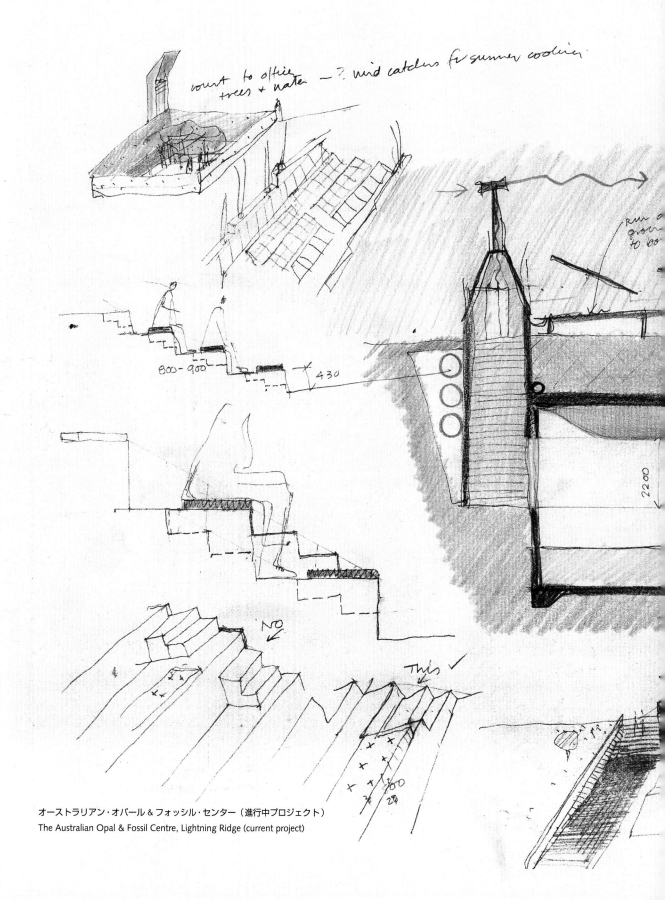

オーストラリアン・オパール & フォッシル・センター（進行中プロジェクト）
The Australian Opal & Fossil Centre, Lightning Ridge (current project)

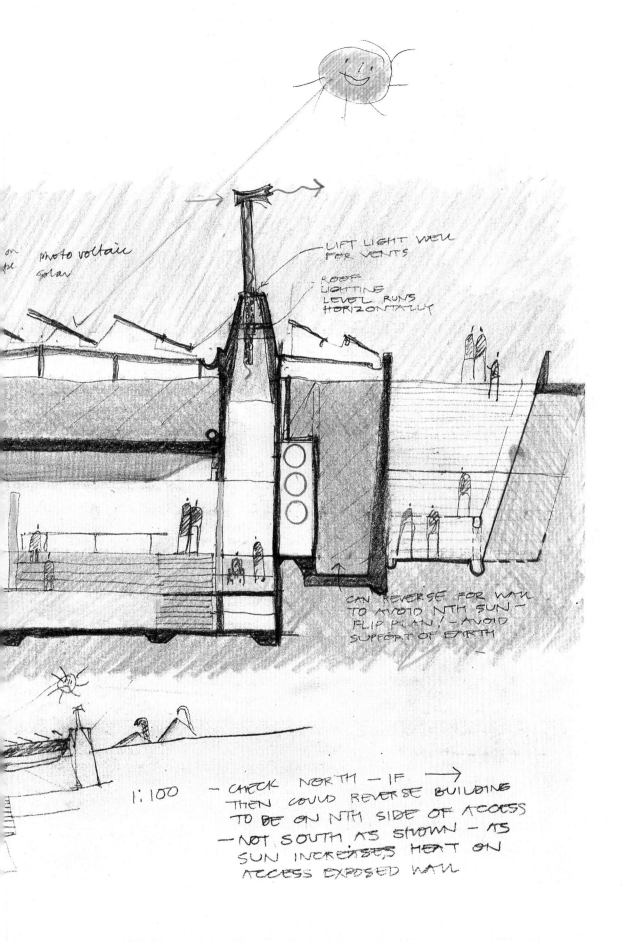

photo voltaic
on
Solar

LIFT LIGHT WELL
FOR VENTS

ROOF
LIGHTING
LEVEL RUNS
HORIZONTALLY

CAN REVERSE FOR WALL
TO AVOID NTH SUN —
FLIP PLAN! — AVOID
SUPPORT OF EARTH

1:100 — CHECK NORTH — IF →
THEN COULD REVERSE BUILDING
TO BE ON NTH SIDE OF ACCESS
— NOT SOUTH AS SHOWN — AS
SUN INCREASES HEAT ON
ACCESS EXPOSED WALL

モスク（進行中プロジェクト）
Mosque (current project)

グレン・マーカット：シンキング・ドローイング／ワーキング・ドローイング
Glenn Murcutt: Thinking Drawing / Working Drawing

目次 Contents

シンキング・ドローイング／ワーキング・ドローイング

マリアム・グーシェ＆キャサリン・ラッセン

図面を通して考える。グレン・マーカットの設計活動で際立つ1点は、手描きの図面以外はあり得ないという主義である。スケッチ、設計図面、施工図面などすべての図面は、マーカットとそしてウェンディ・ルーウィンなどの協働者により描かれる。通常は模型を制作しないことから、彼の図面は、その設計過程を理解する上でよい手がかりとなる。びっしりと説明書された図面は、優先順位がはっきりと示された濃縮された情報の伝達方法として働く。これらの図面は、マーカットの建築的関心事が連綿と改良しつづけられている過程を示している。竣工した建物の写真をともに見ると、図面は彼の深い考案を明示するものである。

パーススケッチと初期のダイアグラムを描くと同時に素材のディテールが検討されてプロジェクトが発展する。建物の形状や配置は、冬期と夏期の太陽高度、卓越風、よい眺めなどを手がかりに記述される。平面は、状況に応じた機能の可変性を模索するダイアグラムとして検討される。それは構造や施工のアイデアとともに発展し、その際に多く描かれるのが縮尺20分の1の断面図である。それらの図面で、マーカットは、建物の空間や機能的序列を定めるとともに、架構方法、構成要素、素材や典型的

Thinking drawing / Working drawing

Maryam Gusheh & Catherine Lassen

Thinking through drawing; a striking aspect of Glenn Murcutt's practice is his insistence on hand drafted drawings. These include sketches, working drawings and construction documents by Murcutt and regular collaborators such as Wendy Lewin. He does not typically make models and the drawings provide an important introduction to his working method. Densely annotated and operating as compressed modes of communication in which priorities are explicitly documented; they register a precise and continuous process of adjustment to a consistent set of architectural preoccupations. In conjunction with photographs of the buildings they demonstrate the rich thought in this built work.

One can see that projects are developed with perspective sketches and early diagrams generally at the same time as ideas about material detail. The form and placement of the building is described with reference to precise sun angles in winter and summer, prevailing winds, and optimum aspect. Plans are frequently explored as maps of interchangeable functional relationships. These are developed in parallel with structural and construction ideas and a recurrent drawing type is the short cross section at a scale of 1:20. Here Murcutt studies the spatial and functional hierarchy of the building simultaneously with its assembly, component parts, materials and typical details. In many of the projects the building appears to architecturally evolve though several iterations of this section

なディテールを考える。多くのプロジェクトにおいて、何通りもの矩計図を描き連ねることで、建物は完成形へ近づいていく。感情が抑えられた経済的なプレゼンテーションである図面は、思考方法であると同時に施工手段である。図面により建て方の優先順位がつけられる。

マーカットが考え抜いたすべての建物要素は、図面によって、建物として総合的に発展する。「平凡な」要素が改良されて再構成されるなど、調整と削減が行われる。1つのプロジェクトで完成した手法は、次のプロジェクトで使用され、新しく描かれ、与件にそって特化される。部分詳細もそうだが、窓の機能とその意匠が発見されて次へ活かされることは、棟の形式の継承へと及んでいる。

注意深いディテールの検討は特に、建物の表層、住み手が調節できる何層かの窓へ向けられる。サザンハイランドの住宅では、北立面のすべての窓平面詳細図が2分の1のスケールで描かれた（pp.190-202参照。本書ではその一部）。多くの既製品と、素材の規格寸法に対する複雑な知識により、それらはプロジェクトに難なく組み込まれる。マーカット設計の多くの住宅に見られる、「リドコ」社の

drawing. Dry and economical, these representations are both a mode of thinking and a medium for constructing the building. They clearly prioritise the thought of construction.

The drawings evidence the thorough architectural development of all parts of the building. This is achieved with repeated adjustment, material reduction and adaptation such that 'ordinary' elements are reframed as refinements. Once developed, strategies are re-used in successive projects, re-drawn and through this process each time particularised as a new condition. This method extends consistently from the scale of individual details through to the discovery and re-use of functional and fenestration components, at times extending to entire building types.

Details are meticulously studied and this attention is particularly devoted to the design of the exterior skin, typically conceived as a series of operable layers. The entire northern façade of the house in the southern highlands, for example, is documented in plan at 1:2 (see pp.190-202). And intricate knowledge of many off-the-shelf parts and standard materials allows them to be systematically integrated into the projects. Murcutt's treatment of 'Lidco' sliding door and window glazing systems, found in many of his houses, is indicative. Every aluminium extrusion is typically drawn in plan

引戸の使い方も示唆的である。押出成形のアルミニウム窓枠は、原寸か、縮尺2分の1の平面図と断面図に描かれて新しい与条件にあわせて考え直され、素材の使用を最小限にして構造の働きを最適化するように調整される。シンプソン＝リー邸の縮尺の大きい図面では、むき出しにされたアルミニウム窓枠は、両端部のパーツが180度回転したものが組み合わされた（p.116参照）。引戸が合わさると強い構造になり風圧に耐え、見えがかりはただ1本の窓枠のように表現される。この重なり合いは、何層にもなる窓や網戸などの合計幅を減らす。独特な、しかし適切な構成として表現される標準断面（スタンダードディテール）は、このように洗練されるのだ。

このような施工図面での思考方法は、より大きな建築要素へも影響を及ぼしている。ビンジーポイントのマグニー邸の窓の、シンプソン＝リー邸への継承がそれを説明している。マグニー邸の断面スケッチでは、キッチンとバスルームでガラス窓と換気方法が検討された（pp.068-069参照）。ここでは連続するハイサイドライトとして扱われたこの建築的な仕掛けは、シンプソン＝リー邸のキッチンで再び考えられて20分の1の図面で示された（pp.108-109、キッチン断面図 pp.114-115、キッチン平面図

and section at half or full scale to study its new architectural situation and adjusted to minimise material use and optimise structural performance. In the documents for the Simpson-Lee House, large scale drawings re-think these components showing stripped glazing extrusions coupled with rotated identical supports (see pp.116-117). This interlocked system offers structural stability and wind resistance and allows two vertical elements to read as a single glazing jamb. The overlapping also reduces the total width of the accumulated layers. Standard sections are in this way refined; re-presented as unfamiliar and yet as appropriate arrangements.

This mode of working/drawing informs the architectural development of larger building components. The evolution of a window from the Bingie Point House to the Simpson-Lee House is informative. A sectional sketch of the earlier project studies a glazing and ventilation strategy for the kitchen and bathing facilities (see pp.068-069). In this case treated as a continuous upper level window, the device is later re-explored as a kitchen bay of the Simpson-Lee House, described in a 1:20 section (see pp.108-109; see also kitchen section p.115, kitchen plan pp.112-113, sketch p.096). In both situations the material treatment is highly abstract; an apparently solid piece of glass inclined outward to provide adjustable horizontal ventilation. The details in both houses individuate the provision of pp.112-113、スケッチ pp.096 参照）。どちらの窓も素材表現は抽象的である。フィックスガラスを傾け、水平な換気窓をとる。このディテールは両邸において、光、風、機能をもたらす要素として南立面に表された。要素の反復は、シンプソン＝リー邸のキッチンのスペースを広げることとなった。傾斜したガラスは拡大されて変形し、ディテールは密になった。結果として、より建築要素を忠実に示す厳密な表現となった。

特定の構成要素が建物の外へと広げられる手法は、マリカ＝アルダートン邸の床から浮かんだ箱としてのベッドやキッチンでさらに検討された。合板の仕切り壁が窓から飛び出すように南の立面を構成し、プライバシーを確保しつつ夏の早朝や午後の日射しの遮蔽をする。その形状や寸法は、太陽角度や造り付けの家具によって規定された（pp.126-127、133 参照）。機能を内包する厚い壁は、深い陰をもたらし、自然換気を可能とする。その後ウェンディ・ルーウィン、レッグ・ラークと協同したボイド・アートセンターにおいて、この手法は、住宅のコンテクストから公共建築の表現へと転換された。

light and air and register a functional component on the southern façade. In its re-iteration the device volumetrically extends the kitchen. The glass plane is amplified and transformed, the resulting detail concentrated. It offers a more elemental and austere expression.

In the Marika-Alderton House floating box-like beds and kitchen bays further the exploration of externally projected functional building parts. Plywood fins extend each window along the southern façade, offering privacy and protection from the early morning and late afternoon summer sun. The fin dimensions are derived in accordance with relevant sun angles and the specific use of the built-in furniture (see pp.126-127 and p.133). The series of blades and functional bays form a thickened operable timber wall, offering deep shade and natural ventilation. In the Boyd Art Centre, designed with Wendy Lewin and Reg Lark, this device is transferred from a domestic situation and re-thought in relation to a civic building for school children.

In an altered physical and programmatic context and collaborative drawing environment the element is reconceived in the light of new architectural possibilities. Solid plywood timber fins, initially developed for privacy and sun control in Australia's extreme north, are re-employed as white painted

敷地環境の違い、建物のプログラムの違い、そして協同で行われた図面の制作は、新しい建築の可能性を開いた。もとはオーストラリア最北の地の日射とプライバシーを制御するために生まれた合板の仕切り壁は、ショールヘブン川への眺めと枠組みする抽象的な白い枠として援用された。ベッドルームの平面図と断面図は、直裁的に見えて詳細では入り組んだスタディがされており、機能にぴったりと沿わせるための寸法調整のやり直しが明らかである（pp.174-179参照）。ボイドセンターでは、小さい仕切り壁は各寝床からの眺めを縁取る。このディテールは繰り返され、引戸を外部に収納する大きい仕切り壁ともなり、宿泊棟の正面立面をめりはりをつけて形づくる。1部屋を2分割する引戸は、仕切り壁の間へとしまわれる。抽象的なベッドの扉や窓の仕切りが集合的に表現されたことで、公共建築としての象徴性が獲得された。

マーカットの仕事の手法、それは原寸での押し出し成形アルミニウムの洗練に始まり、キッチン壁や合板仕切り壁などの、彼が考え続けている建築要素の再考察に至るまでの、前例でのアイデアが後のプロジェクトへと発展するものである。そしてこれは、図面上で、どうやって建てるかについて考えること

abstract frames for individual views of the Shoalhaven River valley. They offer reflected northern light. Precise readjustment is evident in the simple but intricately studied plan and sections of the bedrooms (see pp.174-179). In the Boyd Art Centre small fins bracket and define a view from each bed. The detail is repeated and transformed as a full height hollow plywood blade, which accommodates a sliding door and externally punctuates each bedroom cluster along the main façade. The plan design provides for an operable wall in the bedrooms which can divide each room into two; the larger fin allows the door to completely disappear. Together the series of varying blades symbolically renders the main façade as a public building; a collective of implied beds individuated by the abstraction of external doors and window frames.

Murcutt's working mode, whereby strategies from previous buildings are carried from one project to the next, extends from the 1:1 refinement of an aluminium extrusion to the continual re-working of architectural elements such as a kitchen bay window or a plywood fin. In each case this is achieved through construction thought in drawing. As a continuum, entire house types are re-employed, similarly adjusted and productively re-engaged as new situations. The documents convey a consistent effort and commitment to particularising through specific re-examination of first principles whereby

で達成される。それは、棟の形式を改案することまでも含まれ、変容する連続体として新しい与件に合わせて変えられる。新たな目的に合わせた調整を行い、原則に立ち返って考えることによって、再構成される要素とディテールは変化しつつも一貫したシステムを生み出している。マーカットが、彼の手法の変容していく性質について深く理解していることは、彼の建築を発展させ、形式の再利用が模倣でなく新しい解釈であることを確実にしている。

マーカットの大多数の設計図面は現在、ニューサウスウェールズ州の州立図書館へ寄贈されている。この本のほとんどの図面はそのコレクションに拠る。それらの図面集を見比べるとき、各プロジェクトの違いが浮き彫りにされると同時に、根底に流れる共通の思想をみることができる。図面の公開は、マーカットの仕事、そしてそこに描かれた数々のプロジェクトを通じた考え方などについて、新たに考察することを可能にしている。それは、マーカットの建築的発見、革新性——施工と、特に「平凡さの変容」についての思考について——をより深く理解することにつながるだろう。

reassembled parts and all their details operate as if one apparently shifting yet coherent system. Insight into the transformative nature of this process allows for a better appreciation of the evolution of the architecture, and the understanding that in this work the re-use of types is not imitation but invention through subtle translation.

The majority of drawings from Glenn Murcutt's office are now held in an archive at the State Library of NSW. Drawings in this book are largely sourced from that collection. As a set they convey differences in the development of each project, evidencing collaborations as well as specific emphases. Increasing public availability of these documents provides an opening for re-examining the work and the embedded drawn dialogue between the projects. They offer an insight into Murcutt's conception of architectural discovery and invention; the craft of thought in construction and this particular 'transfiguration of the commonplace.'[1]

[1] The expression is from the title of a book by Arthur Danto, *The Transfiguration of the Commonplace, A Philosophy of Art*, Harvard University Press, Cambridge Massachusetts, 1981.

インタビュー
ジェームズ・テイラー（構造設計者）

グレン・マーカットは、彼の全作品を通じて、ただ2人の構造設計家と協同してきた。すでにリタイアしたディック・テイラーと、その息子ジェームズである。以下は、ジェームズ・テイラーが、マーカットと仕事をすることについて語ったものである。

聞き手：トム・ヘネガン

Q── TOTOギャラリー・間、グレン・マーカット展（2008年6月12日〜8月9日）のタイトルは「シンキング・ドローイング／ワーキング・ドローイング」です。展覧会では、氏が各プロジェクトにおいて、数えきれないほどの図面作成をすることで、より確実により精巧にそのアイデアを発展させていることが示されます。彼は、あなたと楽しんで仕事ができる1つの理由は、あなたが立体的なスケッチを上手に描くことができ──それができるエンジニアは限られていますが──それがアイデアを交わしたり議論したりすることを簡単にしている、と言っています。

A──まず言うべきことは、グレンは実際、構造に対してとてもよい感覚をもっているということです。そ

Interview
James Taylor, structural engineer

Throughout his career, Glenn Murcutt has worked with only two structural engineers—first with Dick Taylor, now retired, and then with his son James. Below, James Taylor reflects on his experiences of working with Murcutt.

Interviewer: Tom Heneghan

Q: The title of Glenn's exhibition at TOTO GALLERY·MA (June 12–August 9, 2008) is "Thinking Drawing / Working Drawing." The intention is to show how he develops his ideas, for each project, through the production of an incredible number of drawings, gradually becoming more and more certain and more refined. He has said that one of the reasons he enjoys working with you is your ability to draw well in three-dimensions—which few structural engineers can do—and that this makes it very easy for him to discuss and exchange ideas with you.

A: The first thing to say is that Glenn actually has a very well refined feeling for structure. I guess,

れから、彼は長く設計を続けているわけですから、プロジェクトにおいて床がどれくらいの厚さになるか、構造のメンバーはどれくらいかを認識できます。これは、明らかな行き止まりに向かって議論をする必要がない、ということです。もちろん、私たちは可能性について話し合いはします。たいてい同じ紙を覗き込み、鉛筆を互いの手にもち、特に接合部分について話します。思うのですが、多くの建築家は、予算を抑えるために210mm の梁成を190mm にできないかなどの副次的な問題に囚われがちです。構造の構成という主題を考えている時に、それは副次的な問題と言えるでしょう。グレンは、初期におけるこのような態度はまったくの時間の無駄と考えています。その他私たちが立ち入らないのは、この計算された梁は……とかね！　重要なのは、柱の接合部やコーナーの見え方、そしてファサードにどのような影響を与えるかということです。スケッチが描けることは、その検討をする時に役立ちます。ジョイント部分や交差部分のディテールをどうするかをはっきりと問題視できるのです。しかし、私のスケッチは、アートなんかではありません。構造と仕上げ、窓や窓枠をラインで描くだけです。それでもプロジェクトが進んでいくのを助けはします。上からや下からのパースペクティブなど、3次元で想像できることは、重要なデザイン要素を押さえながらプロジェクトをより早く進ませます。子どもの頃からこの手の

too, that he has been at his designs long enough for him to appreciate what sort of structural members or thickness of flooring will work in pretty well any given situation. This of course means we don't end up wasting time discussing obvious dead ends. We still discuss options and most of this discussion occurs with pencils in hand and working over the same piece of paper looking at junctions particularly. I think too many architects end up focussing on irrelevant issues such as—is this or that slab 210 thick and why can't it be 190 thick to save lots of money? Well, that's pretty irrelevant to initial conversations when you are trying to look at arrangements. Glenn well appreciates what a waste of time this usually is at the early stages. Another area which we usually quickly leave behind is whether a given steel beam is a...well, whatever! What really matters is the appearance of the connection at columns or corners, and what is the impact on the façade. This is particularly where it is so handy to be able to draw. It becomes readily apparent that what really matters is the treatment of joints and junctions. But, I really have to say that my drawing is anything but art, as such. It is very much sketching of lines of structure and finishes such as windows and reveals, but it does help progress. It is very helpful to be able to visualise in 3D all these sorts of

ものを描くことができたと思います。確かに、私が学校で使っていたテキスト類は、不適切にもドローイングがびっしり描き込まれています！　多量のインクが、これらの教科書という間違った場所で消費されたわけです。

Q——グレンさんは、自然資源の利用を最少に抑えようという姿勢から、彼の建築を可能な限り軽くつくります。これは、エンジニアであるあなたにとってやりがいのある課題であると思われます。

A——グレンの建物は、たいがいスパンと空間が余裕をもってつくられるから「軽い」のです。いずれにせよ住宅は、その方がよく機能するように思います。また、それを可能にしているのは、梁や床を「軽く」したり「ぎゅうぎゅうに押し込んだり」しなくてよい点です。軽く見えるのは、主に、巧みな梁の取り合わせ方とディテールによってです。鉄骨梁と柱のサイズは、広い空間や与えられた屋根形状を支えて、それ自身が「合っている」ことを示す傾向があります。梁や柱どちらも、サイズが小さすぎると空間に合わないのです。とても細い柱は、構造計算があっていても、間違っているように感じたり、確信がもてな

things including perspectives from above or below, as it does enable you to progress faster with the elements that matter. I think I have been able to draw these sort of things pretty much all my life; certainly my school textbooks were overly and inappropriately decorated with drawings! Vast amounts of ink seemed to get in the wrong places in those text books.

Q:Glenn makes his buildings as light as possible, partly out of a concern to minimise the use of natural resources. That must be challenging for you, as his structural engineer.

A:Glenn's buildings are "light" partly because the spans and spaces are usually modest. I think houses function best like this anyway. The other point to make in this setting is that the beams and slabs are not necessarily so "light" or "squeezed." The appearance of lightness is principally achieved with skillful beam connections and detailing. The sizes of steel beams and columns tend to suggest themselves because they feel "right" across a space, or supporting a given roof form. Something that is too thin, either beam or column, just doesn't suit the space. Little pin columns,

いように感じるものです。ですから、デザインの軽さは、簡潔な、整合性のある接合とディテールを達成することに拠っていると言えるでしょう。窓やドア、窓の鴨居や敷居の位置が、梁の芯と整合性があるかを考えることが重要になってきます。これは、グレンの構造の「軽さ」や線を実現するためです。これをするには、ドアや窓や窓の水抜きなどをどうしたらよいか考えがないと困るわけですが。それからグレンは私に、雨がつける汚れについて理解する重要性を教えました。写真撮影の後すぐに雨が降り、建物が斑になったまま取り残されるようでは具合が悪いでしょう。

Q——グレンさんは、ビンジーポイントのマグニー邸をデザインした時、あなたが最初は二の足を踏んだと言われましたが。

A——（ニューサウスウェールズ州の）南にある、ビンジーの家は、本当に興味深い仕事でした。初期デザインから大きく変わった、あの波型の屋根を最初に私にもってきた時、彼が間違った方向に進んでいるのではないかと思いました。彼の感情と繊細さを配慮して、私は穏やかに彼に「グレン、本当に

where very small, can just feel wrong or unconvincing, even if the structural analysis shows that they can be that small. So, lightness in design is much more about achieving crisp, neat connections and details. It becomes important to see how windows and doors and their tracks and slides can be integrated into beam lines. This is an important way to achieve the lines and "lightness" of Glenn's structures. Along the way of course, we have become fairly clever in understanding the possibilities in doors, windows, and water drainage from the door tracks—Glenn has taught me the importance of understanding weathering of materials. It is no good if, immediately after the photo shoot, rain comes and the building is left with unsightly weathering patterns on its external faces.

Q:Glenn has mentioned your initial concern about the design of the Magney House, at Binge Point.

A:The Bingie House, down south, was a really interesting job. In its form it marked a departure from earlier designs, and when Glenn first brought in the sketches and showed me the wave form roof I was concerned he might be on the wrong path. To protect his feelings and sensibilities I

……？」と訊くと、グレンは

「何だ？　ジェームズ？」

「屋根だよ、グレン。本当に？」

「ああ！　無教養なエンジニアよ！　説明するよ！　この家は素晴らしい家になるんだ、そして私の傑作になる！」

と言いました。実際、それはすべてうまくいき、もちろん彼は正しかったのです。デザインは飛躍であったのですが、それは整合性からの飛躍ではありませんでした。私は、（説明を受けて）住宅が、彫刻のようなクオリティをもつ最高に素晴らしいもので、敷地周辺環境の中にぴったりと沿う、唯一の考えうるものなのだと即座に理解しました。グレンと一緒に働いて素晴らしい点の1つは、グレンはユーモアを備えていて、人生の一風変わった面を見ることができることです。しかし、告白をすれば、このユーモアが消えたことが1度だけあり、それは彼がシドニー郊外のモナベールの建物の木造のひどい接合部分を見た時のことです。この日に至るまで、どうやってこのL字型のサポートディテールが私たちの図面に入り込んだのかまったくわからないのですが、確かに図面上にあって、正しく建てられたのです。

gently said to him, "Glenn are you sure........."

"What, James?"

"The roof, Glenn, are you sure..........?"

"Aha! You Philistine engineer! I'll show you! This will be a great house, and my most acclaimed work!"

Well, as it all worked out, he was totally right of course. The design was a departure but it certainly wasn't a departure from sense. I quickly came to see that the house is the most amazing building sculpture, and sits comfortably in its environment in a way unimaginable for any other form of building in that location. One of the great pleasures working with Glenn is his never failing humour and his ability to see the quirky side of life. I must say, however, that once this humour did suffer a moderate to severe setback when he discovered a very tacky timber connection on a building we did in Mona Vale, a Sydney suburb. To this day, I have no idea how this angle bracket detail got onto our drawings but it was certainly there and faithfully built. It wasn't a 'good look', and it wasn't a good reaction from Glenn either! At least this malfunction is now consigned to history of

「結果オーライ」もなければ、グレンの反応もよくないものでした。少なくとも、20年経った今ではこの失敗は歴史となりました（少なくともそう願いましょう）。

Q──グレンさんの仕事の中で特に気に入っているものはありますか？

A──多くのその他の仕事からどれか1つを選ぶのは難しすぎます。すべての仕事に興味深い可能性が豊富にあり、そして常に注意を引く厄介な部分があるものです。しかし、グレンの仕事の中で、残念にも建たなかったものですが、好きなものがあります。それはブロークンヒルの鉱物採鉱ミュージアムです。いくつかの素晴らしい特徴があって、打ち固められた土壁の上に「マルカフ」という風を捉える装置があり、そして片流れの屋根が敷地上部にそびえていました。もしかしたら、そして願わくば、将来このデザインに触発された誰かがどこかでこれを建てるかもしれませんね。

over 20 years ago (well hopefully anyway).

Q: What has been your favourite project by Glenn?

A: It would be too hard to pinpoint any one job as my favourite over all the others. Every job has a wealth of interesting possibilities and always there will be a quirky corner to engage your attention. I do, however, have a favourite job of Glenn's that never got built, which was such a shame. This was the Broken Hill Mining Museum which incorporated some fantastic features, and was a really bold concept with big earth rammed walls topped with 'malqaf' ventilation with an angled roof soaring over the lot. Perhaps, and hopefully someone in the future will be inspired to build this one somewhere.

Douglas Murcutt House

1969-72 Belrose, Sydney, New South Wales

海抜150m。温暖気候。夏の気温は25度前後で、
北東の涼しい風も吹くが、稀に40度を記録する。
冬の気温は18度前後、冷たい西南西の風が吹き、
10度まで下がる。水はけの悪い粘土層に建つ。

Altitude: 150m above sea level. Temperate climate.
Summer, circa 25 deg C, infrequently up to 40 deg C
with north-east cooling winds. Winter, circa 18 deg C
with cold west-south-west winds and lows of 10 deg C.
Clay soil with poor drainage.

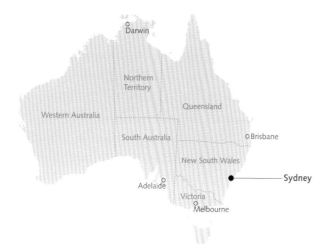

Douglas Murcutt House

住宅へのエントランスの初期スケッチ。交差する高い自立壁とその上部に浮かぶ水平屋根の構成で、ミース・ファン・デル・ローエのコートヤードハウス形式の影響が見える。

Early studies of the entrance to the house, showing the design conceived as a series of tall intersecting walls surmounted by a floating roof plane, indicating the influence of Mies van der Rohe's experiments with courtyard houses.

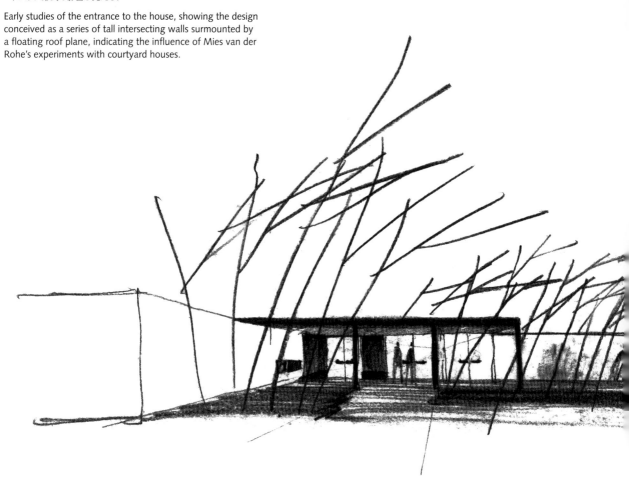

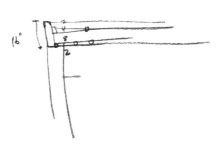

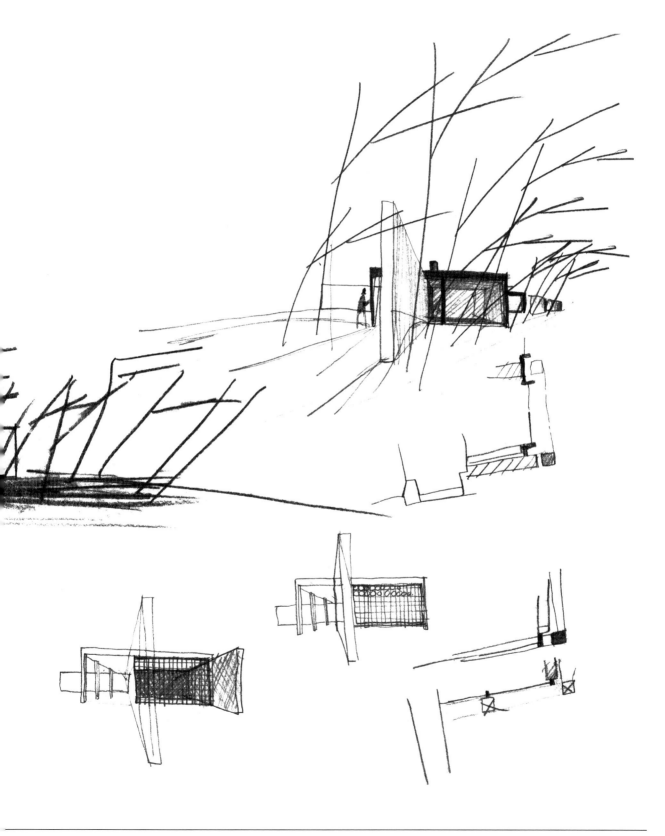

初期の平面スタディ。寝室とピアノ・レッスン室は、南の庭の塀に
あわせて並列に配置された。ダイニングは池に面し、明るい北側
の庭の半分はワイヤーに這わせた蔓性植物で日除けとしている。
南半球では太陽は北の空から照る。

Early plan study showing the bedrooms and music room
aligned with the southern garden wall, the dining room
facing onto a pond, and half of the sunny northside
garden shaded by a roof of cables grown with vines. In the
southern hemisphere the sun shines from the northern sky.

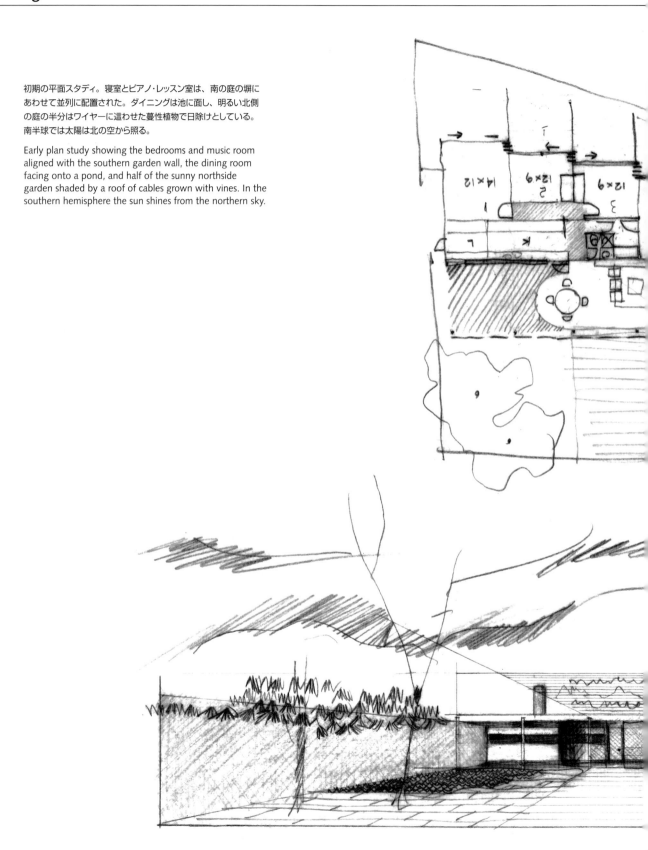

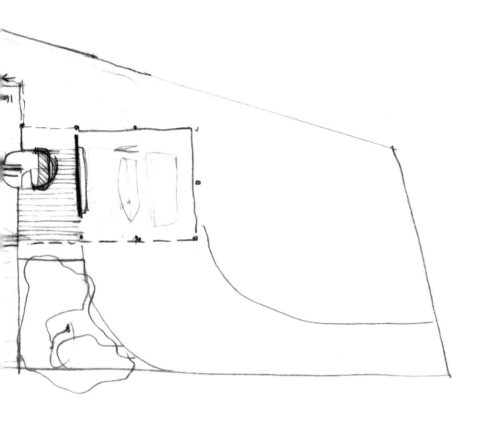

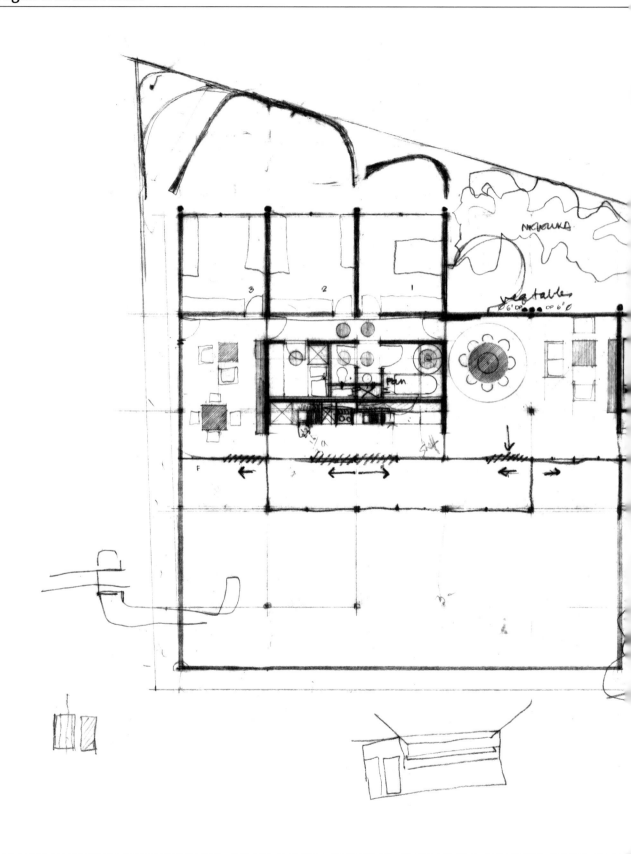

最終形平面に近いスケッチで、ワトル（アカシア）、メラルーカなどの
樹木、野菜などの植栽計画も提案されている。マーカットは平面図
に常に家具を描き、部屋の正確な広さと使い方を確認する。

Sketch study of the simplified final plan, showing proposed
planting of the gardens with Wattle, Melaleuca and vegetables.
Murcutt always draws furniture on plans to get a correct sense
of the scale of the rooms and of their ways of use.

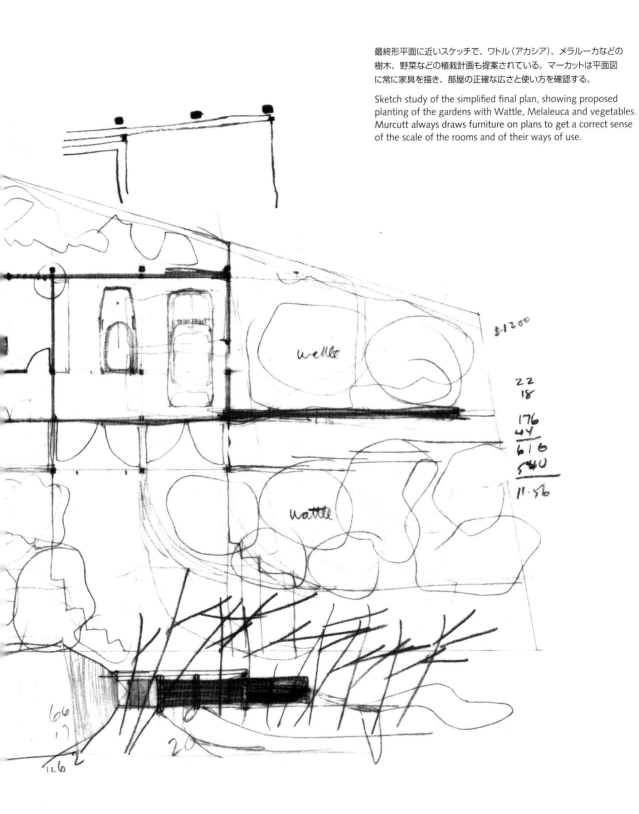

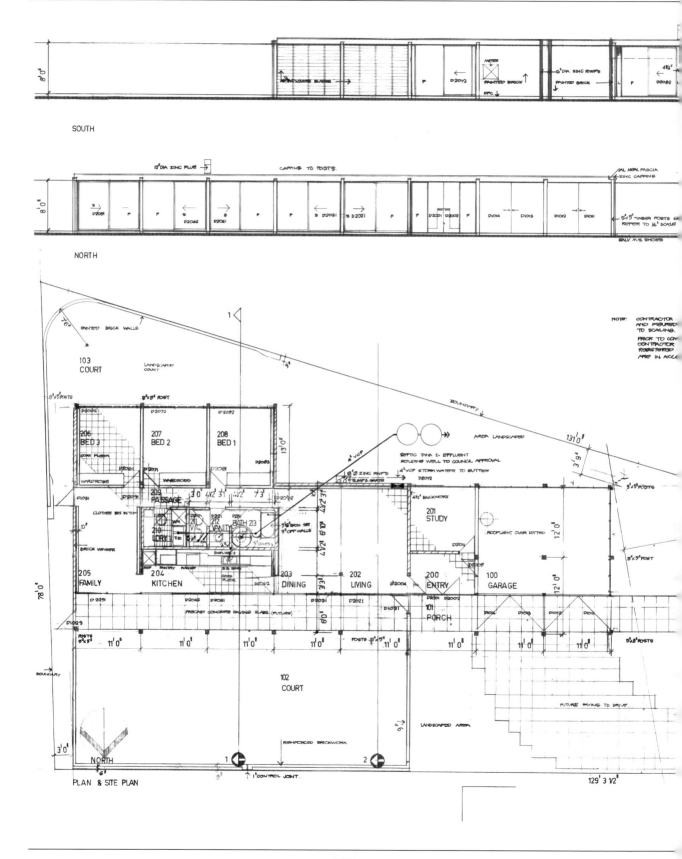

SOUTH

NORTH

PLAN & SITE PLAN

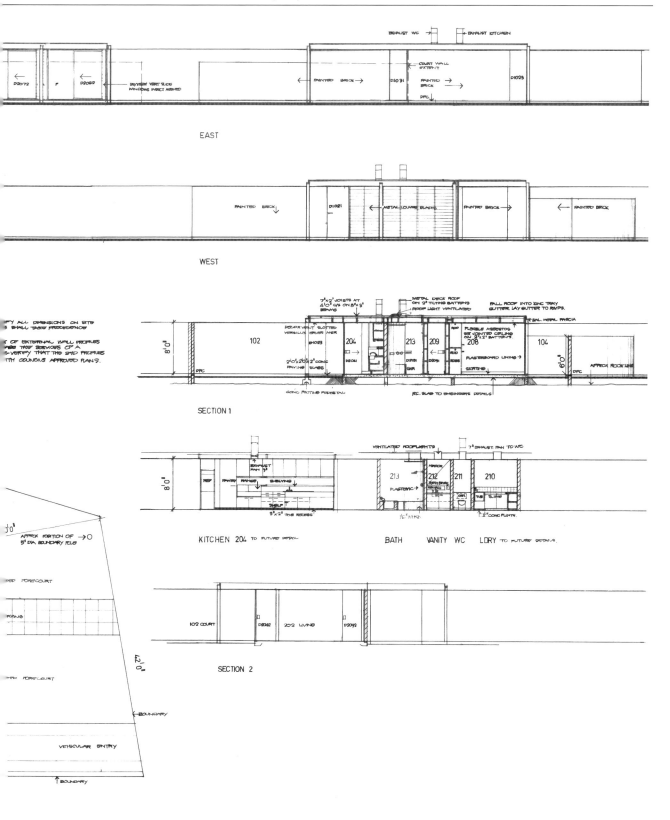

EAST

WEST

SECTION 1

KITCHEN 204 to future detail.

BATH　VANITY　WC　LDRY to future details.

SECTION 2

0　　1　　2　　　　　5m

Marie Short / Glenn Murcutt House

1974-75 / 1980 Kempsey, New South Wales

海抜20m。温暖気候でも暑く、亜熱帯に近い。多雨。
夏の気温は26度前後で、北東の風により涼しさがもたらされる。
冬の気温は18度前後。水はけの悪い粘土層に建つ。

Altitude: 20m above sea level. Warm-temperate/sub-tropical
climate. High rainfall. Summer, circa 26 deg C cooled by
north-east winds. Winter circa 18 deg C. Clay soil with poor
drainage.

Darwin

Northern
Territory

Queensland

Western Australia

South Australia

o Brisbane

New South Wales ●━━━━━ **Kempsey**

Adelaide

o Sydney

Victoria
Melbourne

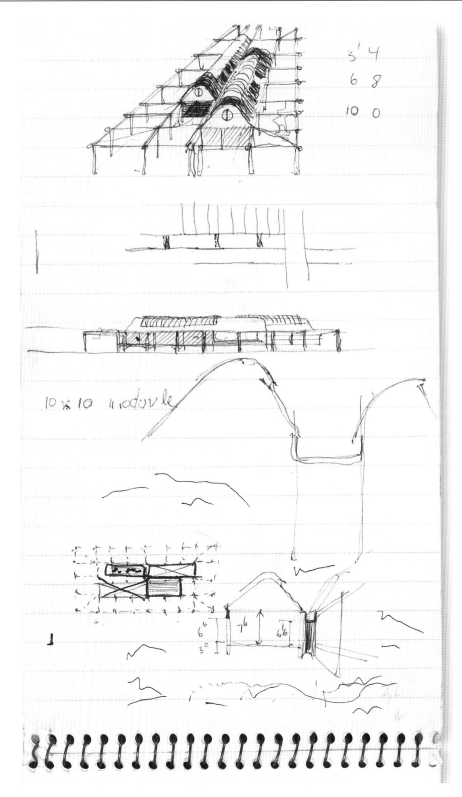

初期スケッチ。プロジェクトは既存住宅の改築として始まったが、マーカットは、改築と同じコストで建てられるとして新築を提案した。

Early sketches for the new house. The project was originally conceived as an alteration to the original farmhouse on the property. Murcutt proposed a new building which could be realised for the same cost as the proposed extensions.

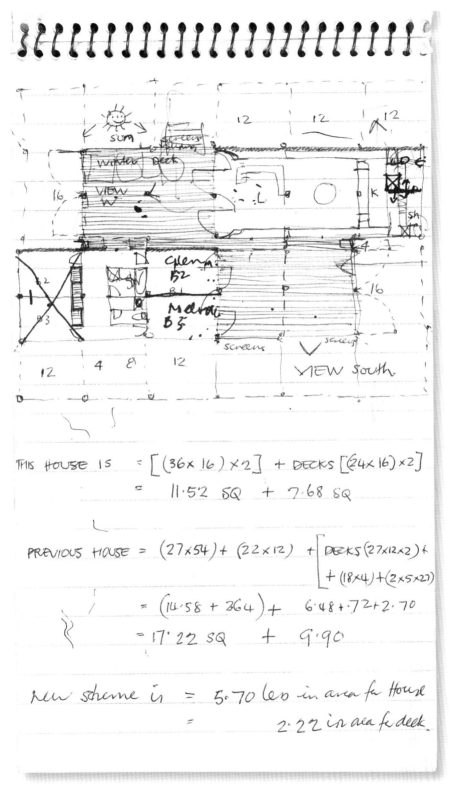

THIS HOUSE IS $= [(36 \times 16) \times 2] + DECKS [(24 \times 16) \times 2]$

$= 11.52$ SQ $+ 7.68$ SQ

PREVIOUS HOUSE $= (27 \times 54) + (22 \times 12) + [DECKS (27 \times 12 \times 2) +$
$+ (18 \times 4) + (2 \times 5 \times 27)]$

$= (14.58 + 2.64) + 6.48 + .72 + 2.70$

$= 17.22$ SQ $+ 9.90$

new scheme is $= 5.70$ less in area fa House
$= 2.22$ in area fa deck.

雁行配置の2棟とする初期スケッチ。同じ柱間寸法を繰り返す手法で、ここでは12フィート、後に10フィートに変更された。
Early plan of the slipped double pavilions. Organisation is conceived in terms of the repetitive structural bay, here as twelve feet, later revised to a ten foot module.

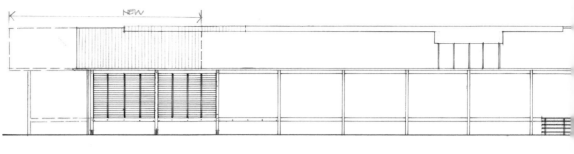

NORTH

SOUTH

PLAN

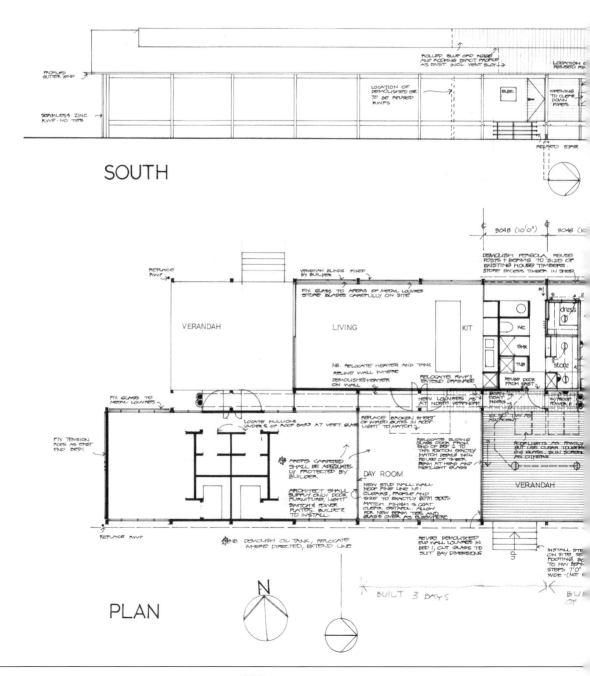

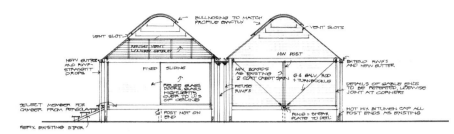

EAST

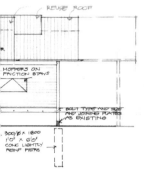

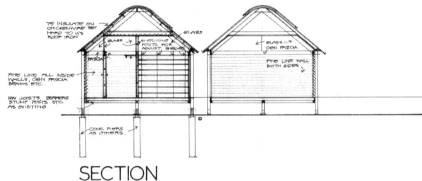

SECTION

— ALL VARIATIONS TO SIZE OF HOUSE DONE ON SITE DURING EARLY STAGES OF FOOTING POUR —

SAME BUILDER DID STAGES OF CONSTRUCTION,

1980年の改築。寝室とリビングを補完するため2棟とも増築された。タローウッドのベランダはボルトが外され新位置へ動かされた。1975年の住宅からは（寝室棟と居室棟という構成が）再構成されたがディテールは保持している。

Alterations, 1980. Each pavilion was extended, providing additional bedroom and living space. An additional bay is marked in a written note. The tallowwood veranda was unbolted and moved to its new location. The design reframes the building's spatial relationships but maintains its material detail.

1980　ALTERATIONS AND ADDITIONS TO FARMHOUSE
glenn murcutt araia architect
august 1980

0　1　2　　　　5m

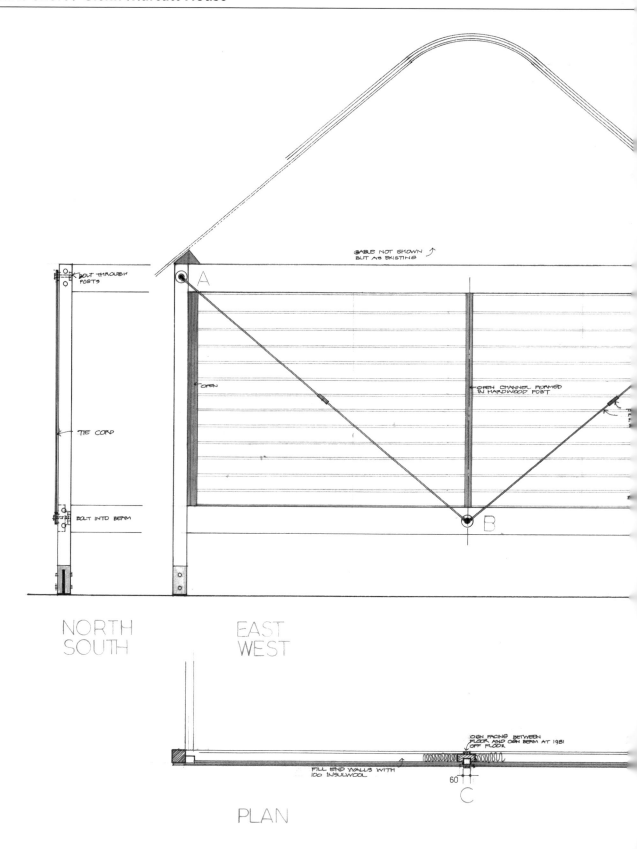

GABLE NOT SHOWN ↗
BUT AS EXISTING

BOLT THROUGH
POSTS

A

OPEN

OPEN CHANNEL FORMED
IN HARDWOOD POST

TIE CORD

BOLT INTO BEAM

B

NORTH
SOUTH

EAST
WEST

O/W FACING BETWEEN
FLOOR AND O/W BEAM AT 1981
OFF FLOOR

FILL END WALLS WITH
100 INSULWOOL

60

C

PLAN

棟端部立面と筋交いのディテール。1980年。
End façade and bracing detail, 1980.

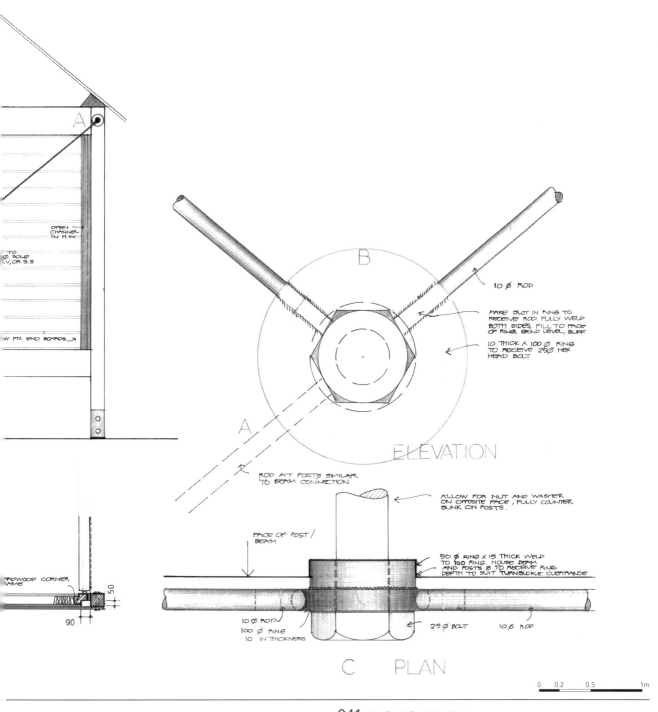

OPEN
CHANNEL
IN H.W

TO
Ø SOLID
L.V, OR S.S

W FIX END BOARDS

10 Ø ROD

MAKE SLOT IN RING TO
RECEIVE ROD, FULLY WELD
BOTH SIDES, FILL TO FACE
OF RING, GRIND LEVEL, BUFF

10 THICK X 100 Ø RING
TO RECEIVE 25 Ø HEX
HEAD BOLT

B

A

ELEVATION

ROD AT POSTS SIMILAR
TO BEAM CONNECTION

ALLOW FOR NUT AND WASHER
ON OPPOSITE FACE, FULLY COUNTER
BUNK ON POSTS.

FACE OF POST /
BEAM

50 Ø RING X 15 THICK WELD
TO 100 RING, HOUSE BEAM
AND POSTS B, TO RECEIVE RING
DEPTH TO SUIT TURNBUCKLE CLEARANCE

HARDWOOD CORNER
JAMIE

50

90

10 Ø ROD
100 Ø RING
10 IN THICKNESS

25 Ø BOLT

10 Ø ROD

C

C   PLAN

0   0.2   0.5   1m

架構方式と施工ディテールを示す断面詳細図。

Section drawing showing typical construction details and assembly system.

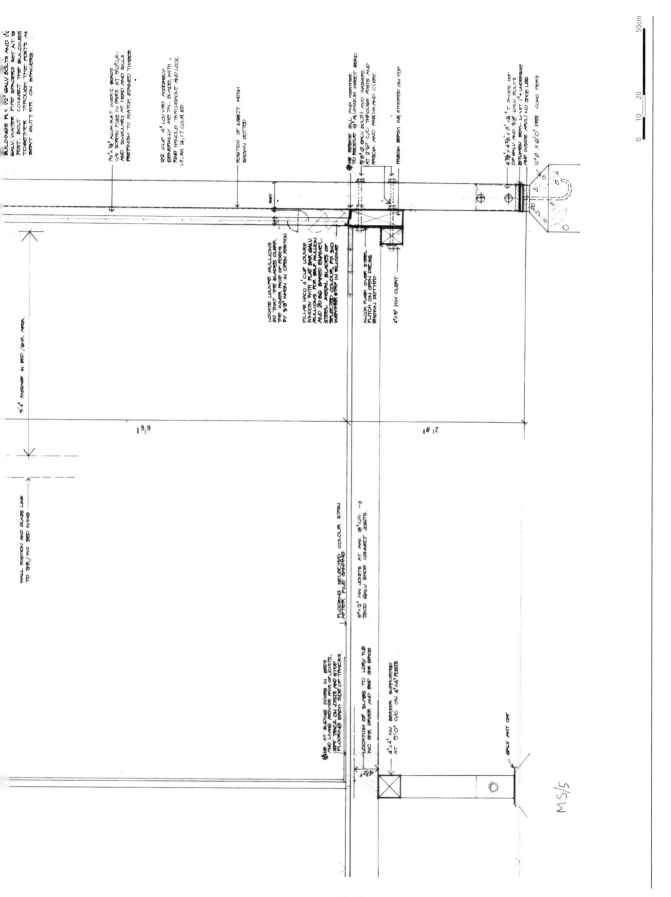

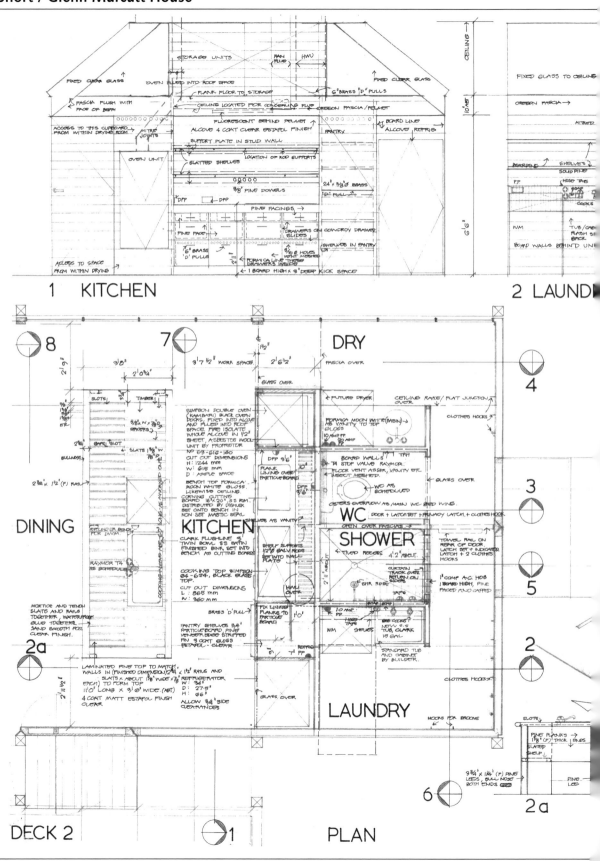

1 KITCHEN

2 LAUNDRY

8 7 DRY 4

DINING

KITCHEN

WC

SHOWER

3

5

2a

LAUNDRY

2

DECK 2 1 PLAN 6 2a

キッチン、バス、ランドリーの平面詳細
図と断面図。1974-75年。

Plans and sections of kitchen, bathing
and laundry facilities, 1974-75.

3 TOILET　　4 DRY　　5 SHOWER

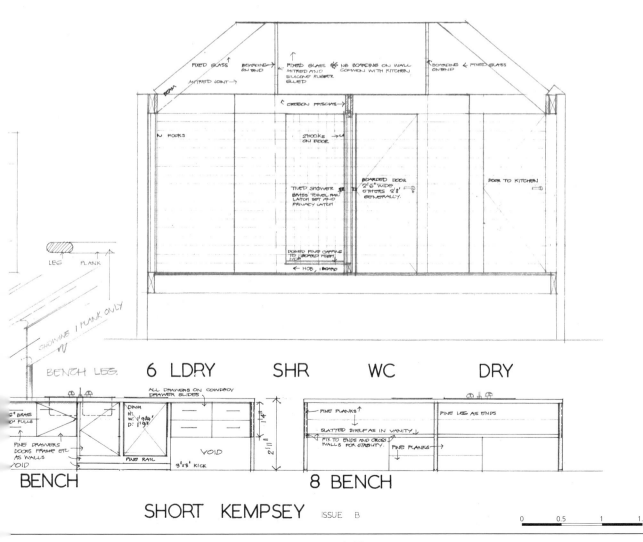

6 LDRY　　SHR　　WC　　DRY

BENCH　　　　8 BENCH

SHORT　KEMPSEY　ISSUE　B

0　　0.5　　1　　1.5m

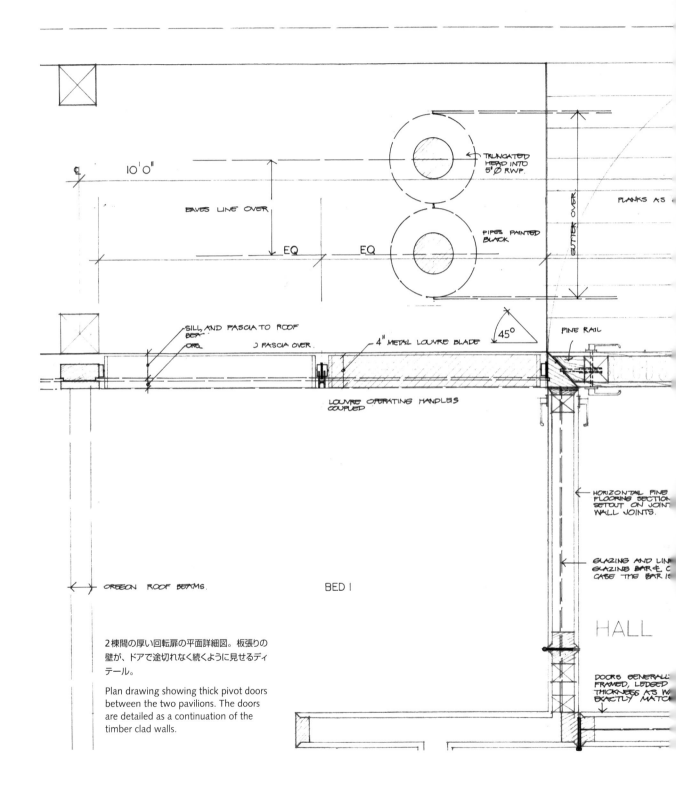

10' 0"

EAVES LINE OVER

EQ   EQ

TRUNCATED
HEAD INTO
5' Ø RWP.

PIPES PAINTED
BLACK

GUTTER OVER

PLANKS AS

SILL AND FASCIA TO ROOF
BEA
ORE   J FASCIA OVER

4" METAL LOUVRE BLADE

45°

PINE RAIL

LOUVRE OPERATING HANDLES
COUPLED

HORIZONTAL PINE
FLOORING SECTION
SETOUT ON JOINT
WALL JOINTS.

GLAZING AND LIN
GLAZING BAR ¢ C
CASE TIME BAR IS

OREGON ROOF BEAMS.

BED I

HALL

DOORS GENERALL
FRAMED, LEDGED
THICKNESS AS W
EXACTLY MATCH

2棟間の厚い回転扉の平面詳細図。板張りの
壁が、ドアで途切れなく続くように見せるディ
テール。

Plan drawing showing thick pivot doors
between the two pavilions. The doors
are detailed as a continuation of the
timber clad walls.

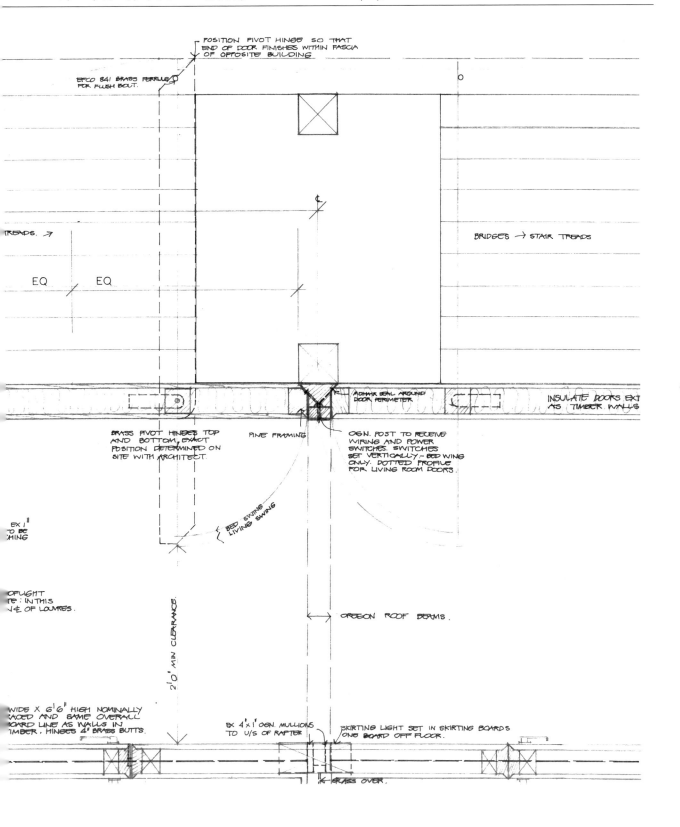

POSITION PIVOT HINGE SO THAT
END OF DOOR FINISHES WITHIN FASCIA
OF OPPOSITE BUILDING

EFCO 841 BRASS FERRULE
FOR FLUSH BOUT.

TREADS. →

EQ   EQ

BRIDGES → STAIR TREADS

MOHAIR SEAL AROUND
DOOR PERIMETER

INSULATE DOORS EXT
AS TIMBER WALLS

BRASS PIVOT HINGES TOP
AND BOTTOM, EXACT
POSITION DETERMINED ON
SITE WITH ARCHITECT.

PINE FRAMING

OGN. POST TO RECEIVE
WIRING AND POWER
SWITCHES. SWITCHES
SET VERTICALLY - BED WING
ONLY. DOTTED PROFILE
FOR LIVING ROOM DOORS.

EX 1"
TO BE
CHING

BED SWING
LIVING SWING

ROOFLIGHT
TE: IN THIS
N∉ OF LOUVRES.

2'0" MIN CLEARANCE

OREGON ROOF BEAMS.

WIDE X 6'6" HIGH NOMINALLY
RACED AND SAME OVERALL
BOARD LINE AS WALLS IN
TIMBER, HINGES 4" BRASS BUTTS.

EX 4"x1" OGN. MULLIONS
TO U/S OF RAFTER

SKIRTING LIGHT SET IN SKIRTING BOARDS
ONE BOARD OFF FLOOR.

GLASS OVER.

0   10   20   30cm

外付けの金属ルーバーをもつ天窓の断面詳細図。冬の太陽高度の
角度に固定された羽が、春分、秋分の太陽高度でオーバーラップ
して、春分を過ぎた後は直射日光を入れない。

Section details of skylight showing fixed metal louvers above
glazing. The angle of the louvers is determined in relation to
the mid summer and mid winter sun angles.

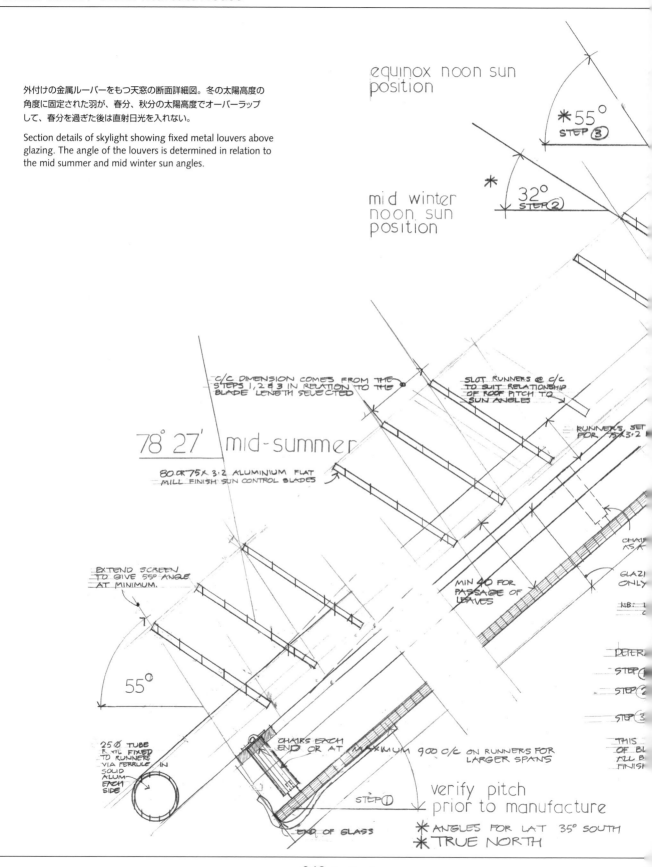

equinox noon sun position

＊ 55° STEP ③

mid winter noon sun position

＊ 32° STEP ②

c/c DIMENSION COMES FROM THE STEPS 1, 2 & 3 IN RELATION TO THE BLADE LENGTH SELECTED

SLOT RUNNERS @ c/c TO SUIT RELATIONSHIP OF ROOF PITCH TO SUN ANGLES

RUNNERS SET FOR 75×3·2

78° 27' mid-summer

80 OR 75×3·2 ALUMINIUM FLAT MILL FINISH SUN CONTROL BLADES

EXTEND SCREEN TO GIVE 55° ANGLE AT MINIMUM.

MIN 40 FOR PASSAGE OF LEAVES

55°

25 Ø TUBE RAIL FIXED TO RUNNERS VIA FERRULE IN SOLID ALUM— EACH SIDE

CHAIRS EACH END OR AT MAXIMUM 900 c/c ON RUNNERS FOR LARGER SPANS

STEP ①

verify pitch prior to manufacture

END OF GLASS

＊ ANGLES FOR LAT 35° SOUTH
＊ TRUE NORTH

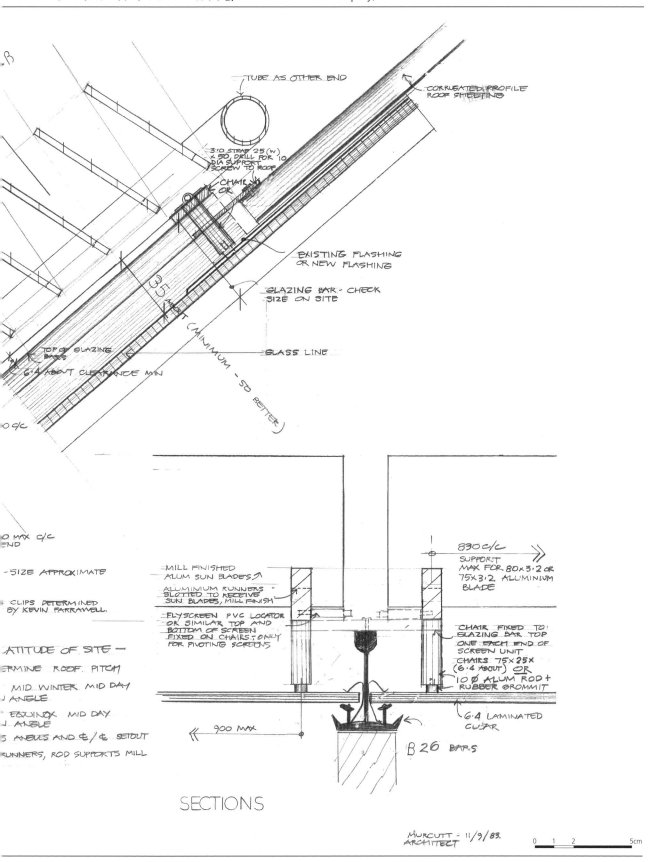

TUBE AS OTHER END

CORRUGATED PROFILE
ROOF SHEETING

3.10 STRAP 25 (W)
× 50, DRILL FOR 10
DIA SUPPORT
SCREW TO ROOF

CHAIR
OR

EXISTING FLASHING
OR NEW FLASHING

GLAZING BAR - CHECK
SIZE ON SITE

TOP OF GLAZING
BARS

GLASS LINE

6.4 ABOUT CLEARANCE MIN

O C/C

MAX C/C
END

SIZE APPROXIMATE

CLIPS DETERMINED
BY KEVIN FARRAWELL.

LATITUDE OF SITE —

ERMINE ROOF PITCH

MID WINTER MID DAY
ANGLE.

EQUINOX MID DAY
ANGLE.

ANGLES AND ℄/℄ SETOUT
RUNNERS, ROD SUPPORTS MILL

MILL FINISHED
ALUM SUN BLADES

ALUMINIUM RUNNERS -
SLOTTED TO RECEIVE
SUN BLADES, MILL FINISH

FLYSCREEN PVC LOCATOR
OR SIMILAR TOP AND
BOTTOM OF SCREEN
FIXED ON CHAIRS: ONLY
FOR PIVOTING SCREENS

830 C/C

SUPPORT
MAX FOR 80×3·2 OR
75×3·2 ALUMINIUM
BLADE

CHAIR FIXED TO
GLAZING BAR TOP
ONE EACH END OF
SCREEN UNIT
CHAIRS 75×25×
(6·4 ABOUT) OR
10 Ø ALUM ROD +
RUBBER GROMMIT

6·4 LAMINATED
CLEAR

900 MAX

B 26 BARS

SECTIONS

MURCUTT - 11/9/83.
ARCHITECT

0   1   2   5cm

Fredericks / White House

1981-82 / 2001-04 Jamberoo, New South Wales

海抜500m。海岸からの影響を受ける温暖気候。
熱帯雨林に取り囲まれている。良好な雨量。南西のコジオスコ山
からの、冬の冷たい風から守られる山の裏にある。
夏の気温は26度、冬の気温は23度前後だが、最低気温は
5度まで下がる。火山灰土壌、花崗岩地質。

Altitude: 500m above sea level. Temperate climate with
coastal influence. Rainforest environment. Good rainfall.
Sited in the lee of an escarpment which protects it from cold
south-west winter winds off Mount Kosciusko.
Summer, circa 26 deg C. Winter, circa 23 deg C
with lows of 5 deg C. Volcanic and granite soils.

OCT 26 '81

PLANS ENCLOSED DO NOT WORK F
YOUR SITE + OPERATION, - THIS
I THINK - HAVE SPENT SOME TIM
THIS SAT + SUNDAY - HOPE YOU AN
COL LIKE IT.

REGARDS, Glenn

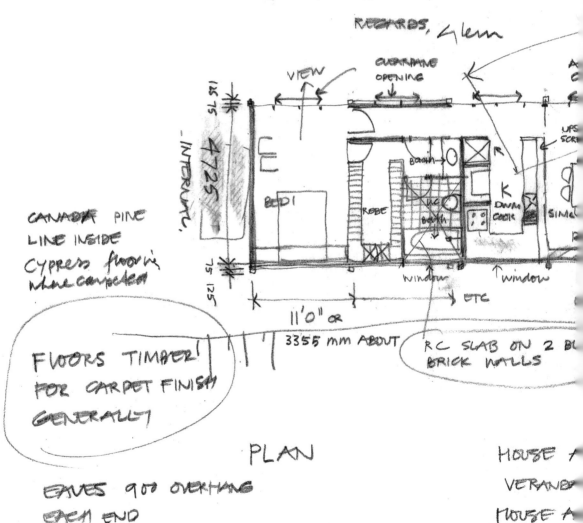

CANADA PINE
LINE INSIDE
Cypress floorie
where completed

FLOORS TIMBER!
FOR CARPET FINISH
GENERALLY

PLAN

EAVES 900 OVERHANG
EACH END

1981年の初期スケッチ。農家から遺された暖炉の位置に網戸付きの玄関ポーチをとる1棟の構成。

Early plan sketch, 1981. The building was initially conceived as a single pavilion with an open screened entrance porch at an existing fireplace.

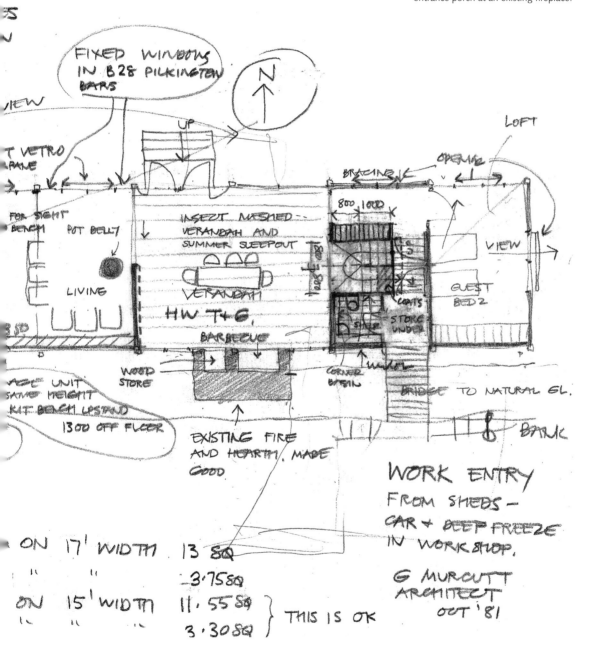

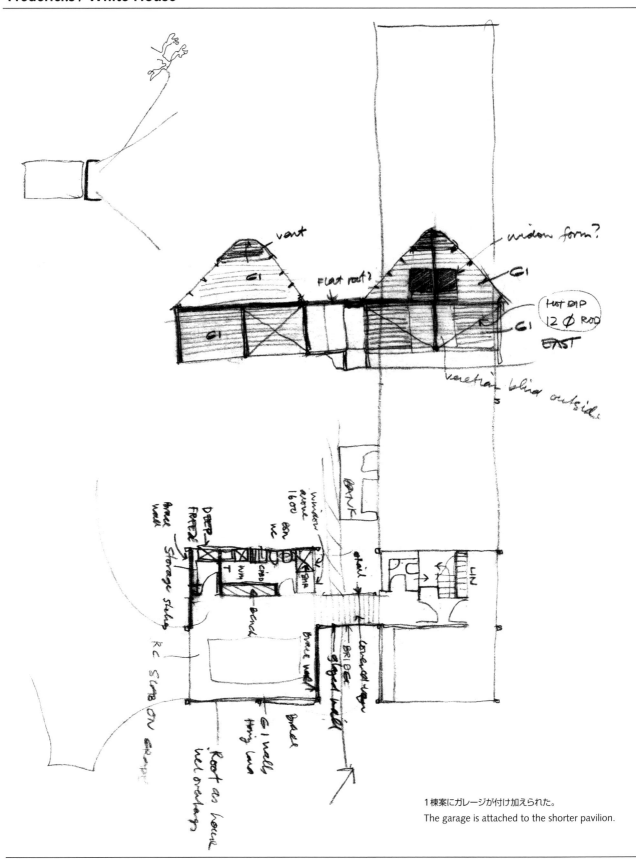

1棟案にガレージが付け加えられた。
The garage is attached to the shorter pavilion.

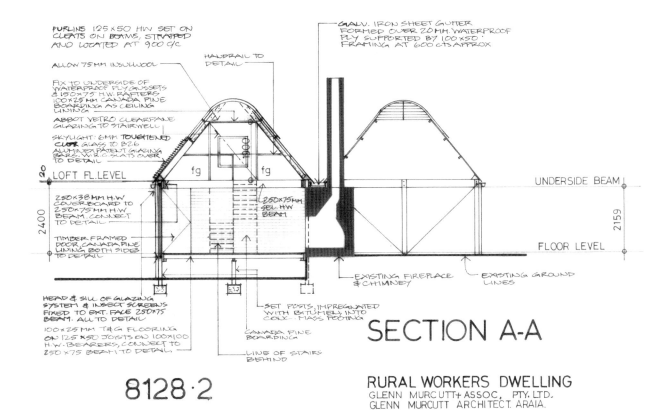

PURLINS 125 × 50 HW SET ON CLEATS ON BEAMS, STRAPPED AND LOCATED AT 900 C/C

ALLOW 75MM INSULWOOL

FIX TO UNDERSIDE OF WATERPROOF PLY GUSSETS 150×75 H.W. RAFTERS 100×25 MM CANADA PINE BOARDING AS CEILING LINING

ABBOT VETRO CLEARPANE GLAZING TO STAIRWELL

SKYLIGHT: 6MM TOUGHENED CLEAR GLASS TO B2.6 ALUMINEX PATENT GLAZING BARS. W.R.C. SLATS OVER TO DETAIL

HANDRAIL TO DETAIL

GALV. IRON SHEET GUTTER FORMED OVER 20 MM. WATERPROOF PLY SUPPORTED BY 100×50 FRAMING AT 600 CTS APPROX

LOFT FL. LEVEL

fg   fg

250×38 MM H.W COVERBOARD TO 250×75 MM H.W BEAM. CONNECT TO DETAIL

250×75 MM SEL. HW BEAM

TIMBER FRAMED DOOR, CANADA PINE LINING BOTH SIDES TO DETAIL

UNDERSIDE BEAM

2159

FLOOR LEVEL

EXISTING FIREPLACE & CHIMNEY

EXISTING GROUND LINES

2400

20

HEAD & SILL OF GLAZING SYSTEM & INSECT SCREENS FIXED TO EXT. FACE 250×75 BEAM. ALL TO DETAIL

100×25 MM T&G FLOORING ON 125×50 JOISTS ON 100×100 H.W. BEARERS, CONNECT TO 250×75 BEAM TO DETAIL.

SET POSTS IMPREGNATED WITH BITUMEN, INTO CONC. MASS FOOTING

CANADA PINE BOARDING

LINE OF STAIRS BEHIND

8128·2

SECTION A-A

RURAL WORKERS DWELLING
GLENN MURCUTT + ASSOC. PTY. LTD.
GLENN MURCUTT ARCHITECT. ARAIA.

NOVEMBER 1981

既存暖炉を通る1981年の断面図。マリー・ショート／グレン・マーカット邸で試された多くのアイデアを再度試みている。断面形状は、ロフトスペースを確保するために垂直方向に伸ばされた。

Section drawing through existing fireplace, 1981.
The project reworks many of the ideas initially tested in Marie Short/Glenn Murcutt House. Here the roof profile is steeper and allows for an upper loft.

0   1   2   5m

Fredericks / White House

1981年の平面図。柱間を1ユニットとして多様な機能が並列
された。フレデリックス邸においてベランダはリビングルーム
として実現した。

Plan, 1981. The repetitive module accommodates a
variety of domestic activities. The open screened veranda
was not realised in the initial building.

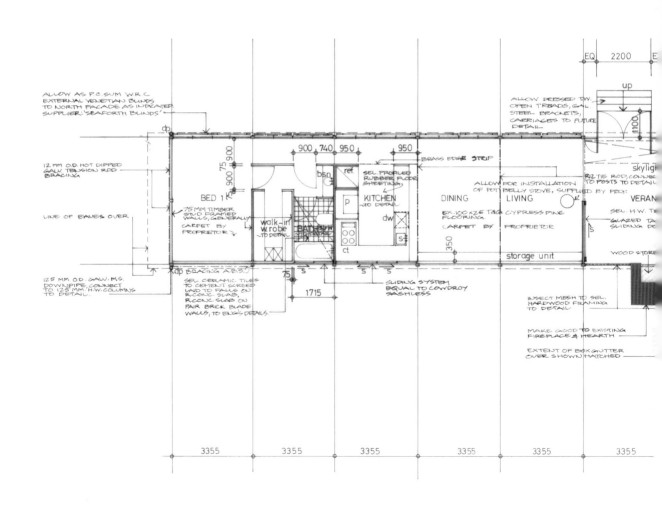

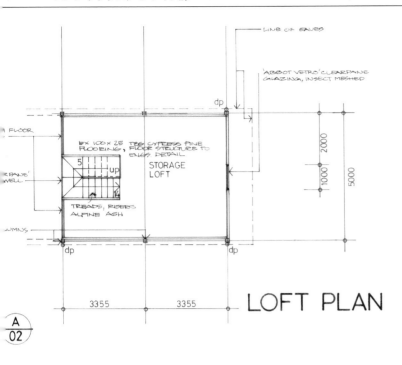

LOFT PLAN

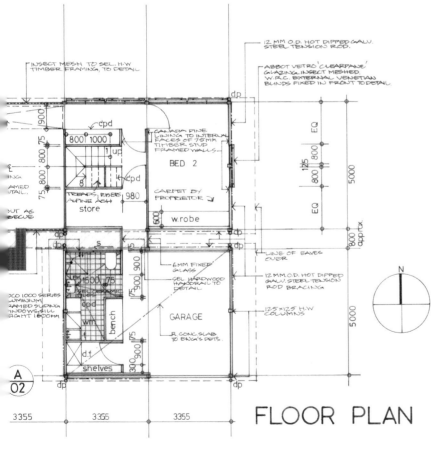

RURAL WORKERS DWELLING
GLENN MURCUTT+ASSOC. PTY. LTD.
GLENN MURCUTT ARCHITECT. ARAIA

FLOOR PLAN

8128·1   NOVEMBER 1981

0   1   2   5m

Fredericks / White House

2001-04年改築平面図。半屋内ベランダを付与するために西に2スパン分動いて、1981年案では実現しなかったベランダが実現した。

Alterations, 2001-04. The northern pavilion was extended by two bays to the west to provide an additional bedroom and a veranda.

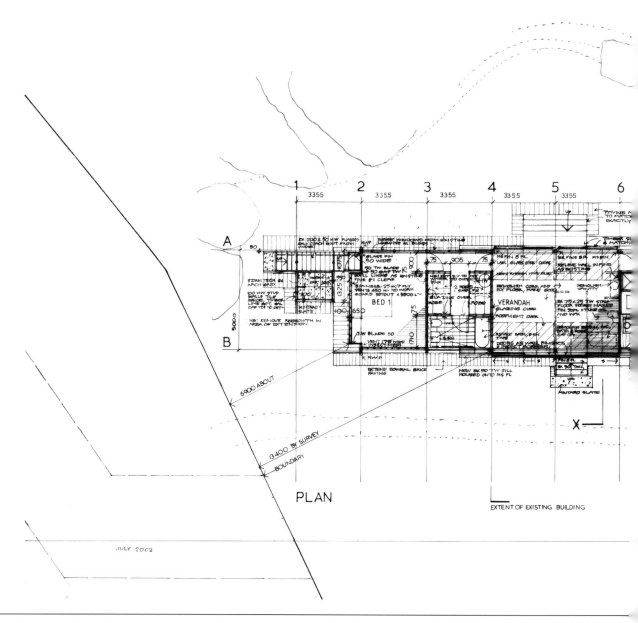

PLAN

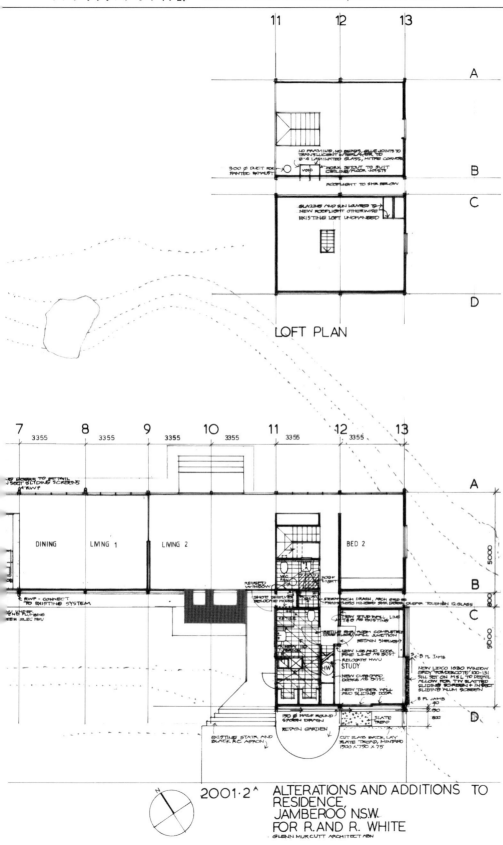

LOFT PLAN

ALTERATIONS AND ADDITIONS TO
RESIDENCE,
JAMBEROO N.S.W.
FOR R. AND R. WHITE
GLENN MURCUTT ARCHITECT ABN

2001·2^

0   1   2   5m

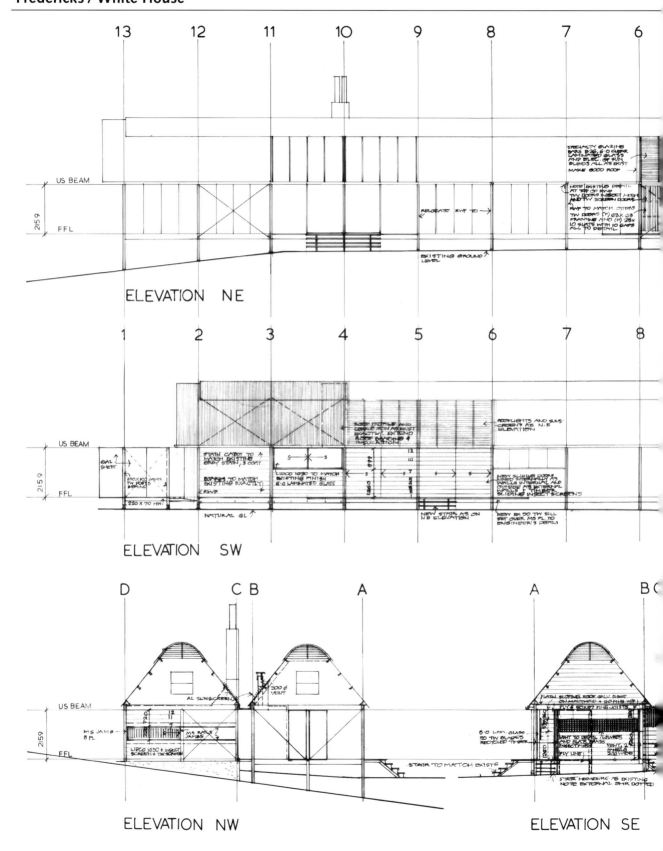

ELEVATION NE

ELEVATION SW

ELEVATION NW

ELEVATION SE

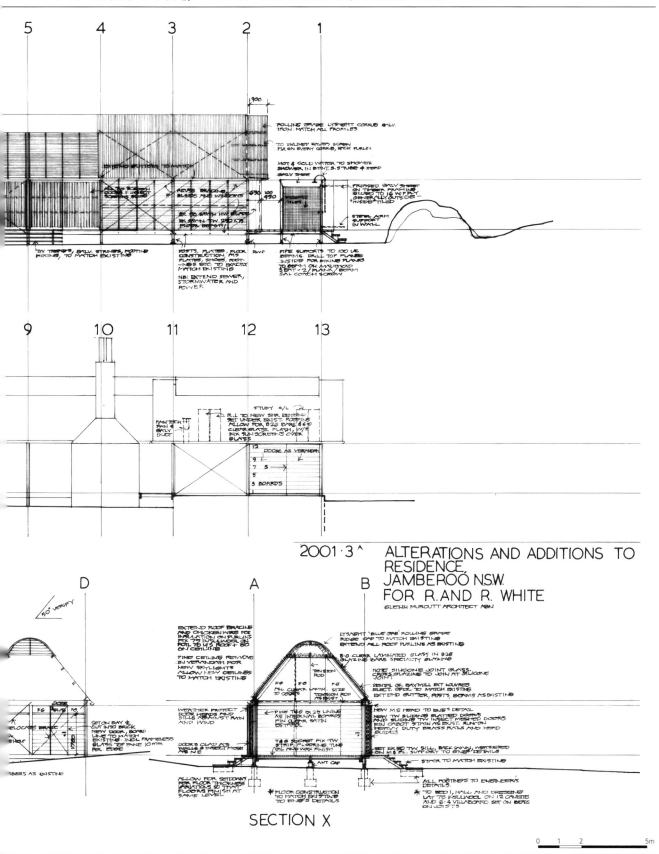

2001·3 ^ ALTERATIONS AND ADDITIONS TO RESIDENCE, JAMBEROO N.S.W. FOR R. AND R. WHITE

GLENN MURCUTT ARCHITECT ABN

SECTION X

Fredericks / White House

ホワイト邸西立面図（View A）と室内展開図（View X）。右下は
増築寝室から屋外シャワーをつなぐブリッジ部分の平面詳細図。

West elevation of White House (View A) and interior elevation
of new bedroom (View X). Below, right is detailed plan of
bridge connecting the bedroom and the external shower.

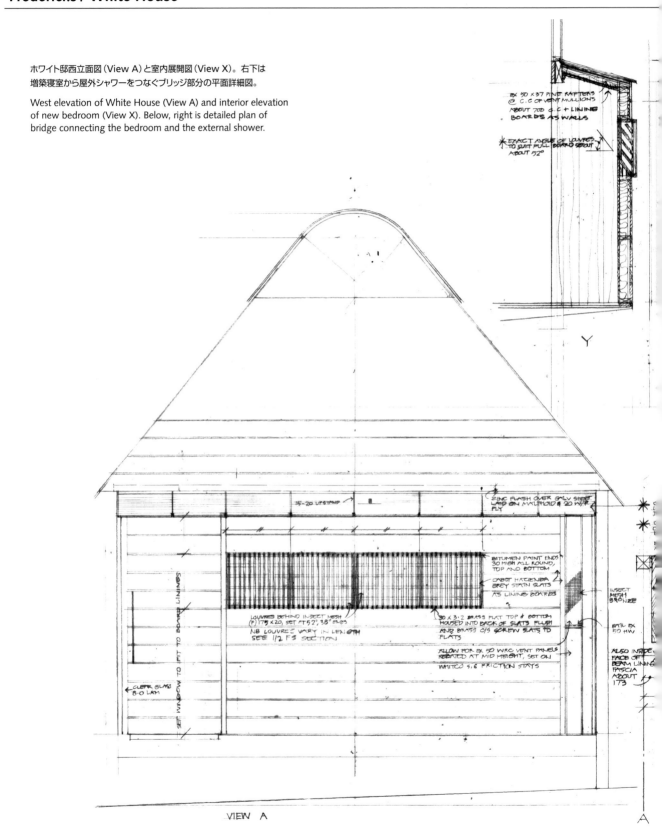

VIEW A

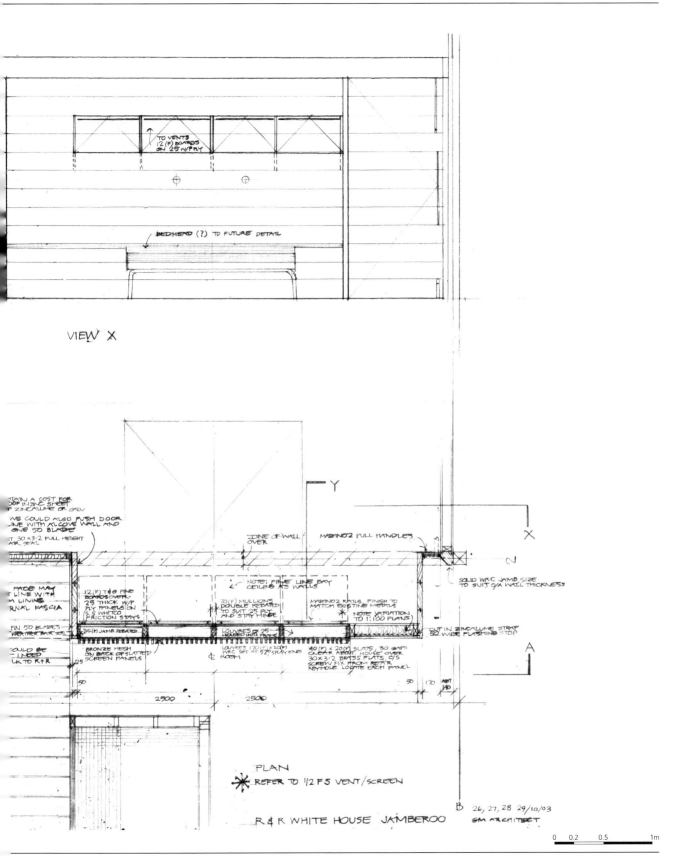

TO VENTS
12 (F) BOARDS
ON 25 W/PLY

BEDHEAD (?) TO FUTURE DETAIL

VIEW X

Y

X

OBTAIN A COST FOR
ROOF IN ZINC SHEET
OF ZINCALUME OR GALV

WE COULD ALSO PUSH DOOR
IN LINE WITH ALCOVE WALL AND
ONE 50 BLADE

PT 30 x 3.2 FULL HEIGHT
AIR SEAL

FACE MAY
LINE WITH
INTERNAL FASCIA

FIN 50 BLADES
WEATHER BAR 30.2

COULD BE
PINNED
LINK TO R+R

ZONE OF WALL
OVER

MABINO2 PULL HANDLES

12 (F) T+G PINE
BOARDS OVER
25 THICK W/P
PLY PANELS ON
S.S WHITCO
FRICTION STAYS

70 (F) MULLIONS
DOUBLE REBATED
TO SUIT 25 PLY
AND STAY HINGE

36 (F) JAMB REBATED

LOUVRES @ 25°
HOUSED INTO FRAME

BRONZE MESH
ON BACK OF SLATTED
SCREEN PANELS

LOUVRES 170 (F) x 20 (F)
WRC SET AT 52° SPLAY ENDS

MABINO2 RAILS, FINISH TO
MATCH EXISTING METALS

NOTE VARIATION
TO 1:100 PLANS

NOTE: FINE LINE B/Y
CEILING AS WALLS

SOLID WRC JAMB, SIZE
TO SUIT O/A WALL THICKNESS

CUT IN ZINCALUME STRAP
50 WIDE FLASHING STOP

40 (F) X 20 (F) SLATS, 30 GAPS
CLEAR ABOUT HOUSE OVER
30 X 3.2 BRASS FLATS C/S
SCREW FIX FROM REAR
KEYHOLE LOCATE EACH PANEL

A

50   2500   2500   50   170   ABT
                                                              140

PLAN
REFER TO 1/2 F5 VENT/SCREEN

R & R WHITE HOUSE JAMBEROO

B 26, 27, 28 29/10/03
GM ARCHITECT

0   0.2   0.5   1m

Magney House

1982-84 / 1999 Bingie Point, New South Wales

海抜50m。海岸からの影響を受ける温暖な気候。
年間降雨量1,000mm 程度。夏の平均気温は20度で、北東の
海風が吹く。冬は15度前後だが、コジオスコ山から
とても冷たい風が吹き、5度まで下がることもある。花崗岩地質。

Altitude: 50m above sea level. Temperate climate with coastal influence. Rainfall approx 1,000mm per year. Summer, circa 20 deg C with north-east on-shore breezes. Winter, circa 15 deg C with extremely cold winds from south-west off Mt. Kosciusko and lows of 5 deg C. Granite soils.

Darwin

Northern Territory

Queensland

Western Australia

South Australia

○ Brisbane

New South Wales

Adelaide

○ Sydney

Victoria

● —— **Bingie Point**

Melbourne

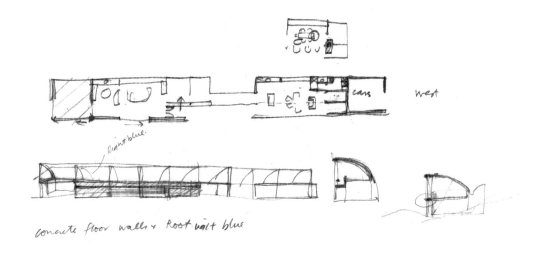

light blue.

concrete floor walls + Roof walt blue

west

cars

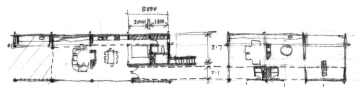

5000

300 1800

3·7

2·1

PLAN

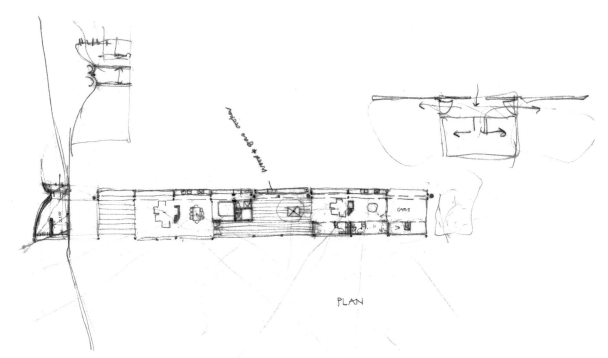

CARS

PLAN

ベランダを東端と中央に配置した、カーブ屋根の初期のアイデア。

Early design ideas, some showing a semi-circular vault
roof and a veranda on the east end of the house as well as
in the center.

谷樋をダブルかシングルにするかの検討。ドア上部の
カーブも合わせて発展している。

Studies of double-gutter and single-gutter options,
and of the relationship between the form of a single-
gutter and the curved head of the doors, below.

屋根の素材、構造、南面の高窓の断面スケッチ。
固定ガラスの下部、ドアの高さに、網戸付きの水平
換気窓を設けるディテールも併せて検討している。

Section sketch showing roofing materials,
structure and south facing fixed upper glazing.
Details explore adjustable horizontal vents with
insect mesh at door head height.

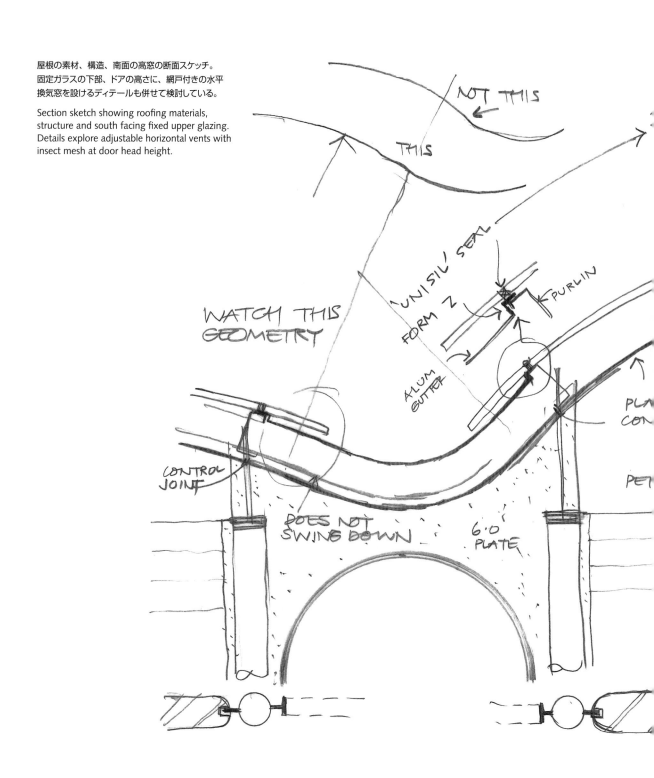

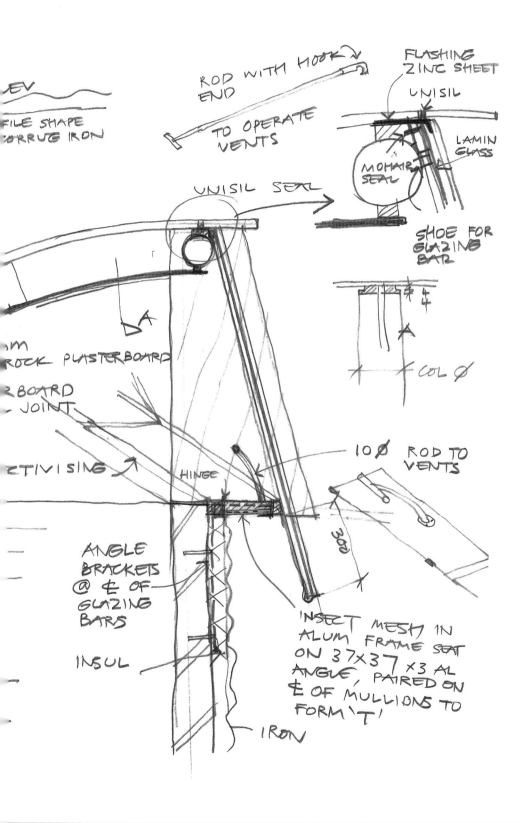

EV

FILE SHAPE
ORRUG IRON

ROD WITH HOOK
END

TO OPERATE
VENTS

FLASHING
ZINC SHEET

UNISIL

MOHAIR
SEAL

LAMIN
GLASS

UNISIL SEAL

SHOE FOR
GLAZING
BAR

m
ROCK PLASTERBOARD

RBOARD
JOINT

TIVISING

COL ∅

10 ∅ ROD TO
VENTS

HINGE

ANGLE
BRACKETS
@ ₵ OF
GLAZING
BARS

INSUL

300

INSECT MESH IN
ALUM FRAME SEAT
ON 37 X 37 X 3 AL
ANGLE, PAIRED ON
₵ OF MULLIONS TO
FORM 'T'

IRON

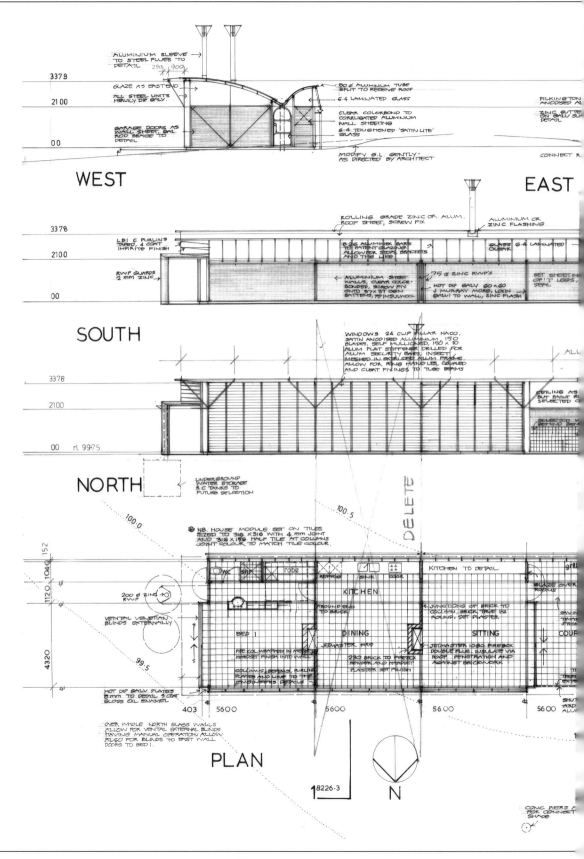

WEST

EAST

SOUTH

NORTH

PLAN

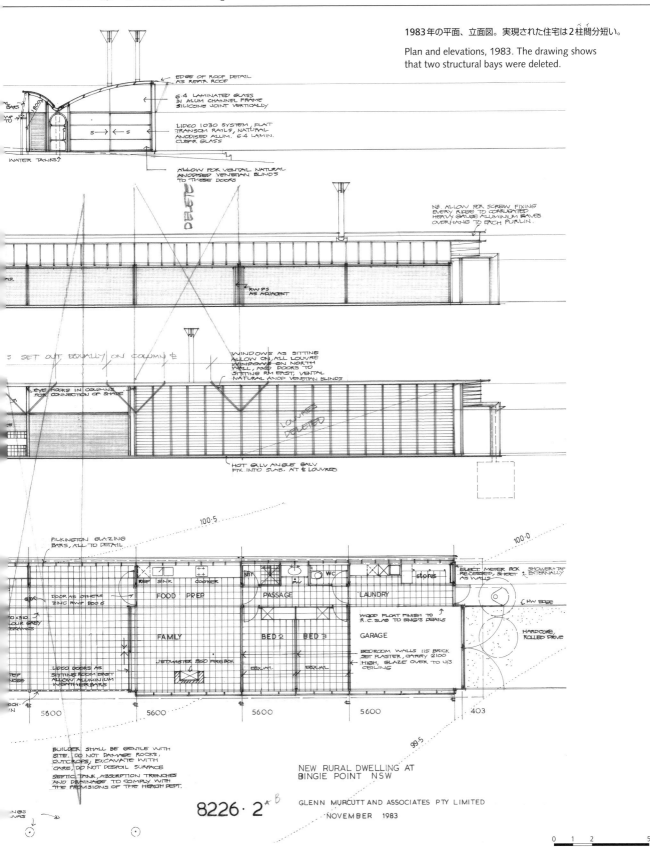

1983年の平面、立面図。実現された住宅は2柱間分短い。

Plan and elevations, 1983. The drawing shows
that two structural bays were deleted.

50 Ø ZINC OR ALUMINIUM TUBE SLEEVED
OVER ROOF SHEETING

BUILDER TO SUPPLY AND FIX
ALUMINIUM PELMET 110 x 4 mm

VENTAL NATURAL ANODISED
ALUMINIUM EXTERNAL BLINDS
OVER LOUVRED WALLING, ONE
BLIND PER TWO LOUVRE BAYS

FIXED GLASS ABOVE
TRANSOM

STRUCTURE INCL PIPE FRAMES
PURLINS, BEAMS, BRACING ETC
TO ENGINEER'S DETAILS, HOT DIP
GALV FINISHED

LAMINATED OR TOUGHENED
GLASS TO DETAIL

TUBE SET TO CONNECT TO
STIFFENERS ON LOUVRE ASSEMBLY

LIDCO 1030 DOOR SERIES
SATIN ANODISED ALUMINIUM
OFFSET 'D' MOUNT 1100 TO ₵
OFF FLOOR - SWITCHES SAME.

VENTAL TO THIS LEVEL
- NO LOUVRES AT WALL
BUT LIDCO 1030 DOORS
1 FIXED + 1 SLIDE EACH BAY

VENTAL SATIN ANODISED
ALUMINIUM VENETIAN BLIND
ASSEMBLY ZONE

NOTE CAREFULLY ALL SETOUT
FACES RELATE TO TILE GRID

150   160   4160

LOUVRE WINDOWS, STIFFENER
AND SECURITY BAR + INSECT SCREEN
ZONE

BRICK FIRE CASING INSULATED
AND HARDSET PLASTERED
CLASSIC CERAMICS 315 x 315 x 8
NOMINAL GREY CERAMIC FLOOR TILING

rl 99·75

HOT DIP GALV ANGLE TO
ENGINEER'S DETAILS

ALLOW FOR 100 HARDCORE
50 SAND, TERMITE TREAT
WHOLE AREA OF SLAB.
LAY HEAVY DUTY FORTECON
AND SLAB TO ENGINEER'S
DETAILS

NOTE HOW POSITION OF
WALLS ARE DETERMINED
BY FULL AND HALF TILES
₵

SITTING

← FLUE T
OUTER

COMPLY
REQUIRE
FLASH V

9330 r

基準断面詳細図。オリジナルは縮尺20分の1で描かれた。
マーカットはこの縮尺で空間の関係性、素材や工法のディ
テールを同時に検討する。

Typical cross section originally drawn at 1:20.
The scale allows the spatial relationships as well as
the material/structural detail to be studied in the
one drawing.

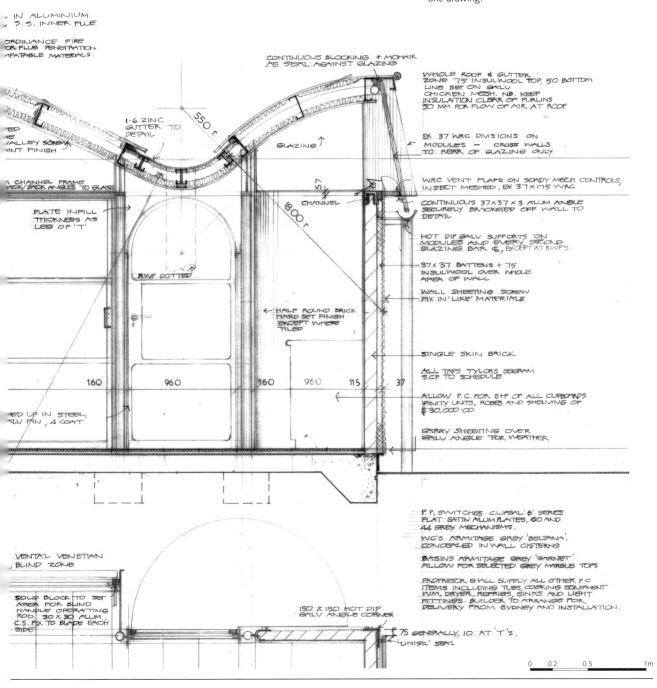

- IN ALUMINIUM
- 5.5. INNER FLUE

ORDINANCE FIRE
OR FLUE PENETRATION
PATABLE MATERIALS.

CONTINUOUS BLOCKING + MOHAIR
AS SEAL AGAINST GLAZING

WHOLE ROOF & GUTTER
ZONE 75 INSULWOOL TOP, 50 BOTTOM
LINE SET ON GALV
CHICKEN MESH. NB. KEEP
INSULATION CLEAR OF PURLINS
50 MM FOR FLOW OF AIR, AT ROOF

1.6 ZINC
GUTTER TO
DETAIL

550 f.

EX 37 WRC DIVISIONS ON
MODULES – CROSS WALLS
TO REAR OF GLAZING ONLY

ED
ME
VALLEY SCRIM
NT FINISH

GLAZING →

57

WRC VENT FLAPS ON SOADY MECH CONTROLS,
INSECT MESHED, EX 37×175 WRC

A CHANNEL FRAME
CK/BACK ANGLES TO GLASS

1800 f.

CHANNEL

CONTINUOUS 37×37×3 ALUM ANGLE
SECURELY BRACKETED OFF WALL TO
DETAIL

PLATE INFILL
THICKNESS AS
LEG OF 'T'

HOT DIP GALV SUPPORTS ON
MODULES AND EVERY SECOND
GLAZING BAR ⅊, EXCEPT AT RWPS.

37×37 BATTENS + 75
INSULWOOL OVER WHOLE
AREA OF WALL

RWP DOTTED

WALL SHEETING SCREW
FIX IN 'LIKE' MATERIALS

← HALF ROUND BRICK
HARD SET FINISH
EXCEPT WHERE
TILED

SINGLE SKIN BRICK

ALL TAPS TYLORS SEGRAM
S.C.P TO SCHEDULE.

160   960   160   960   115   37

ALLOW P.C. FOR SFF OF ALL CUPBOARDS
VANITY UNITS, ROBES AND SHELVING OF
$30,000·00

ED UP IN STEEL,
LV FIN, 4 COAT

CARRY SHEETING OVER
GALV ANGLE FOR WEATHER.

P.P, SWITCHES CLIPSAL 'B' SERIES
FLAT SATIN ALUM PLATES, 60 AND
44 GREY MECHANISMS.

WC'S ARMITAGE GREY 'BELTANA',
CONCEALED IN WALL CISTERNS

BASINS ARMITAGE GREY 'GARNET'
ALLOW FOR SELECTED GREY MARBLE TOPS

PROPRIETOR SHALL SUPPLY ALL OTHER P.C
ITEMS INCLUDING TUBS, COOKING EQUIPMENT,
WM, DRYER, REFRIGS, SINKS AND LIGHT
FITTINGS. BUILDER TO ARRANGE FOR
DELIVERY FROM SYDNEY AND INSTALLATION.

VENTAL VENETIAN
, BLIND ZONE

SOLID BLOCK TO SET
AREA FOR BLIND
HANDLE OPERATING
ROD. 30×30 ALUM
C.S. FIX TO BLADE EACH
SIDE

150×150 HOT DIP
GALV ANGLE CORNER

75 GENERALLY, 10 AT 'T's.

'UNISIL' SEAL

0   0.2   0.5   1m

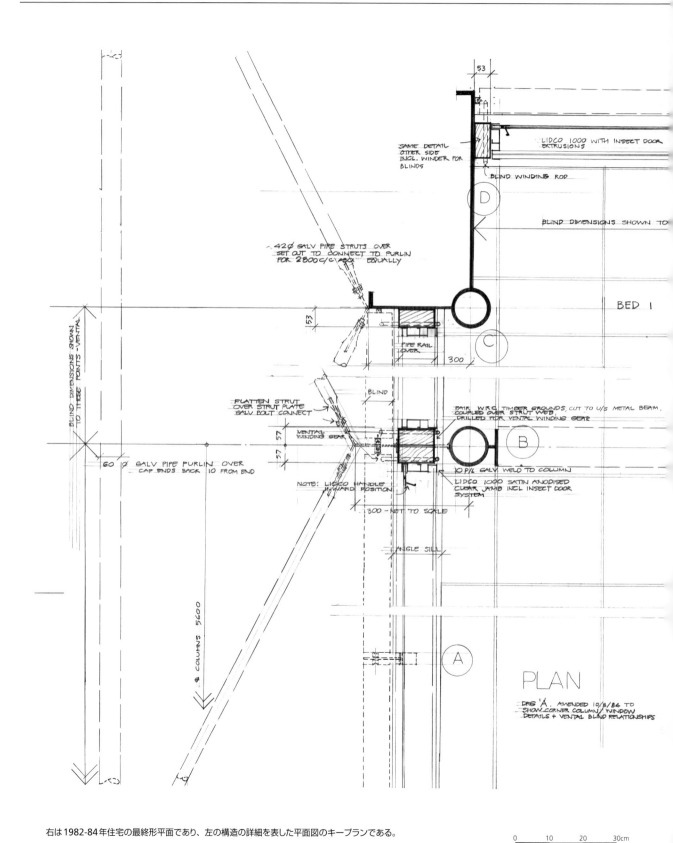

SAME DETAIL
OTHER SIDE
INCL. WINDER FOR
BLINDS

LIDCO 1000 WITH INSECT DOOR
EXTRUSIONS

BLIND WINDING ROD

D

BLIND DIMENSIONS SHOWN TO

42Ø GALV PIPE STRUTS OVER
SET OUT TO CONNECT TO PURLIN
FOR 2800 C/C APART EQUALLY

BED 1

53

C

PIPE RAIL
OVER

300

FLATTEN STRUT
OVER STRUT PLATE
GALV BOLT CONNECT

BLIND

PAIR WRC TIMBER GROUNDS, CUT TO U/S METAL BEAM,
COUPLED OVER STRUT WEB,
DRILLED FOR VENTAL WINDING GEAR

VENTAL
WINDING GEAR

57
57

B

60 Ø GALV PIPE PURLIN OVER
CAP ENDS BACK 10 FROM END

10 P/L GALV WELD TO COLUMN

NOTE: LIDCO HANDLE
INWARD POSITION

LIDCO 1000 SATIN ANODISED
CLEAR JAMB INCL INSECT DOOR
SYSTEM

300 - NOT TO SCALE

ANGLE SILL

⅊ COLUMNS 5600

BLIND DIMENSIONS SHOWN
TO THESE POINTS - VENTAL

A

PLAN

DRG 'A'. AMENDED 10/8/84 TO
SHOW CORNER COLUMN / WINDOW
DETAILS + VENTAL BLIND RELATIONSHIPS

右は1982-84年住宅の最終形平面であり、左の構造の詳細を表した平面図のキープランである。

0   10   20   30cm

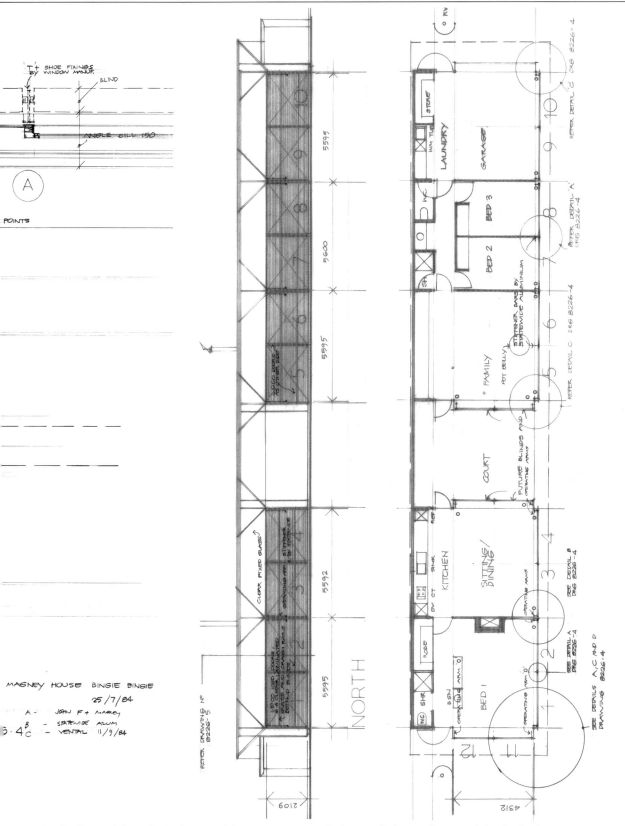

The plan illustrated shows the final version of the 1982-84 project and references the large scale structural plan details adjacent.

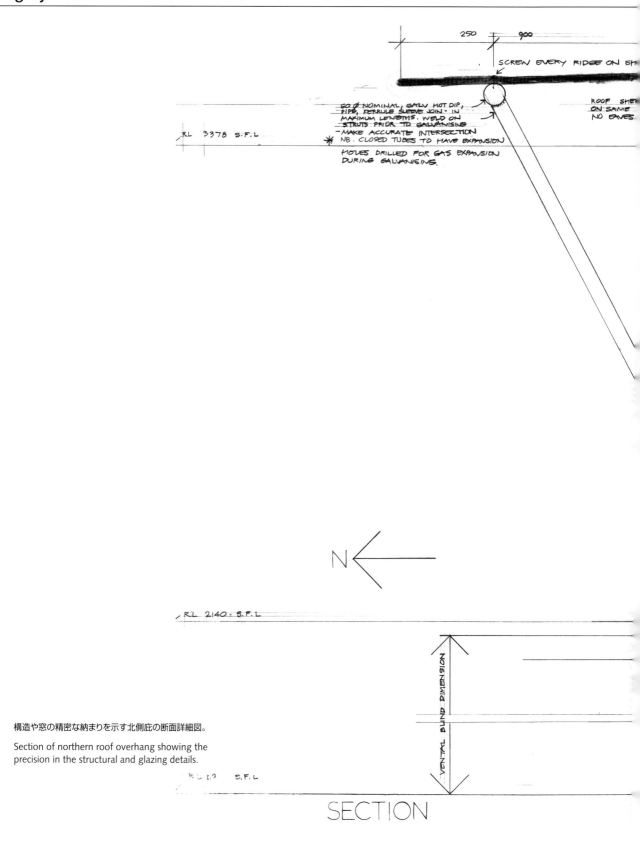

250   900

SCREW EVERY RIDGE ON SH

ROOF SHE
ON SAME
NO EAVES

RL 3378 S.F.L

60 Ø NOMINAL, GALV HOT DIP,
PIPE, FERRULE SLEEVE JOIN · IN
MAXIMUM LENGTHS. WELD ON
STRUTS PRIOR TO GALVANISING
— MAKE ACCURATE INTERSECTION
NB · CLOSED TUBES TO HAVE EXPANSION
HOLES DRILLED FOR GAS EXPANSION
DURING GALVANISING.

N

RL 2140 · S.F.L

VENTAL BLIND DIMENSION

構造や窓の精密な納まりを示す北側庇の断面詳細図。

Section of northern roof overhang showing the
precision in the structural and glazing details.

RL t.0 S.F.L

SECTION

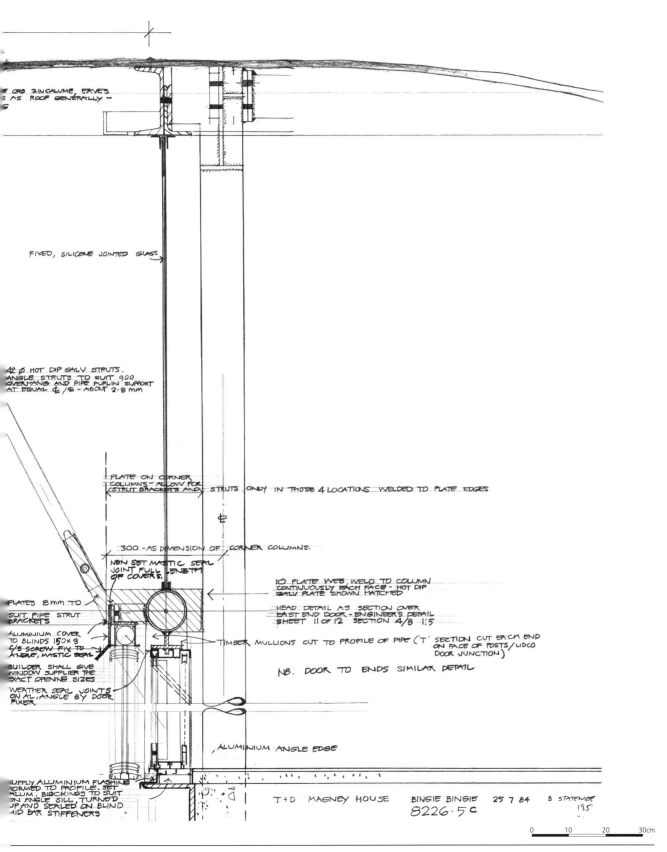

E ORB ZINCALUME, EAVES
S AS ROOF GENERALLY —

FIXED, SILICONE JOINTED GLASS

42 Ø HOT DIP GALV STRUTS,
ANGLE STRUTS TO SUIT 900
OVERHANG AND PIPE PURLIN SUPPORT
AT EQUAL ℄ /℄ - ABOUT 2·8 mm

PLATE ON CORNER
COLUMNS - ALLOW FOR
STRUT BRACKETS AND   STRUTS ONLY IN THOSE 4 LOCATIONS WELDED TO PLATE EDGES

℄

300 -AS DIMENSION OF CORNER COLUMNS.

NON SET MASTIC SEAL
JOINT FULL LENGTH
OF COVERS.

PLATES 8 mm TO
SUIT PIPE STRUT
BRACKETS

ALUMINIUM COVER
TO BLINDS 150x3
C/S SCREW FIX TO
ANGLE, MASTIC SEAL

BUILDER SHALL GIVE
WINDOW SUPPLIER THE
EXACT OPENING SIZES

WEATHER SEAL JOINTS
ON AL ANGLE BY DOOR
FIXER

10 PLATE WEB WELD TO COLUMN
CONTINUOUSLY EACH FACE - HOT DIP
GALV PLATE SHOWN HATCHED

HEAD DETAIL AS SECTION OVER
EAST END DOOR - ENGINEER'S DETAIL
SHEET 11 OF 12 SECTION 4/8 1:5

TIMBER MULLIONS CUT TO PROFILE OF PIPE ('T' SECTION CUT EACH END
ON FACE OF POSTS/UIDCO
DOOR JUNCTION)

NB. DOOR TO ENDS SIMILAR DETAIL

ALUMINIUM ANGLE EDGE

SUPPLY ALUMINIUM FLASHING
FORMED TO PROFILE, SET
ALUM. BLOCKINGS TO SUIT
ON ANGLE SILL, TURNED
UP AND SEALED ON BLIND
MID BAR STIFFENERS

T+D MAGNEY HOUSE   BINGIE BINGIE   25 7 84   B STATEWIDE
8226·5 C   19.5

0   10   20   30cm

Magney House

1986-90 Paddington, Sydney, New South Wales

海抜200m。温暖な海岸気候。
夏は平均気温25度、海風が陸上をわたってくる。
冬は18度前後、最低気温12度。砂岩地質。

Altitude: 200m above sea level. Temperate coastal climate.
Summer, circa 25 deg C with cooling on-shore breezes.
Winter circa 18 deg C with lows of 12 deg C. Sandstone soil.

Magney House

1988年の初期計画の断面詳細図。後により経済的な案に変更された。

Section drawing of early scheme, 1988. This was later revised in favour of a more economical solution.

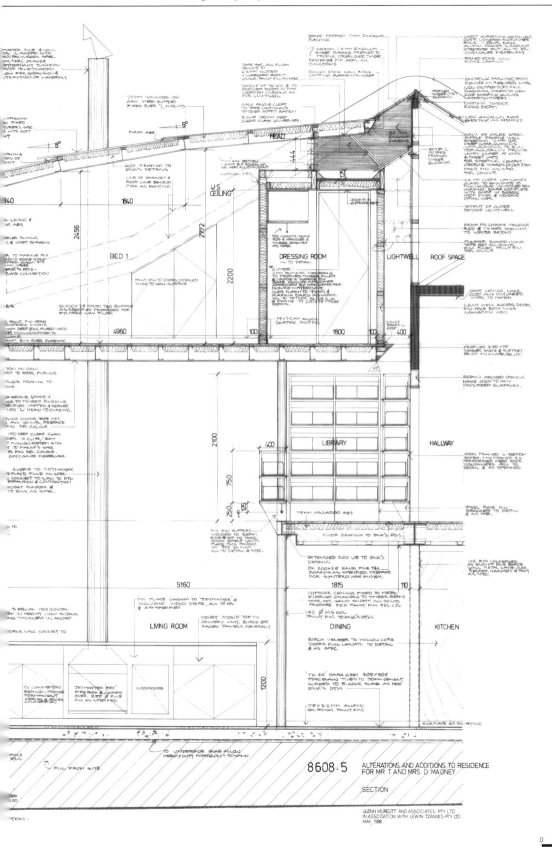

ALTERATIONS AND ADDITIONS TO RESIDENCE
FOR MR T. AND MRS D. MAGNEY

8608·5

SECTION

GLENN MURCUTT AND ASSOCIATES PTY LTD
IN ASSOCIATION WITH LEWIN TZANNES PTY LTD
MAY, 1988.

0   0.5   1   1.5m

実現された平面図。

Plans of the realised project.

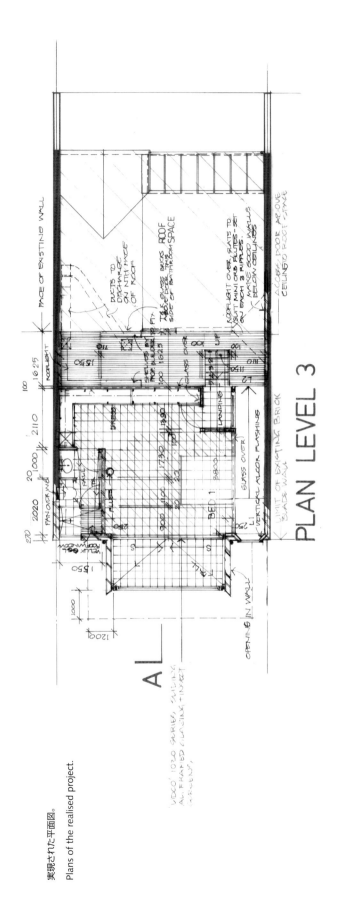

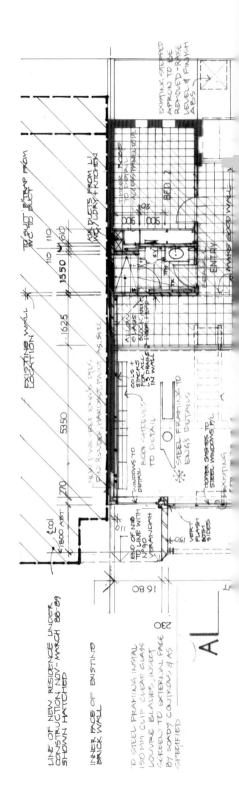

PLAN LEVEL 3

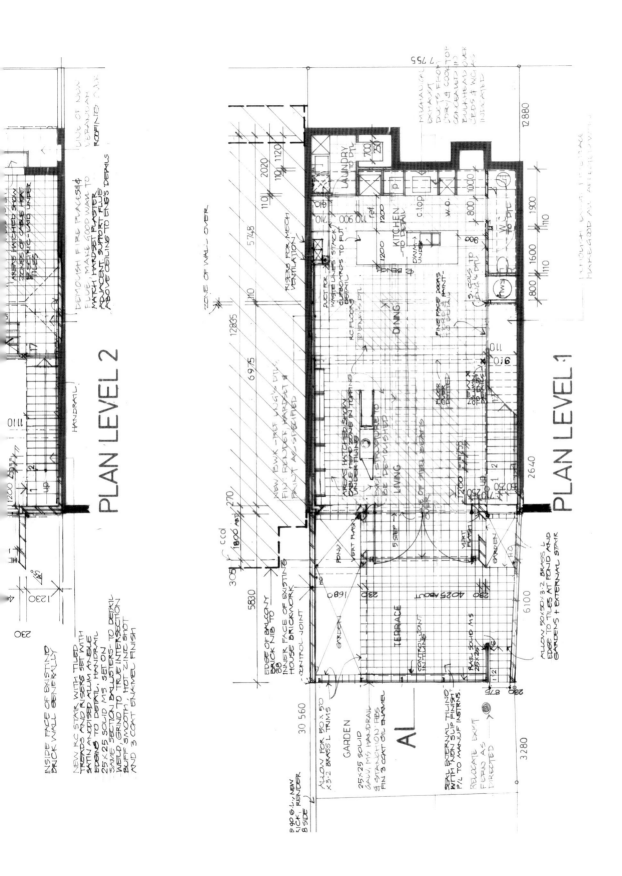

PLAN LEVEL 2

PLAN LEVEL 1

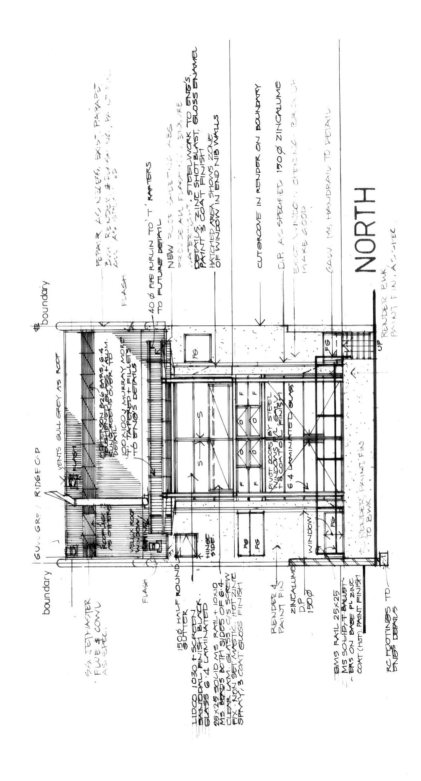

実現された長手断面図と北立面図。初期案でも見られた
ライトウェル（光井戸）がさらに大きくなり、寝室は玄関ホールから
数段上がったレベルになった。

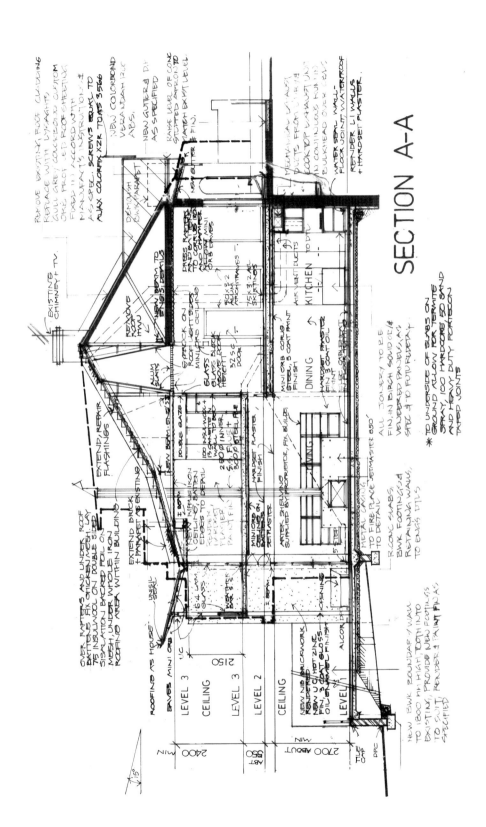

SECTION A-A

Long section and northern elevation of the realised project.
The roof light, visible in the early scheme, is now emphasized, and
the bedroom was set few steps up from the entry.

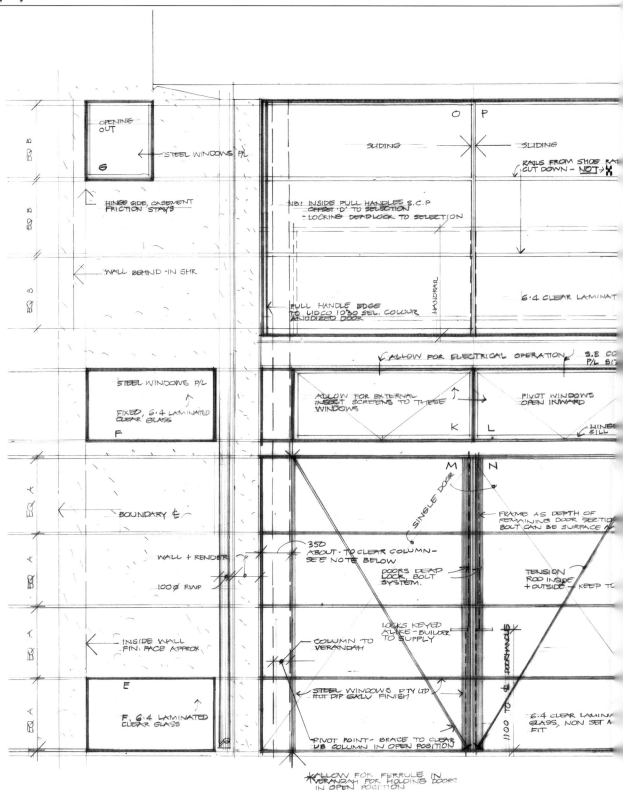

OPENING
OUT

G

←—STEEL WINDOWS P/L

←— HINGE SIDE, CASEMENT
FRICTION STAYS

←— WALL BEHIND - IN SHR

STEEL WINDOWS P/L

FIXED, 6·4 LAMINATED
CLEAR GLASS

F

←— BOUNDARY ℄

←— WALL + RENDER

100 ⌀ RWP

←— INSIDE WALL
FIN. FACE APPROX

E

F. 6·4 LAMINATED
CLEAR GLASS

SLIDING   O P   SLIDING

RAILS FROM SHOE R⌐
CUT DOWN - NOT·X

NB! INSIDE PULL HANDLES S.C.P
OFFSET 'D' TO SELECTION
- LOCKING DEADLOCK TO SELECTION

HANDRAIL

6·4 CLEAR LAMINAT

PULL HANDLE EDGE
TO LIDCO 1030 SEL. COLOUR
ANODIZED DOOR

←ALLOW FOR ELECTRICAL OPERATION   S.E CO
P/L B17

ADLOW FOR EXTERNAL
INSECT SCREENS TO THESE
WINDOWS

PIVOT WINDOWS
OPEN INWARD

K   L   HINGE
SILL

SINGLE DOOR

M   N

FRAME AS DEPTH OF
REMAINING DOOR SECTION
BOLT CAN BE SURFACE M

350
ABOUT - TO CLEAR COLUMN -
SEE NOTE BELOW

DOORS DEAD
LOCK, BOLT
SYSTEM.

TENSION
ROD INSIDE
+ OUTSIDE - KEEP TO

LOCKS KEYED
ALIKE - BUILDER
TO SUPPLY

DOOR HANDLE

COLUMN TO
VERANDAH

STEEL WINDOWS PTY LTD
HOT DIP GALV FINISH

1100 TO ⌀

6·4 CLEAR LAMINA
GLASS, NON SET M
FIT

PIVOT POINT - BRACE TO CLEAR
UB COLUMN IN OPEN POSITION

←ALLOW FOR FERRULE IN
VERANDAH FOR HOLDING DOORS
IN OPEN POSITION

ELEVATION NORTH   EXTERNAL VIEW

北立面詳細図。

North façade glazing drawing showing elevations
and material specifications.

FIXED WINDOW
6·4 CLEAR LAMIN-
ATED GLASS IN
STEEL WINDOWS P/L

H

EQUAL C

EQUAL C

I

FIXED GLASS IN
STEEL WINDOWS P/L
FRAME - DOTTED +
HATCHED - 6·4
CLEAR LAMINATED

LEVEL 3 FIN FLOOR

2150 (VERIFY)

310

LEVEL 2 FIN FLOOR

495 (VERIFY)

310

STEEL DOOR SUPPORT UB

BOUNDARY ₵

RWP 100 ∅

STEEL WINDOWS P/L
UNITS E F G H I J K L M + N
- LIDCO DOORS O + P.

✳ NB: ALL STEEL WINDOWS P/L
- WINDOWS HOT DIP GALV. FINISH
- PAINTING BY BUILDER

- ALL DIMENSIONS SHOWN ARE
BELIEVED TO BE CORRECT, IT
IS THE RESPONSIBILITY OF
THE BUILDER AND WINDOW
FABRICATORS TO VERIFY THEM
FROM ACTUAL DIMENSIONS ON SITE

- INSECT SCREENS BY OTHERS

2700 (VERIFY)

STEEL WINDOWS P/L
OPENING WINDOW OUT
INSECT MESHED

J HINGE

CLEAR 6·4 LAMIN
GLASS

FIXED →

64 CLEAR GLASS
LAMINATED

LANDING
BEHIND

LEVEL 1 FIN FLOOR

40

8608·6   T & D MAGNEY
PADDINGTON
GLENN MURCUTT AND ASSOC P/L

0   0.2   0.5   1m

寝室への階段詳細図。
Steel stair details to raised bedroom.

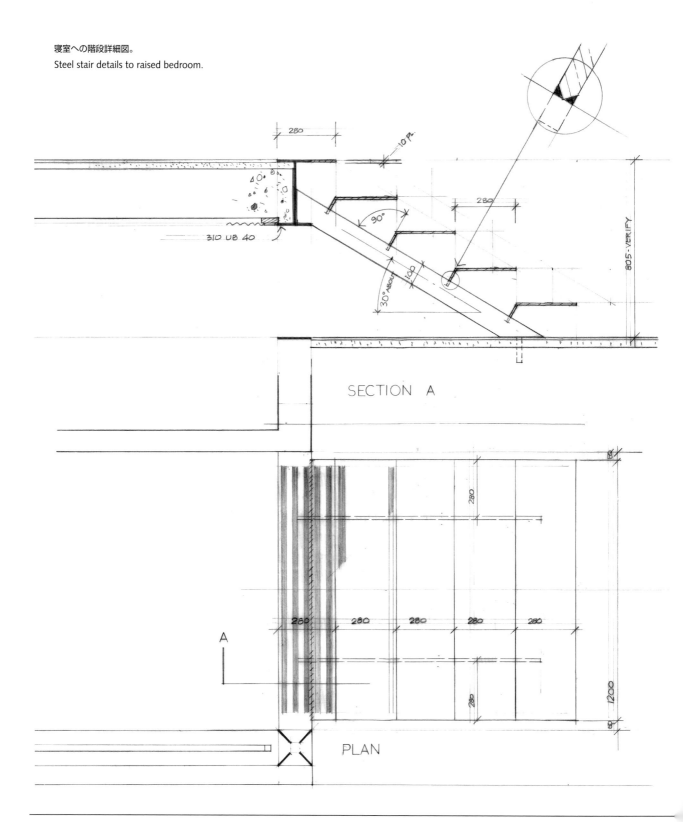

310 UB 40

280

10 P.

90°

280

30° ABOUT

805 - VERIFY

SECTION   A

280

280   280   280   280   280

280

1200

A

PLAN

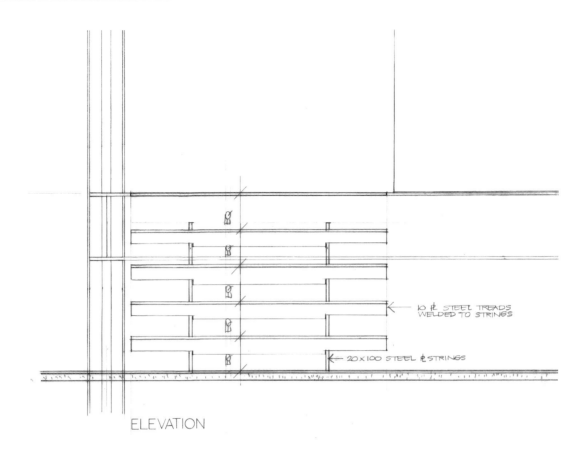

ELEVATION

10 ⅋ STEEL TREADS WELDED TO STRINGS

20 x 100 STEEL ⅋ STRINGS

ALLOW FOR STAIR CONNECTIONS WELDED ONTO STRINGS, ACCURATELY AND TO TRUE GEOMETRY HOT ZINC SPRAY FOR PAINT FINISH

8608·9 B   REVISED STAIR FOR BED
GLENN MURCUTT AND ASSOCIATES PTY LTD ARCHITECTS
JULY 1989

0   10   20   50cm

Simpson-Lee House

1988-93 Mount Wilson, New South Wales

海抜1,000m。温暖気候でも寒い地帯。稀に少量の降雪。
山の陰にあり、西からの冬の冷たい風、夏の熱い風から
守られている。夏の気温は29度、冬は16度前後だが、
最低1度まで下がる。火山灰土壌、砂岩地質。

Altitude: 1,000m above sea level. Cool temperate climate.
Occasional light snowfalls. Sited in the lee of a hill which
protects it from cold westerly winds in winter and hot westerly
winds in summer. Summer circa 29 deg C. Winter circa
16 deg C with lows of 1 deg C. Volcanic and sandstone soils.

Darwin

Northern
Territory

Queensland

Western Australia

South Australia

○ Brisbane

Mount Wilson

New South Wales

Adelaide

○ Sydney

Victoria

Melbourne

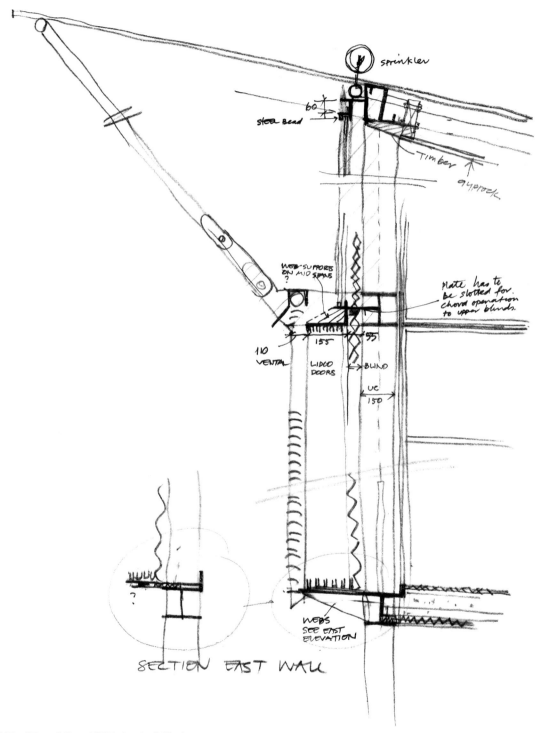

sprinkler

60

steel bead

Timber

gyprock

WEB SUPPORTS
ON M10 SPANS
?

plate has to
be slotted for.
chord operation
to upper blinds.

155   55

110
VENTAL

LIDCO
DOORS

BLIND

UC
150

WEBS
SEE EAST
ELEVATION

SECTION EAST WALL

東立面、ガラススクリーンの断面スケッチ。「リドコ」
社のガラス引戸と外付けの可動ルーバーを鉄骨軸組へ
納めるディテールスケッチ。屋根上方に山火事消火用
スプリンクラーが見える。

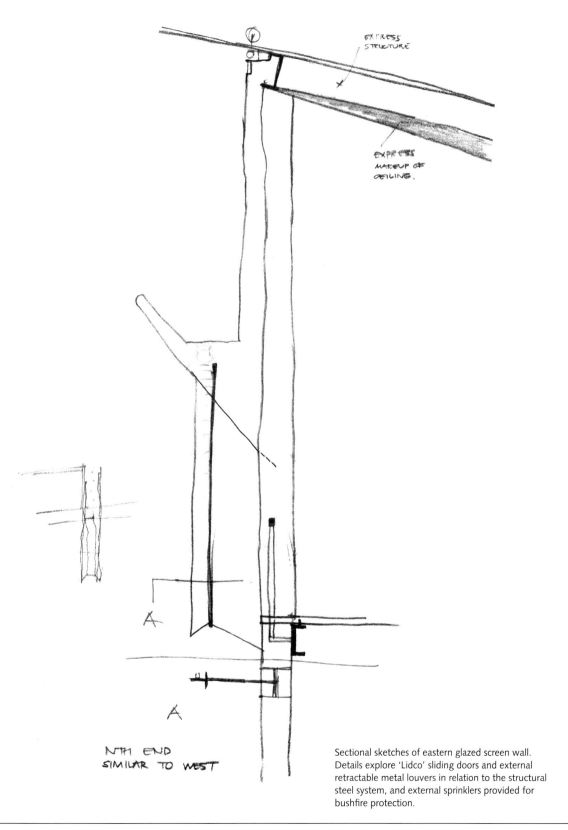

EXPRESS
STRUCTURE

EXPRESS
MAKEUP OF
CEILING.

A

A

NTH END
SIMILAR TO WEST

Sectional sketches of eastern glazed screen wall.
Details explore 'Lidco' sliding doors and external
retractable metal louvers in relation to the structural
steel system, and external sprinklers provided for
bushfire protection.

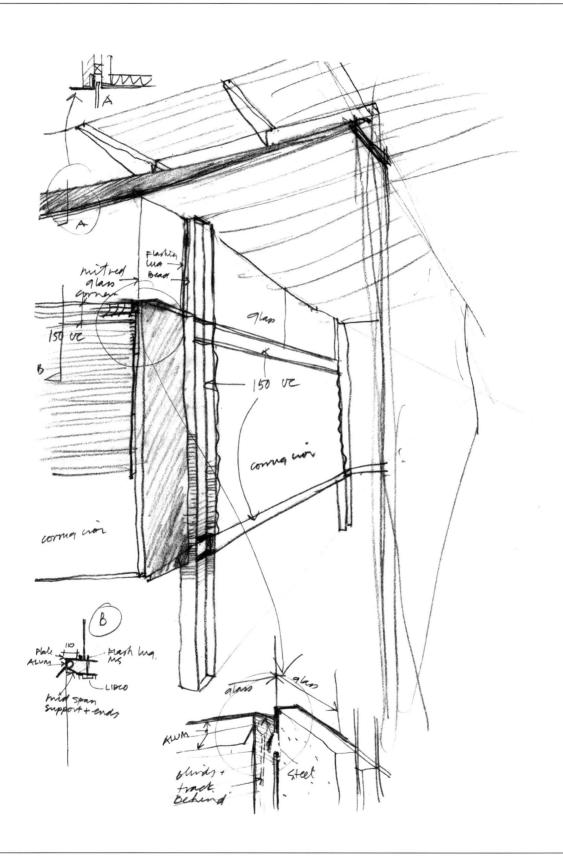

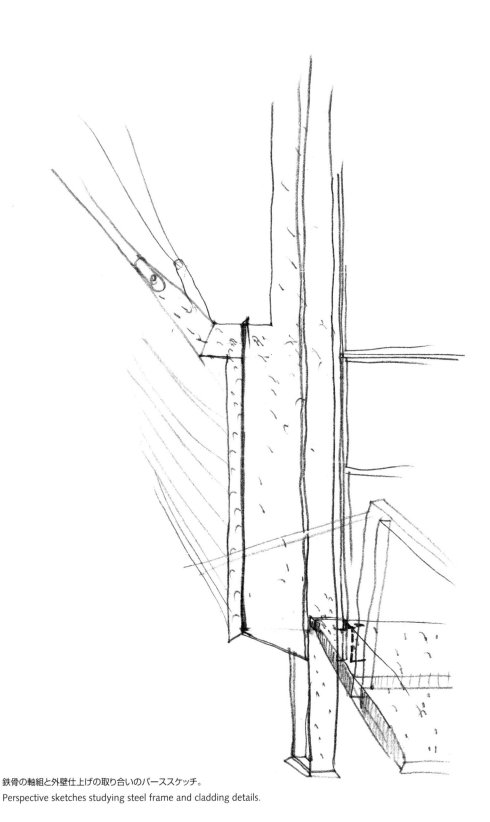

鉄骨の軸組と外壁仕上げの取り合いのパーススケッチ。
Perspective sketches studying steel frame and cladding details.

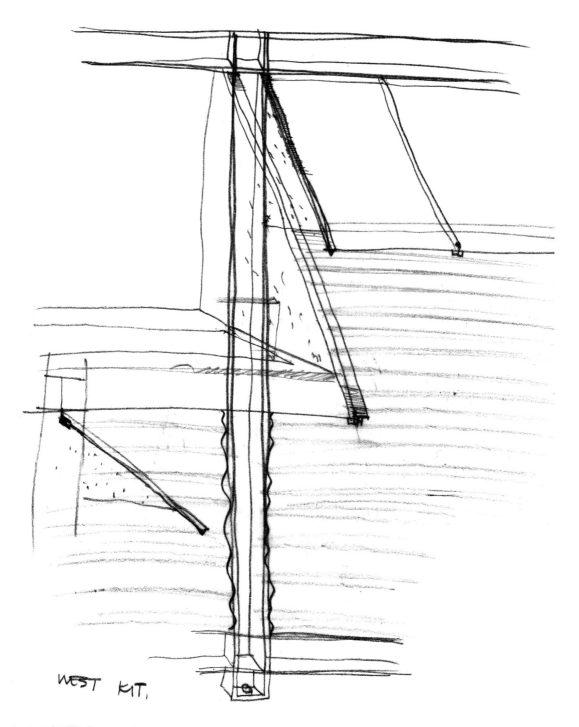

WEST KIT.

キッチンの窓の詳細パーススケッチ。

Perspective sketch studying glazing
detail at kitchen window.

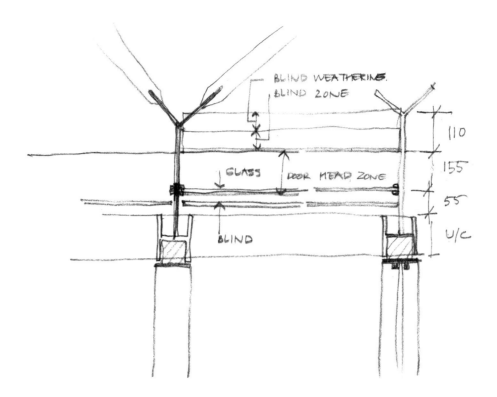

BLIND WEATHERING.
BLIND ZONE

110

155

55

U/C

GLASS   DOOR HEAD ZONE

BLIND

ABOVE EAST HEAD.

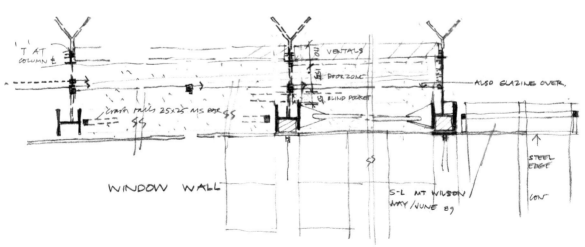

T AT
COLUMN ℄

VENTALS

DOOR ZONE

BLIND POCKET

ALSO GLAZING OVER.

crash rails 25x25 MS bars SS

SS

STEEL
EDGE

CON

S-L MT WILSON /
MAY /JUNE 89

WINDOW WALL

梁伏せ部分の平面詳細スケッチ。東立面の構造と、
上部ガラスとブラインドとの納まり。

Plan sketch details investigating layers of
glazing and blind systems with upper
triangulated steel struts at eastern façade.

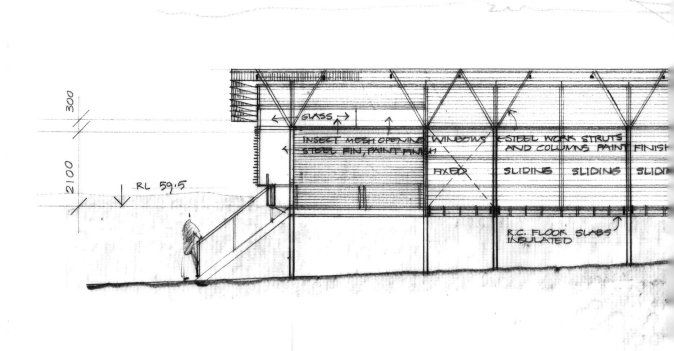

GLASS

INSECT MESH OPENING WINDOWS STEEL WORK STRUTS
STEEL FIN, PAINT FINISH AND COLUMNS PAINT FINISH

FIXED SLIDING SLIDING SLIDI

R.C. FLOOR SLABS
INSULATED

300

2100

RL 59.5

EAST

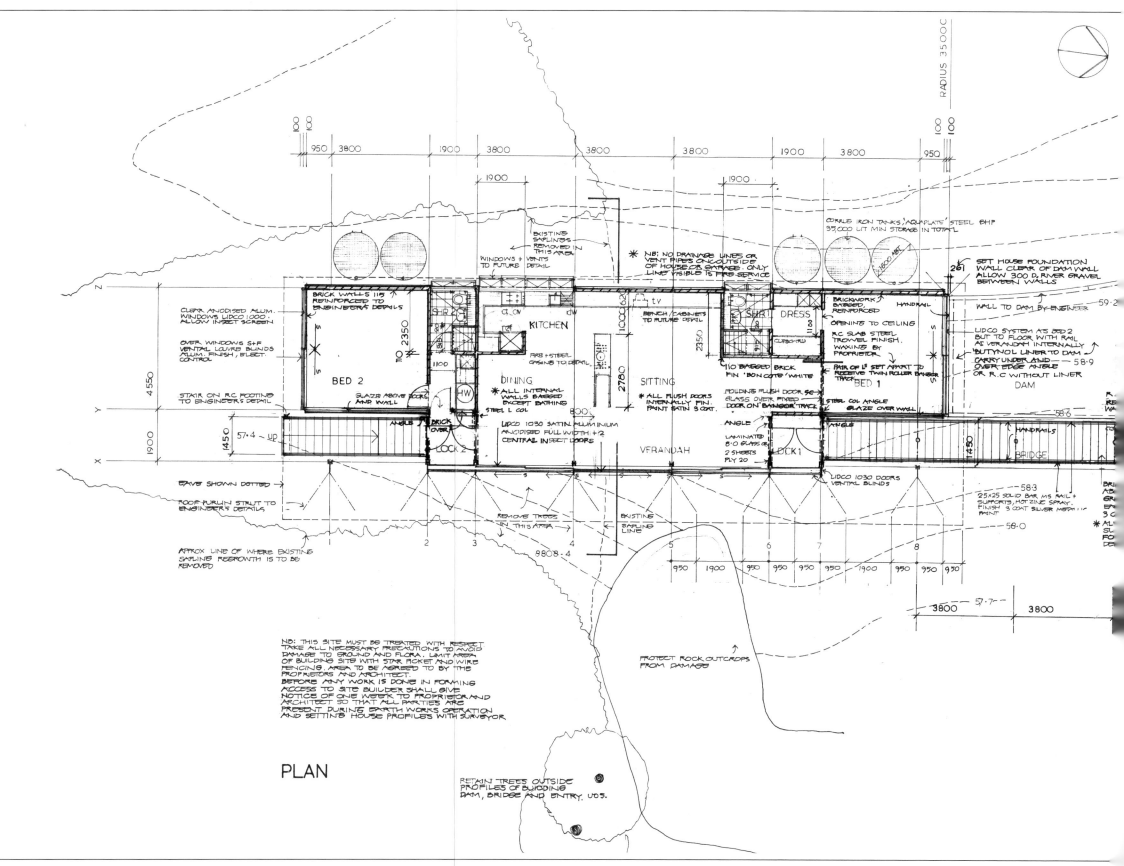

PLAN

FIRE SPRINKLER UPBENDS

← VILLABOARD

GLASS →

← FULL HEIGHT DORENDORF
FIRE + INSULATION SHUTTERS
OVER THIS GLAZING

INSECT MESHWINDOW
NATURAL
ZINCALUME
NON COMBUSTABLE

GLASS

FINISHES + SECTION
AS HOUSE

SLIDING

← VENTAL BLINDS OVER
LIDCO 1030 DOORS

VENTAL BLINDS
OVER SLIDING DOORS
LIDCO 1000/1030

DAM FOR PLANTS + FIRE

STUDIO/
GARAGE

SLIDING   SLIDING   FIXED

0   1   2   3m

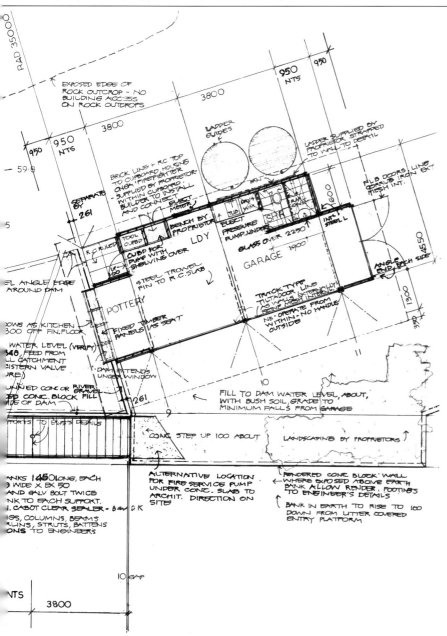

RAD 35000

EXPOSED EDGE OF
ROCK OUTCROP - NO
BUILDING ACCESS
ON ROCK OUTCROPS

950
NTS

950

3800

3800

950   950
NTS

- 59.8

LADDER
GUIDES

LADDER SUPPLIED BY
PROPRIETOR STRAPPED
TO WALL TO DETAIL

BRICK LINE + RC TOP
TO CUPBOARD HOUSING
ONGA FIREFIGHTER
- SUPPLIED BY PROPRIETOR
WITHIN CUPBOARD
BUILDER TO INSTALL
AND CONNECT

FILB DOORS LINE
UP RUB IRON EXT
MESH INT.

SEPARATE
BY
261

ELECT.
METER

FAN

DRY
WM

TUB

PMP

SHR

INT.
STEEL L

ANGLE
END EACH SIDE

TOOL
CUPBD

R.C RULED
L.
50

BENCH BY
PROPRIETOR

LDY

ELECT.
PRESSURE
PUMP UNDER

GLASS OVER 2250
1900

CUPBD FOR
PUMP WITH
SHELVING OVER

4550

L ANGLE EDGE
AROUND DAM

STEEL TROWEL
FIN TO R.C SLAB

GARAGE

1300

POTTERY

FIXED TIMBER
PANELS AS SEAT

TRUCK TYPE
TILT DOOR LINE
AS WALLS EXTERNALLY
REINF MESH INTERNAL
NB · OPERATE FROM
WITHIN - NO HANDLE
OUTSIDE

OWS AS KITCHEN
300 OFF FIN.FLOOR

3570

WATER LEVEL (VERIFY)
348, FEED FROM
L CATCHMENT
CISTERN VALVE
URE.)

DAM EXTENDS
UNDER WINDOW

10

UNNED CONC OR RIVER
GRAVEL
ED CONC. BLOCK FILL
DE OF DAM

261

FILL TO DAM WATER LEVEL, ABOUT,
WITH BUSH SOIL, GRADE TO
MINIMUM FALLS FROM GARAGE

9

PORTS TO ENG'S DETAILS

CONC STEP UP 100 ABOUT

LANDSCAPING BY PROPRIETORS

ANKS 1450 LONG, EACH
WIDE X EX 50
AND GALV BOLT TWICE.
NK TO EACH SUPPORT.
. CABOT CLEAR SEALER - B   D K
GS, COLUMNS, BEAMS
LINS, STRUTS, BATTENS
ONS TO ENGINEER'S

ALTERNATIVE LOCATION
FOR FIRE SERVICE PUMP
UNDER CONC. SLAB TO
ARCHIT. DIRECTION ON
SITE

RENDERED CONC. BLOCK WALL
WHERE EXPOSED ABOVE EARTH
BANK ALLOW RENDER, FOOTINGS
TO ENGINEER'S DETAILS

BANK IN EARTH TO RISE TO 100
DOWN FROM LITTER COVERED
ENTRY PLATFORM

10 GAP

NTS

3800

8808·2^F
NEW HOUSE MT. WILSON

GLENN MURCUTT AND ASSOCIATES PTY LTD ARCHITECTS
OCTOBER 1989
AMENDED NOVEMBER 1990

0   1   2   5m

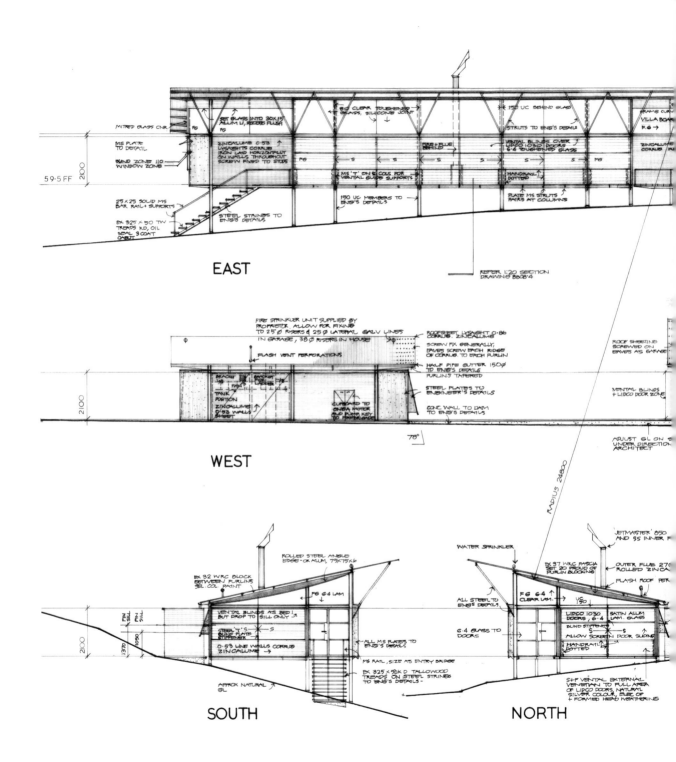

EAST

WEST

SOUTH

NORTH

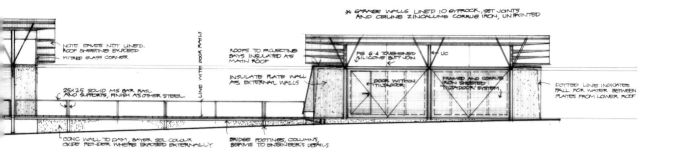

NOTE EAVES NOT LINED. ROOF SHEETING EXPOSED

MITRED GLASS CORNER

LINE WITH DOOR RAILS

25X25 SOLID MS BAR RAIL AND SUPPORTS, FINISH AS OTHER STEEL

CONC WALL TO DAM, BAYER SEL COLOUR OXIDE RENDER WHERE EXPOSED EXTERNALLY

ROOFS TO PROJECTING BAYS INSULATED AS MAIN ROOF

INSULATE PLATE WALL AS EXTERNAL WALLS

BRIDGE FOOTINGS, COLUMNS, BEAMS TO ENGINEER'S DETAILS

✱ GARAGE WALLS LINED 10 GYPROCK, SET JOINTS AND CEILING ZINCALUME CORRUG IRON, UNPAINTED

FG 6·4 TOUGHENED SILICONE BUTT JOIN

UC

DOOR WITHIN TILT DOOR

FRAMED AND CORRUG IRON SHEETED TILT DOOR SYSTEM

DOTTED LINE INDICATES FALL FOR WATER BETWEEN PLATES FROM LOWER ROOF

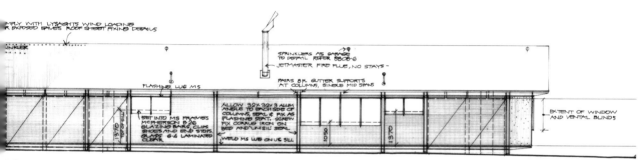

COMPLY WITH LYSAGHTS WIND LOADING OR EXPOSED EAVES ROOF SHEET FIXING DETAILS

RINKLER

FLASHING LUG MS

SET INTO MS FRAMES MCPHERSON B26 GLAZING BARS, CLIPS SHOES AND END STOPS GLASS 6·4 LAMINATED CLEAR

NB TANKS EACH HAVE STOP VALVE, ALL CONNECTED. OVERFLOWS TO RUN INTO DAM

SPRINKLERS AS GARAGE TO DETAIL REFER BBOB·6

JETMASTER FIRE FLUE, NO STAYS

PAIRS 8 R. GUTTER SUPPORTS AT COLUMNS, SINGLE MID SPANS

ALLOW 32X 32X 3 ALUM ANGLE TO EACH SIDE OF COLUMNS, SEAL & FIX AS FLASHING SEAT, SCREW FIX CORRUG IRON ON BED AND LINE SILL SEAL

WELD MS LUG ON UC SILL

1050

1370

EXTENT OF WINDOW AND VENTAL BLINDS

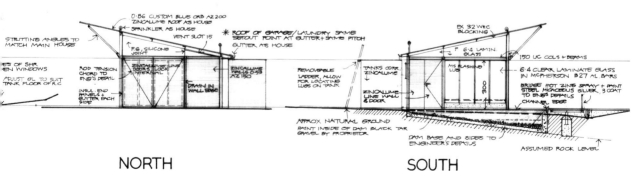

STRUTTING ANGLES TO MATCH MAIN HOUSE

ES OF SHR EN WINDOWS

ADJUST EL TO SUIT TANK FLOOR OF R.C

0·86 CUSTOM BLUE ORB AZ 200 ZINCALUME ROOF AS HOUSE

SPRINKLER AS HOUSE

VENT SLOT 15

FG, SILICONE JOINT

ROD TENSION CHORD TO ENG'S DETAIL

INSUL. END PANELS + GUTTER EACH SIDE

ZINCALUME LINE DOOR & COLOUR INTERNAL

ZINCALUME WALL 53 AZ 150

✱ ROOF OF GARAGE/LAUNDRY SAME SETOUT POINT AT GUTTER + SAME PITCH GUTTER AS HOUSE

DRAIN IN WALL EDGE

REMOVEABLE LADDER, ALLOW FOR LOCATING LUGS ON TANK

TANKS CORR. ZINCALUME

ZINCALUME LINE WALL & DOOR

APPROX NATURAL GROUND PAINT INSIDE OF DAM BLACK TAR GRAVEL BY PROPRIETOR

8X 32 WRC BLOCKING

F 6·4 LAMIN. GLASS

MS FLASHING LUG

300

150 UC COLS + BEAMS

6·4 CLEAR LAMINATE GLASS IN MCPHERSON B27 AL BARS

BRIDGE HOT ZINC SPRAY + PAINT STEEL MICACEOUS SILVER, 3 COAT TO ENG'S DETAILS

CHANNEL EDGE

DAM BASE AND SIDES TO ENGINEER'S DETAILS

ASSUMED ROCK LEVEL

NORTH

SOUTH

0 1 2 5m

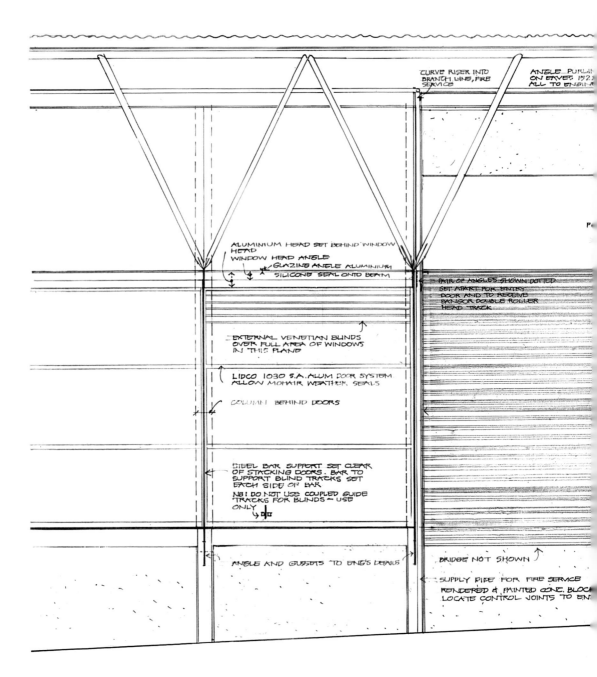

CURVE RISER INTO
BRANCH LINE, FIRE
SERVICE

ANGLE PURLIN
ON EAVES 152
ALL TO ENGIN

ALUMINIUM HEAD SET BEHIND WINDOW
HEAD
WINDOW HEAD ANGLE
GLAZING ANGLE ALUMINIUM
SILICONE SEAL ONTO BEAM

PAIR OF ANGLES SHOWN DOTTED
SET APART FOR ENTRY
DOOR AND TO RECEIVE
BANGOR DOUBLE ROLLER
HEAD TRACK

EXTERNAL VENETIAN BLINDS
OVER FULL AREA OF WINDOWS
IN THIS PLANE

LIDCO 1030 S.A. ALUM DOOR SYSTEM
ALLOW MOHAIR WEATHER SEALS

COLUMN BEHIND DOORS

STEEL BAR SUPPORT SET CLEAR
OF STACKING DOORS. BAR TO
SUPPORT BLIND TRACKS SET
EACH SIDE OF BAR
NB! DO NOT USE COUPLED GUIDE
TRACKS FOR BLINDS — USE
ONLY

ANGLE AND GUSSETS TO ENG'S DETAILS

BRIDGE NOT SHOWN

SUPPLY PIPE FOR FIRE SERVICE
RENDERED & PAINTED CONC. BLOCK
LOCATE CONTROL JOINTS TO EN

EAST

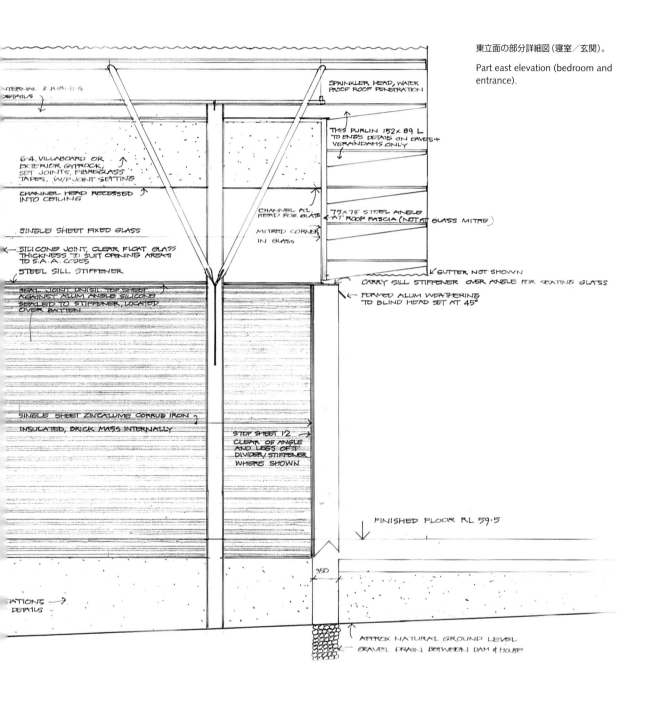

東立面の部分詳細図（寝室／玄関）。

Part east elevation (bedroom and entrance).

INTERNAL Z PURLINS DETAILS

SPRINKLER HEAD, WATER PROOF ROOF PENETRATION

THIS PURLIN 152 x 89 L TO ENDS DETAILS ON EAVES + VERANDAHS ONLY

6·4. VILLABOARD OR EXTERIOR GYPROCK, SET JOINTS, FIBREGLASS TAPES, W/P JOINT SEATING

CHANNEL HEAD RECESSED INTO CEILING

SINGLE SHEET FIXED GLASS

CHANNEL AL. HEAD FOR GLASS

75 x 75 STEEL ANGLE AT ROOF FASCIA (NOT AT GLASS MITRE)

MITRED CORNER IN GLASS

SILICONE JOINT, CLEAR FLOAT GLASS THICKNESS TO SUIT OPENING AREAS TO S.A.A. CODES

STEEL SILL STIFFENER

GUTTER NOT SHOWN

CARRY SILL STIFFENER OVER ANGLE FOR SEATING GLASS

SEAL JOINT UNISIL TOP SHEET AGAINST ALUM ANGLE SILICONE SEALED TO STIFFENER, LOCATED OVER BATTEN

FORMED ALUM WEATHERING TO BLIND HEAD SET AT 45°

SINGLE SHEET ZINCALUME CORRUG IRON INSULATED, BRICK MASS INTERNALLY

STOP SHEET 12 CLEAR OF ANGLE AND LEGS OF DIVIDER / STIFFENER WHERE SHOWN

FINISHED FLOOR RL 59·5

350

ATIONS DETAILS

APPROX NATURAL GROUND LEVEL GRAVEL DRAIN BETWEEN DAM & HOUSE

HOUSE   MT WILSON

0   0.2   0.5   1m

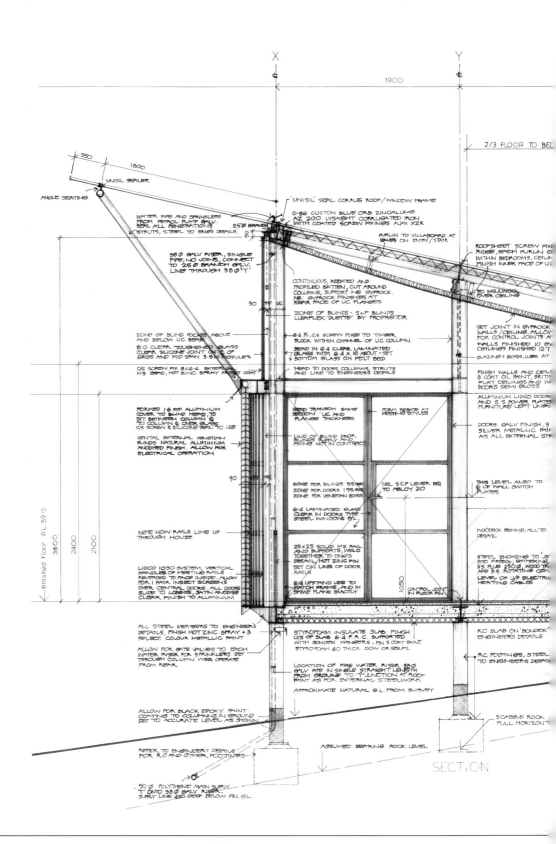

SECTION

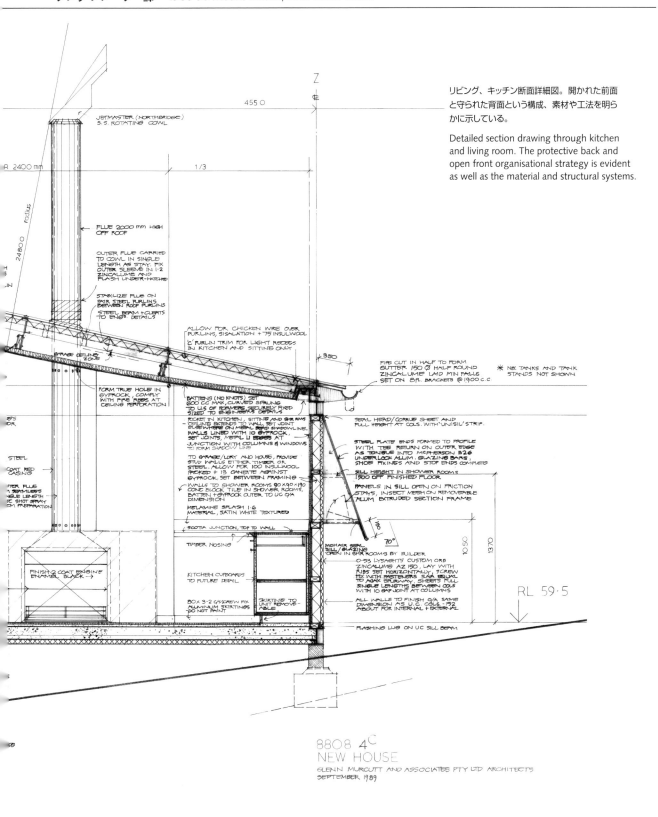

リビング、キッチン断面詳細図。開かれた前面
と守られた背面という構成、素材や工法を明ら
かに示している。

Detailed section drawing through kitchen
and living room. The protective back and
open front organisational strategy is evident
as well as the material and structural systems.

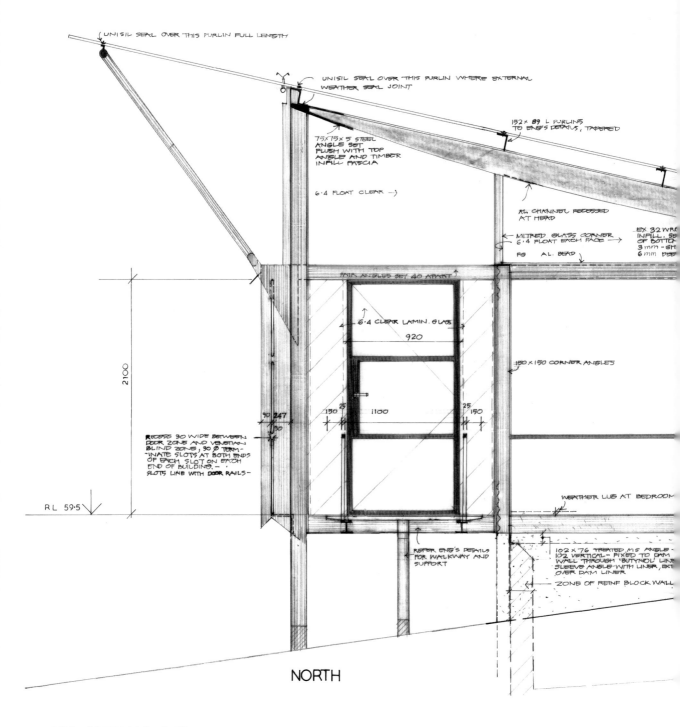

(UNISIL SEAL OVER THIS PURLIN FULL LENGTH

UNISIL SEAL OVER THIS PURLIN WHERE EXTERNAL
WEATHER SEAL JOINT

152 × 89 L PURLINS
TO ENG'S DETAILS, TAPERED

75×75×5 STEEL
ANGLE SET
FLUSH WITH TOP
ANGLE AND TIMBER
INFILL FASCIA

6·4 FLOAT CLEAR →

AL. CHANNEL RECESSED
AT HEAD

MITRED GLASS CORNER
6·4 FLOAT EACH FACE →

EX 32 WRC
INFILL. SE
3 mm - 6M
6 mm DEE

FG   AL. BEAD

PAIR ANGLES SET 40 APART

6·4 CLEAR LAMIN. GLASS

920

180 × 150 CORNER ANGLES

2100

90 | 247
50

RECESS 30 WIDE BETWEEN
DOOR ZONE AND VENETIAN
BLIND ZONE, 30 Ø TERM-
-INATE SLOTS AT BOTH ENDS
OF EACH SLOT ON EACH
END OF BUILDING. -
SLOTS LINE WITH DOOR RAILS-

150 | 25 | 1100 | 25 | 150

RL 59·5 ↓

WEATHER LUG AT BEDROOM

REFER ENG'S DETAILS
FOR WALKWAY AND
SUPPORT

102 × 76 TREATED M.S ANGLE -
102 VERTICAL - FIXED TO DAM
WALL THROUGH 'BUTYNOL' LINE
SLEEVE ANGLE WITH LINER, EXT
OVER DAM LINER

ZONE OF REINF BLOCK WALL

NORTH

居住棟の北立面図と寝室窓の断面詳細図。

Elevation at north end of living pavilion and sectional details at
northern glazed openings.

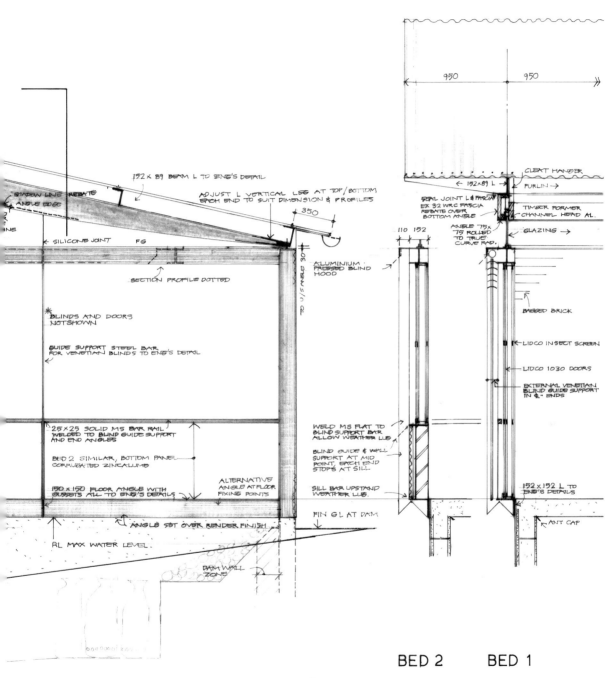

950   950

CLEAT HANGER

152×89 BEAM L TO ENG'S DETAIL

152×89 L

PURLIN →

ADJUST L VERTICAL LEG AT TOP/BOTTOM
EACH END TO SUIT DIMENSION & PROFILES

350

SHADOW LINE REBATE
ANGLE EDGE

SEAL JOINT L & FASCIA
EX 32 WRC FASCIA
REBATE OVER
BOTTOM ANGLE

TIMBER FORMER
CHANNEL HEAD AL.

SILICONE JOINT   FG

ANGLE 75×
75 ROLLED
TO TRUE
CURVE RAD.

GLAZING →

SECTION PROFILE DOTTED

110 152

ALUMINIUM
PRESSED BLIND
HOOD

TO U/S ANGLE 30°

BLINDS AND DOORS
NOT SHOWN

BAGGED BRICK

GUIDE SUPPORT STEEL BAR
FOR VENETIAN BLINDS TO ENG'S DETAIL

← LIDCO INSECT SCREEN

← LIDCO 1030 DOORS

25×25 SOLID MS BAR RAIL
WELDED TO BLIND GUIDE SUPPORT
AND END ANGLES

WELD MS FLAT TO
BLIND SUPPORT BAR
ALLOW WEATHER LUG

EXTERNAL VENETIAN
BLIND GUIDE SUPPORT
IN ₵ ENDS

BED 2 SIMILAR, BOTTOM PANEL
CORRUGATED ZINCALUME

BLIND GUIDE & WALL
SUPPORT AT MID
POINT, EACH END
STOPS AT SILL

150×150 FLOOR ANGLE WITH
GUSSETS ALL TO ENG'S DETAILS

ALTERNATIVE
ANGLE AT FLOOR
FIXING POINTS

SILL BAR UPSTAND
WEATHER LUG.

152×152 L TO
ENG'S DETAILS

ANGLE SET OVER RENDER FINISH

FIN GL AT DAM

ANT CAP

RL MAX WATER LEVEL.

DAM WALL
ZONE

BED 2   BED 1

8808·7 ^{B} HOUSE MT WILSON

$\frac{01}{91}$ GLENN MURCUTT AND ASSOC P/L ARCHITECTS

0   0.2   0.5   1m

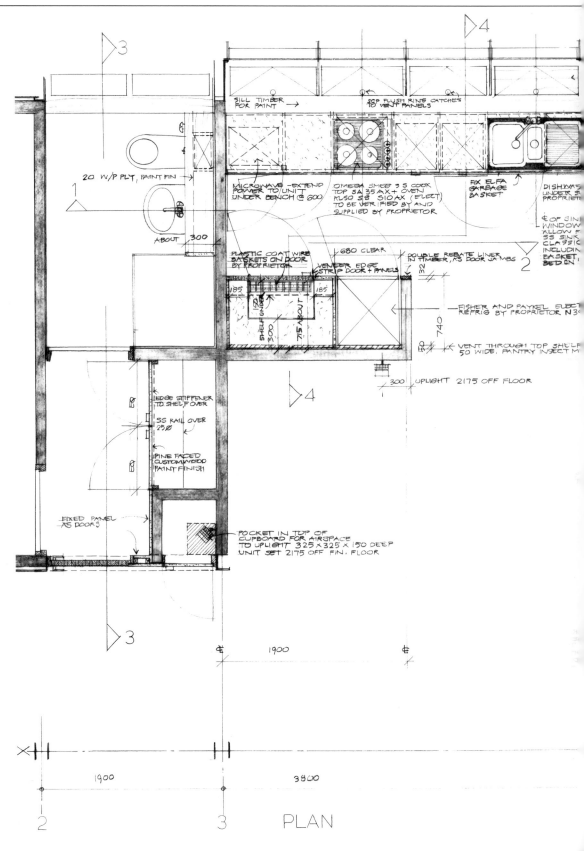

20 W/P PLY, PAINT FIN →

1

ABOUT 300

SILL TIMBER
FOR PAINT →

SCP FLUSH RING CATCHES
TO VENT PANELS

MICROWAVE - EXTEND
POWER TO UNIT
UNDER BENCH @ 600

OMEGA SMEE 3 S COOK
TOP SA 35 AX + OVEN
ALSO S/6 510 AX (ELECT)
TO BE VERIFIED BY AND
SUPPLIED BY PROPRIETOR

FIX ELFA
GARBAGE
BASKET

DISHWAS
UNDER S
PROPRIET

¢ OF SIN
WINDOW
ALLOW F
SS SINK
CLASSIC
INCLUDIN
BASKET
BED ON

PLASTIC COAT WIRE
BASKETS ON DOOR
BY PROPRIETOR

680 CLEAR

DOUBLE REBATE LINER
IN TIMBER, AS DOOR JAMBS

VENEER EDGE
STRIP DOOR + PANELS

2

185

185

32

SHELF UNDER   300   715 ABOUT

300

740

FISHER AND PAYKEL ELEC
REFRIG BY PROPRIETOR N3

VENT THROUGH TOP SHELF
50 WIDE. PANTRY INSECT M

4

300   UPLIGHT 2175 OFF FLOOR

EDGE STIFFENER
TO SHELF OVER

SS RAIL OVER
25Ø

PINE FACED
CUSTOMWOOD
PAINT FINISH

FIXED PANEL
AS DOORS →

POCKET IN TOP OF
CUPBOARD FOR AIRSPACE
TO UPLIGHT 325 X 325 X 150 DEEP
UNIT SET 2175 OFF FIN. FLOOR

3

1900

1900

3800

2   3   PLAN

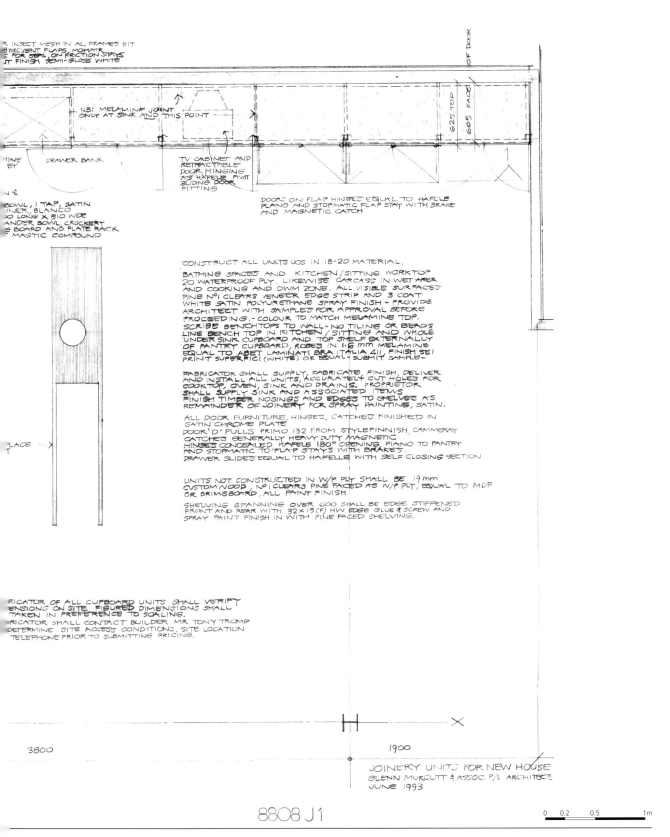

INSECT MESH IN AL. FRAMES FIT
WRC VENT FLAPS, MOHAIR
FOR SEAL ON FRICTION STAYS
JT FINISH SEMI-GLOSS WHITE

NB: MELAMINE JOINT
ONLY AT SINK AND THIS POINT

DRAWER BANK

TV CABINET AND
RETRACTABLE
DOOR HINGING
AS HAFELE PIVOT
SLIDING DOOR
FITTING

DOORS ON FLAP HINGES EQUAL TO HAFELE
PLANO AND STOPMATIC FLAP STAY WITH BRAKE
AND MAGNETIC CATCH

625 TOP
605 FACE

OF DOOR

BOWL, 1 TAP, SATIN
INER, BLANCO
O LONG X 510 WIDE
ANDER BOWL CROCKERY
BOARD AND PLATE RACK
MASTIC COMPOUND

PLACE

CONSTRUCT ALL UNITS UOS IN 18-20 MATERIAL,

BATHING SPACES AND KITCHEN/SITTING WORKTOP
20 WATERPROOF PLY, LIKEWISE CARCASS IN WET AREA
AND COOKING AND DWM ZONE, ALL VISIBLE SURFACES
PINE N°1 CLEARS VENEER EDGE STRIP AND 3 COAT
WHITE SATIN POLYURETHANE SPRAY FINISH - PROVIDE
ARCHITECT WITH SAMPLES FOR APPROVAL BEFORE
PROCEEDING.- COLOUR TO MATCH MELAMINE TOP,
SCRIBE BENCHTOPS TO WALL - NO TILING OR BEADS
LINE BENCH TOP IN KITCHEN/SITTING AND WHOLE
UNDER SINK CUPBOARD AND TOP SHELF EXTERNALLY
OF PANTRY CUPBOARD, ROBES IN 1.6 MM MELAMINE
EQUAL TO ABET LAMINATI BRA ITALIA 411 FINISH SEI
PRINT SUPERFICI (WHITE) OR EQUAL - SUBMIT SAMPLE-

FABRICATOR SHALL SUPPLY, FABRICATE, FINISH, DELIVER
AND INSTALL ALL UNITS, ACCURATELY CUT HOLES FOR
COOKTOP, OVEN, SINK AND DRAINS, PROPRIETOR
SHALL SUPPLY SINK AND ASSOCIATED ITEMS
FINISH TIMBER NOSINGS AND EDGES TO SHELVES AS
REMAINDER OF JOINERY FOR SPRAY PAINTING, SATIN,

ALL DOOR FURNITURE, HINGES, CATCHES FINISHED IN
SATIN CHROME PLATE
DOOR 'D' PULLS PRIMO 132 FROM STYLEFINNISH, CAMMERAY
CATCHES GENERALLY HEAVY DUTY MAGNETIC
HINGES CONCEALED, HAFELE 180° OPENING, PIANO TO PANTRY
AND STOPMATIC TO FLAP STAYS WITH BRAKES.
DRAWER SLIDES EQUAL TO HAFELLE WITH SELF CLOSING SECTION

UNITS NOT CONSTRUCTED IN W/P PLY SHALL BE 19 mm
CUSTOMWOOD, N°1 CLEARS PINE FACED AS W/P PLY, EQUAL TO MDF
OR BRIMSBOARD, ALL PAINT FINISH.

SHELVING SPANNING OVER 600 SHALL BE EDGE STIFFENED
FRONT AND REAR WITH 32 X 15 (F) HW EDGE GLUE & SCREW AND
SPRAY PAINT FINISH IN WITH PINE FACED SHELVING.

RICATOR OF ALL CUPBOARD UNITS SHALL VERIFY
ENSIONS ON SITE, FIGURED DIMENSIONS SHALL
TAKEN IN PREFERENCE TO SCALING.
RICATOR SHALL CONTACT BUILDER MR TONY TROMP
DETERMINE SITE ACCESS CONDITIONS, SITE LOCATION
TELEPHONE PRIOR TO SUBMITTING PRICING.

3800

1900

JOINERY UNITS FOR NEW HOUSE
GLENN MURCUTT & ASSOC. P/L ARCHITECT
JUNE 1993

8808 J1

0 0.2 0.5 1m

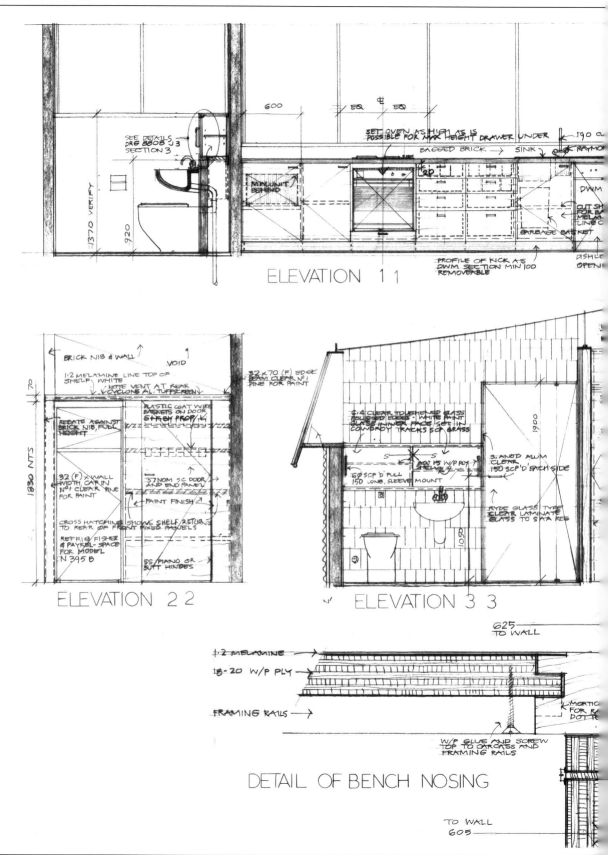

SEE DETAILS
DRG 8808 J3
SECTION 3

600

EQ ⊄ EQ

SET OVEN AS HIGH AS IS
POSSIBLE FOR MAX HEIGHT DRAWER UNDER

190 a

BAGGED BRICK

SINK

MOUNT
BEHIND

1370 VERIFY

920

PROFILE OF KICK AS
DWM SECTION MIN 100
REMOVEABLE

DWM

CUT SH
FOR EV
MELA
LINE C

GARBAGE BASKET

ASHLE
OPEN

ELEVATION 11

BRICK NIB & WALL   VOID

1:2 MELAMINE LINE TOP OF
SHELF WHITE
NOTE VENT AT REAR
VCYCLONE AL TUFFSCREEN

32 x 70 (F) EDGE
BEAM CLEAR N°1
PINE FOR PAINT

PLASTIC COAT WIRE
BASKETS ON DOOR
S+B BY PROP/K

REBATE AGAINST
BRICK NIB, FULL
HEIGHT

32 (F) X WALL
WIDTH, CARIN
N°1 CLEAR PINE
FOR PAINT

37 NOM SC DOOR
AND END PANEL

PAINT FINISH

CROSS HATCHING SHOWS SHELF RETURNS
TO REAR OF FRONT FIXED PANELS

REFRIG FISHER
& PAYKEL SPACE
FOR MODEL
N 395 B

SS PIANO OR
BUTT HINGES

1830 NTS

70

ELEVATION 22

6.4 CLEAR TOUGHENED GLASS
POLISHED EDGES - WHITE PAINT
GLASS INNER FACE SET IN
COWBOY TRACKS SC GLASS

3. ANOD ALUM
CLEAR
150 SCP'D EACH SIDE

60 SCP D' PULL
150 LONG, SLEEVE MOUNT

SOT 15 W/P PLY
SHELVES

1900

1050

RYDE GLASS TYPE
CLEAR LAMINATE
GLASS TO S+A RES

ELEVATION 33

625
TO WALL

1:2 MELAMINE

18-20 W/P PLY

FRAMING RAILS

MORTI
FOR R
DOT

W/P GLUE AND SCREW
TOP TO CARCASS AND
FRAMING RAILS

DETAIL OF BENCH NOSING

TO WALL
605

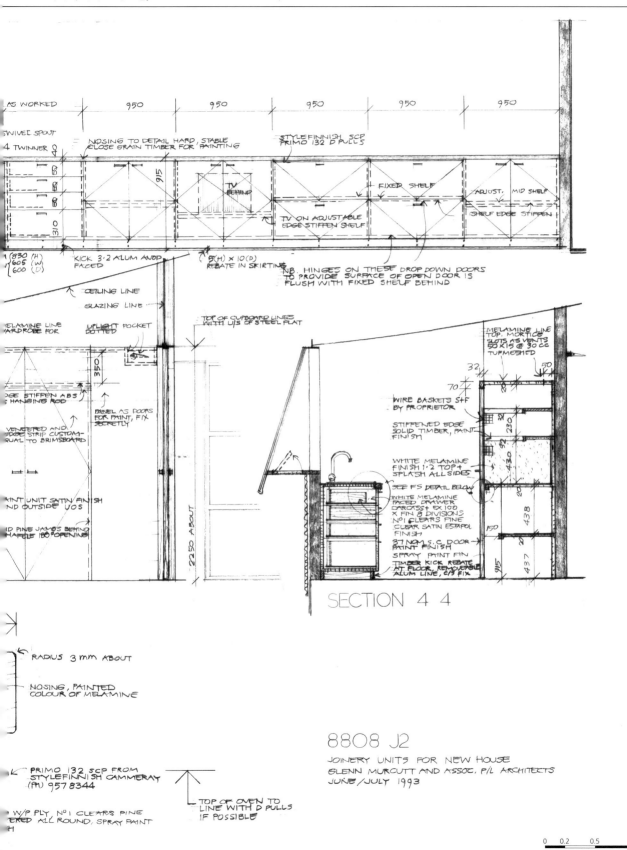

AS WORKED

950　950　950　950　950

SWIVEL SPOUT

4 TWINNER

915

310

NOSING TO DETAIL HARD, STABLE
CLOSE GRAIN TIMBER FOR PAINTING

STYLE FINNISH SCP
PRIMO 132 D PULLS

TV BEHIND

FIXED SHELF

ADJUST. MID SHELF

TV ON ADJUSTABLE
EDGE STIFFEN SHELF

SHELF EDGE STIFFEN

(830 (H)
(605 (W)
(600 (D)

KICK 3·2 ALUM ANOD.
FACED

(5 (H) × 10 (D)
REBATE IN SKIRTING

N.B. HINGES ON THESE DROP DOWN DOORS
TO PROVIDE SURFACE OF OPEN DOOR IS
FLUSH WITH FIXED SHELF BEHIND

CEILING LINE

GLAZING LINE

MELAMINE LINE
WARDROBE FOR

UPLIGHT POCKET
DOTTED

TOP OF CUPBOARD LINES
WITH U/S OF STEEL FLAT

MELAMINE LINE
TOP, MORTICE
SLOTS AS VENTS
50 × 15 @ 30 CC
TUFMESHED

350

32

70

50

EDGE STIFFEN ABS
HANGING ROD

PANEL AS DOORS
FOR PAINT, FIX
SECRETLY

WIRE BASKETS S+F
BY PROPRIETOR

STIFFENED EDGE
SOLID TIMBER, PAINT
FINISH

230

VENEERED AND
EDGE STRIP CUSTOM-
QUAL TO BRIMSBOARD

WHITE MELAMINE
FINISH 1·2 TOP +
SPLASH ALL SIDES

430

438

SEE FS DETAIL BELOW

PAINT UNIT SATIN FINISH
AND OUTSIDE UOS

2250 ABOUT

WHITE MELAMINE
FACED DRAWER
CARCASS + EX 100
× FIN 8 DIVISIONS
N°1 CLEARS PINE
CLEAR SATIN ESTAPOL
FINISH

D PINE JAMBS BEHIND
HAFELE 180°OPENING

37 NOM S.C. DOOR
PAINT FINISH

SPRAY PAINT FIN

150

915

437

TIMBER KICK REBATE
AT FLOOR, REMOVEABLE
ALUM LINE, C/S FIX

SECTION 4 4

RADIUS 3 mm ABOUT

NOSING, PAINTED
COLOUR OF MELAMINE

8808 J2

JOINERY UNITS FOR NEW HOUSE
GLENN MURCUTT AND ASSOC. P/L ARCHITECTS
JUNE/JULY 1993

PRIMO 132 SCP FROM
STYLE FINNISH CAMMERAY
(PH) 957 8344

W/P PLY N°1 CLEARS PINE
ERED ALL ROUND, SPRAY PAINT
H

TOP OF OVEN TO
LINE WITH D PULLS
IF POSSIBLE

0　0.2　0.5　1m

「リドコ」社製ガラス引戸、水抜き穴、鉄骨柱への取り付
きを示した平面詳細図。右手の玄関ロビーの奥行きに3
枚の引戸が収納される。

Large scale plan detail showing 'Lidco' sliding glazed
screens, drainage holes and connection to structural
steel column. The dimensions of the entry lobby
accommodate three sliding screens, allowing the glazed
wall to be completely slid away.

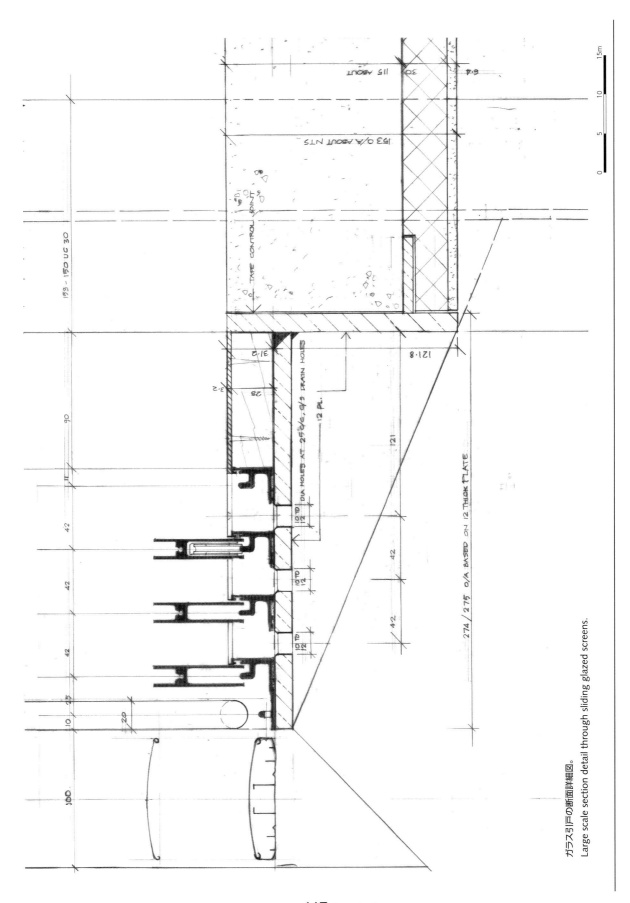

ガラス引戸の断面詳細図。
Large scale section detail through sliding glazed screens.

Marika-Alderton House

1991-94 Eastern Arnhem Land, Northern Territory

海抜3m。季節風のもたらす雨期がある熱帯気候。
熱帯低気圧接近時の満潮浸水深さ500mm。雨期の夏、乾期の冬。
夏の気温は33度前後、北西の熱い風が吹く。冬は南東の風が吹き、
25度を下らず、冬の夜の最低気温は20度。砂質、水はけは良い。

Altitude: 3m above sea level. Monsoonal tropical climate.
Subject to occasional tidal flooding 500mm deep during
cyclones. Wet summers, dry winters. Summer, circa 33 deg C,
hot north-west winds. Winter south-east winds, temperatures
rarely below 25 deg C with lows of 20 deg C on winter nights.
Sandy soil with good drainage.

Eastern Arnhem Land

Darwin

Northern
Territory

Western Australia

Queensland

South Australia

○ Brisbane

New South Wales

Adelaide

○ Sydney

Victoria

Melbourne

淡水池と浜辺の間にある砂地からもち上げられた高床の住居として
考えられた、初期の地理的断面スケッチ。マーカットは、周辺の
多様な植生と卓越風も書き留めている。

Early site study/sectional sketch showing the house as a raised
pavilion on a sand spit between a freshwater lagoon and the beach.
Murcutt notes the presence of various vegetation types
and prevailing winds.

EUCALYPTS
PALMS (WALKING STICK ?)
CYCADS
BRACYCHITON (KURRAJONG ?) RED

++++

Fresh
Mang

Yirrkala Thoughts.

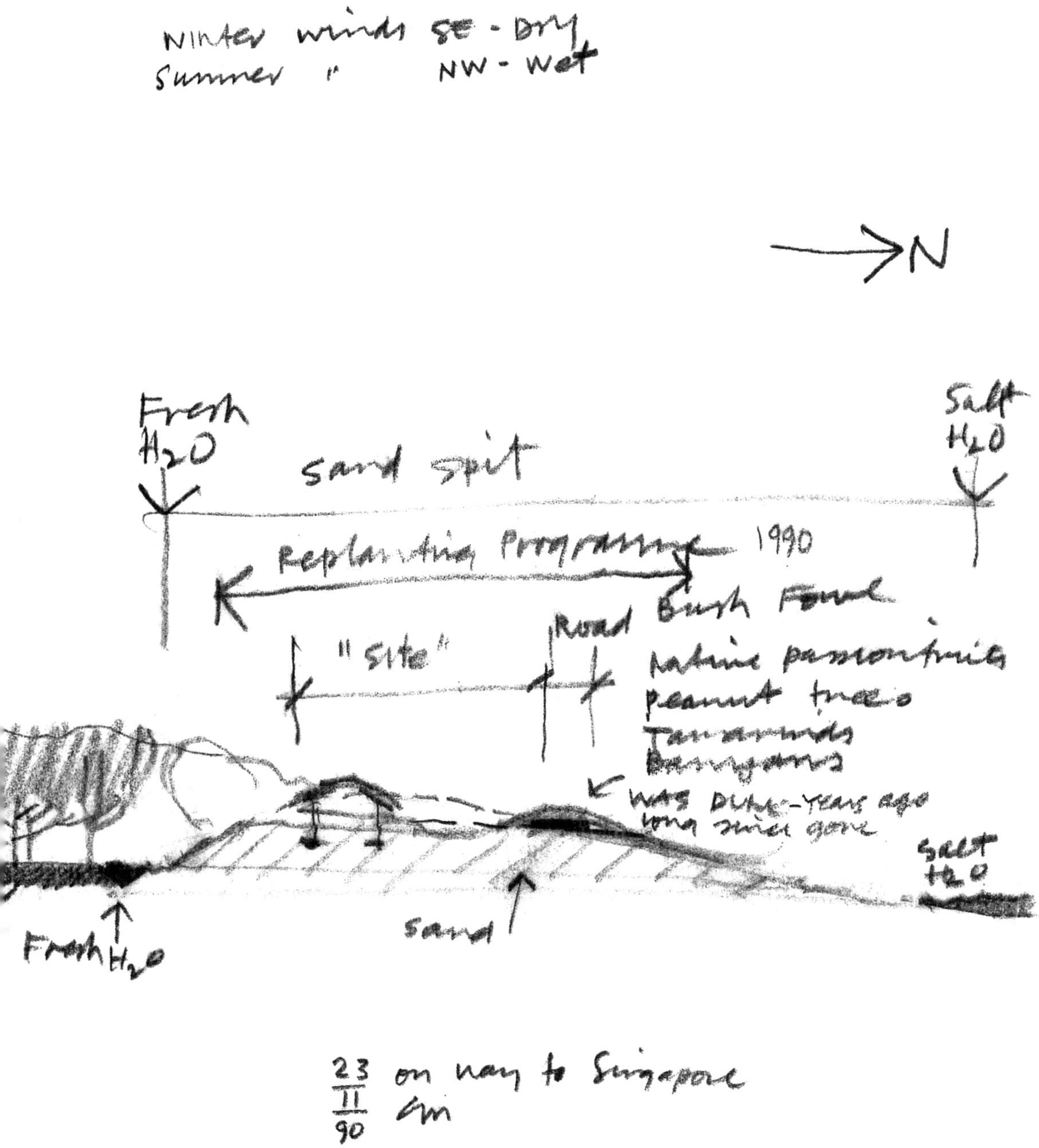

Winter winds SE - Dry
Summer " NW - Wet

$\rightarrow$ N

Fresh
H_2O

Salt
H_2O

sand spit

Replanting Programme — 1990

"Site"

Road Bush Food

native passionfruits
peanut trees
Tamarinds
Banyans

WAS DUNE - Years ago
long since gone

SALT
H_2O

Fresh H_2O

sand

$\frac{23}{\frac{II}{90}}$ on way to Singapore
GM

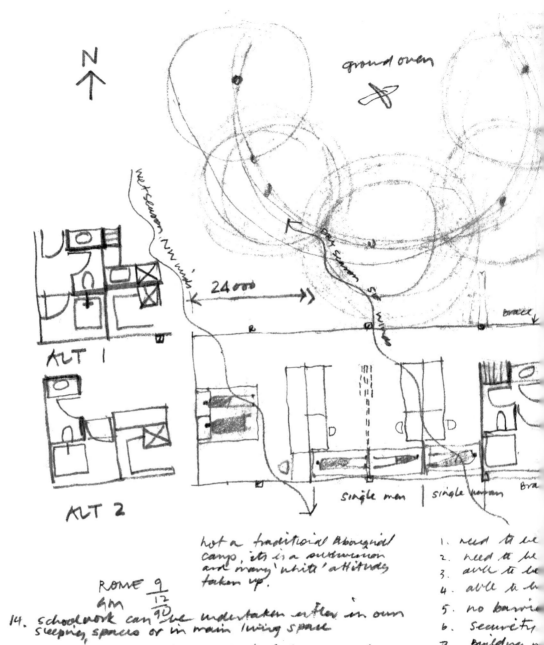

N

ground oven

wet season NW winds

24 000

ground oven

dry summer

SW winds

brace

ALT 1

ALT 2

single man | single woman | Bra

not a traditional Aboriginal camp, it's a subdivision and many 'white' attitudes taken up.

ROME 9
        6m 12
            90

14. schoolwork can be undertaken either in own sleeping spaces or in main living space

15 Provides standard of comfort of European house

1. need to be
2. need to be
3. able to be
4. able to be
5. no barrie
6. security
7. building in winter
8. house no
9. Food all
10. off grou
11. Timber f
12. no brea
13. consum

平面ダイアグラムと、マーカットが施主家族との対話から記した
機能的な必要事項と周辺環境への配慮。

Diagrammatic plan sketches with notes indicating functional
priorities and environmental considerations that Murcutt
developed in discussion with the client family.

"Efficient use of funds is certainly one of the criteria the Department
(of construction) uses to judge the performance of an Aboriginal housing association.
Specifically Aboriginal people, trying to develop their own skills in
specifically Aboriginal way, it can be a devastating weapon"
M HEPPELL

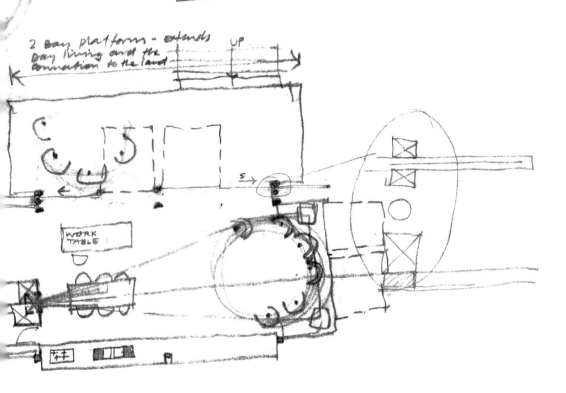

2 Bay platform - extends
Day living and the
connection to the land

UP

S

WORK
TABLE

...e to see activities outside here going on
to see horizon + weather changes and movements of people.
shade at look out - a "shade house" -
...tected from rain and yet not doll house up

...etween this and other buildings
...occupants whilst inside and particularly when asleep.
...act as a protector — summer, for there to be no sun and in
...e rule to open to north for warmth.
...welcome all comers - afford rejection - off ground helps and mobile
...be securely stored, out of sight + well ventilated. walls also help privacy
...rits in floors being less gritty + no blown sand
...smooth + can be cleaned
...ay which might give rise, if incorporated, to belief of entry of evil spirits
...ods can be stored safely, out of dust, sand + heat + wet, dogs cats + kids

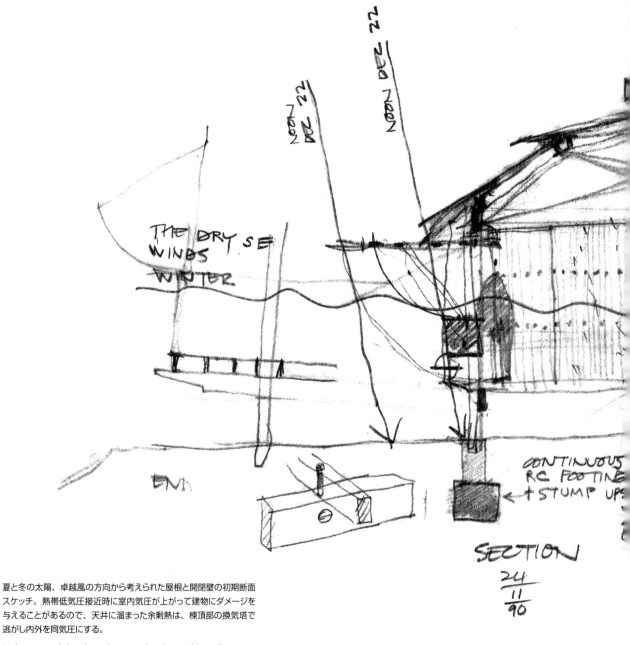

夏と冬の太陽、卓越風の方向から考えられた屋根と開閉壁の初期断面スケッチ。熱帯低気圧接近時に室内気圧が上がって建物にダメージを与えることがあるので、天井に溜まった余剰熱は、棟頂部の換気塔で逃がし内外を同気圧にする。

Early sectional sketch studying roof and operable wall systems in relation to summer and winter sun angles as well as prevailing breezes. Built-up heat is discharged via 'venturi' rotating ventilators in the roof which equalize internal and external air pressures during cyclones, minimizing the danger of damage.

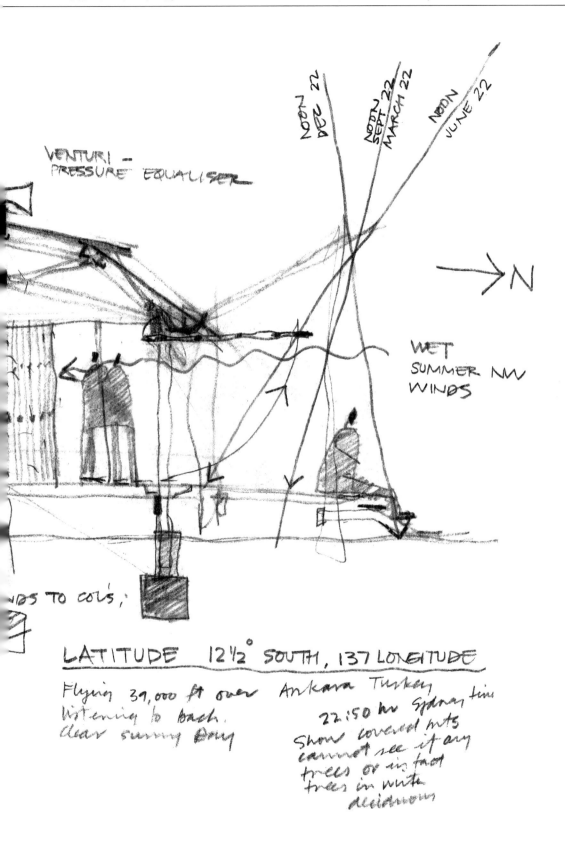

NOON DEC 22

NOON SEPT 22
MARCH 22

NOON JUNE 22

→N

VENTURI –
PRESSURE EQUALISER

WET
SUMMER NW
WINDS

...DS TO COL'S;

LATITUDE 12½° SOUTH, 137 LONGITUDE

Flying 39,000 ft over Ankara Turkey
listening to Bach.
clear sunny day

22:50 hr Sydney time
snow covered mts
cannot see if any
trees or in fact
trees in white
deciduous

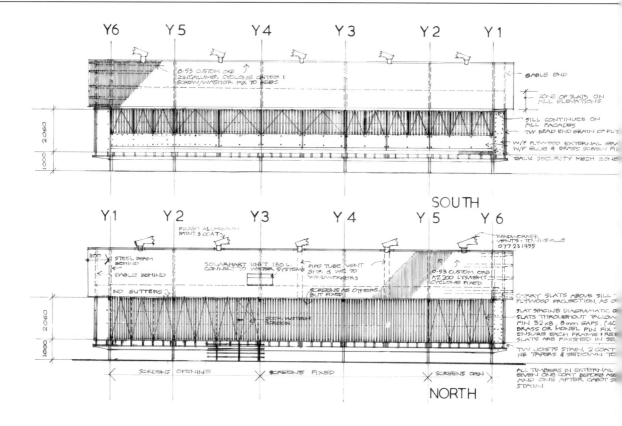

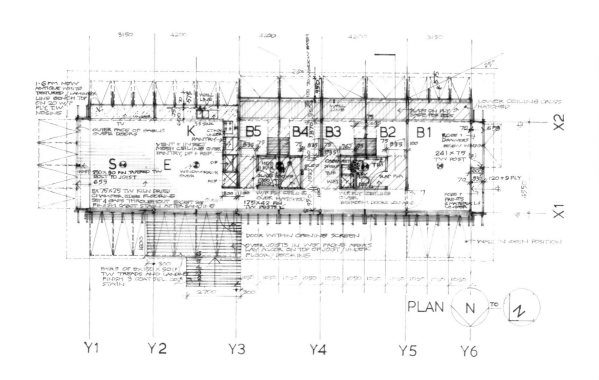

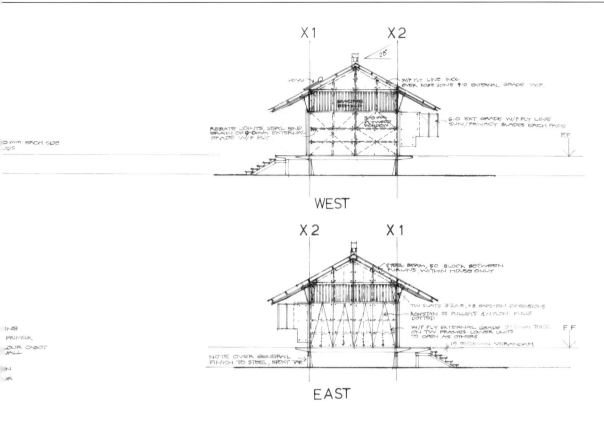

WEST

EAST

DOORS : TO BED 1, 820 X 2035 TIMBER LOUVRE, VENT. TO BEDS 2-5, 765 X 2035 " " W/P EXTERNAL GRADE

DOOR LOCKS + FURNITURE : STYLE-FINNISH ABLOY. ALLOW LOCKSETS KEYED ALIKE AND DBLT LOCK + INTERNAL SNIB ENTRY. TO WC & SHOWER ALLOW FOR PRIVACY LOCKS, ALL S.C.P. FINISH. TO ALL DOORS TO ROOMS, SHR & WC ALLOW FOR STYLE-FINNISH S.C.P. LEVER 20 CUPBOARD 'D' PULLS STYLE-FINNISH SCP PRIMO 142, HEAVY DUTY MAGNETIC LOCKS. HINGES 112 PAIR./DOOR INTERNALLY S.S. CUPBOARD HINGES S.S./BRASS 180° OPENING OFFSET PIVOT OR BUTT HINGES ON JAMB. DRAWER SLIDES BLUM. (ST. FINNISH 02 9576344)

WALL LINING : GENERALLY 75 & 100 X 50 STUD FRAMED WALLS TO COMPLY WITH ASA TIMBER FRAMING INCL PLATES, NOGGING, BRACING AND HOLDING DOWN FOR CATEGORY 1 TERRAIN CYCLONE. INTERNAL WALLS LINED WITH 6.0 MM EXTERNAL GRADE W/P. SEALED END GRAIN EXTERNAL PLY AS INTERNAL BUT THICKNESS TO ENGINEER'S DETAILS, SCREWS BRASS + GLUE

TIMBER FINISHES : FINISH SANDING + 3 COAT CLEAR SATIN POLYURETHANE INTERNALLY + 2 COAT OF SELECTED COLOUR CABOT STAIN OVER 1 COAT CABOT SEALER EXTERNALLY

: WINDWORKER VENTILATOR RIDGE MOUNT FOR 28° ROOF PITCH. 190 LATE GALV WINDWORKER WITH 3 COATS OF EPOXY PAINT, FROM ZINCALUME

ROOF SHEET : ALLOW FOR LYSAGHTS 0.53 CUSTOM ORB ZINCALUME AZ 200 CORRUGATED IRON IN SINGLE LENGTHS. FIXING SHALL COMPLY WITH TERRAIN CATEGORY 1, ZINCALUME CYCLONE WASHERS & SCREWS. ALLOW FOR ZINCALUME AZ 200 ROLL RIDGE CAP FIXED AS FOR ROOF SHEETING, + THS 14.50 /17 SCREWS + CYCLONE WASHERS.

BOLTS : ALL BOLTS HOT DIP 11% HARD GALV INCL WASHERS SIZED TO ENG'S DETAILS

TIMBERS : UOS SHALL BE N°1 CLEAR TALLOWOOD (EUCALYPTUS MICROCORYS) K.D. FOR DOORS, SLATS AND JOINERY AND DECKING/FLOORING TO M.C. OF 15% APPROX. FOR LOCAL CONDITIONS. TIMBER SIZING TO ENGINEERS DETAILS

GLAZING : ALLOW OVER SHR ALCOVE 2 SHEETS OF 8.0 CLEAR LAMINATED GLASS AND WC 1 SHEET 8.0 CLEAR LAMINATED. SHEETS 520 X 1550 EACH SILICONED & CLIPPED ONTO JOISTS

PLUMBING
WC : FOWLER PACIFIC COMPACT VIT CHINA WHITE
WC SEAT : FOWLER PREMIER TOP FIX WHITE
BASIN : FOWLER HAMILTON 600 VIT CHINA WHITE - 3 TAP HOLES
WM : BY PROPRIETOR
LAUNDRY TUB : CLARK 70 LIT. SUDSAVER MKII COMPACT SS + WHITE CABINET
REFRIG + DP : BY PROPRIETOR
COOKER + OVEN : ST GEORGE , NOTE COOKTOP COUNTER + SEP OVEN UNDER - WHITE
SINK : CLARK MONACO 9000 F RH 1 TAP HOLE SS PLUSHLINE, CUTTING BOARD, BASKET COLANDER
HWU : SOLARHART 180 LIT. UNIT FOR ROOF MOUNTING
PIPING : COPPER , SIZE AND HARDNESS TO SUIT PRESSURE AND FITTING DEMAND
TAPS + FITTINGS : RAYMOR T4 SERIES, WHITE HANDLES, SCP BRASS SKIRTS
ALLOW FOR STOP VALVES, MIXERS, TWINNER FOR SINGLE HOLE KITCHEN SINK AND 190 MM AERATED CURVED SPOUT; RECESSED SINK SET FOR LAUNDRY WITH WALL MOUNTED 190 MM CURVED SPOUT; FOR BASIN, 110 MM CONICAL SPOUT AERATED; FOR SHOWER MIXER AND 270 MM SCP DOUBLE ELBOW ADJUST, SET ROSS 1800 TO MOUNTING OFF FLOOR, LDRY HOSE COCKS, + SINK SET, 190 SPT.

GARDEN TAPS : ALLOW 4 HOSE COCKS SET ON EACH CORNER OF HOUSE AT REAR OF COLUMNS - OUT OF VIEW, TURN SIDEWAYS. RISER SET AGAINST A WASTE LINE BACK FROM EDGE OF HOUSE

SUPPLY & WASTE LINES : CONNECT TO TOWN WATER AND SEWER LOCATED TO NORTH SIDE OF SITE ALL LINES CONCEALED FROM VIEW, SET MIN 1500 FROM EDGE OF BUILDING COLUMNS. VENTS CARRIED IN WALLS AND SET VERTICAL AND CLEAR OF VENT PIPE TO WINDWORKER BY 30 MM. COMPLY WITH THE REQUIREMENTS OF LOCAL W.S & DRAINAGE AUTHORITY. CONNECTION TO TOWN WATER IN COPPER - NO METER -
ALL WASTE, SUPPLY AND VENT LINES SET VERTICAL, TRAPS SET HARD AGAINST U/S OF FLOOR. WASTE FITTINGS C.P. BRASS BODIES.

TILING : ALLOW FOR TILING WALLS AND HOB TO SHOWER TO 2035, TO LAUNDRY AND TOILET TO 1200, JOHNSON 200 X 100, SATIN ALABASTER, BOND 1/2 ON SET ON 20 BRC SHEET INDUSTRIAL, SRC LAT WALL JUNCTION, W/P GLUE ALL TO LOCAL AUTHORITY REQUIREMENTS.
FLOOR TILED IN SHOWER MIRAGE TK9 SHEET 100 X 100 X 10 OR SQ END.
NB: IN AREAS OF WATER ADJACENT TO SHOWER, KITCHEN SINK, WC, BASIN, N. WALL AND LAUNDRY ALLOW FOR ALCOR LAID OVER JOISTS PRIOR TO NAILING FLOOR. TOILET PAPER HOLDER + 3 TOWEL RAILS SHR + 1 IN WC SCP LANE 770, 970, 820 L.

NB: READ IN CONJUNCTION WITH 1:20 SECTION DRAWING 9006 4^A REFER TO ENGINEERS DRAWING FOR ALL STRUCTURAL ELEMENTS INCLUDING FOOTINGS, COLUMNS, BEAMS, PURLINS, JOISTS, EAVES PURLIN PROFILES AND EXTERNAL GRADE WATERPROOF PLY USED THROUGHOUT.

ALLOW FOR RONSTAN PULLEY BLOCKS IN SS AND SYNTHETIC HORN CLEATS MONEL BOLT OR SCREW LOCATED, SS EYEBOLTS AND HOOKS & NYLON CHORD + SS HINGES SCP BOLTS FOR OPENING SCREENS AND WINDOWS 2/UNIT.

9006·3^B

NEW HOUSE
YIRRKALA
GLENN MURCUTT AND ASSOCIATES PTY LTD ARCHITECTS
JAN 1992

0 1 2   5m

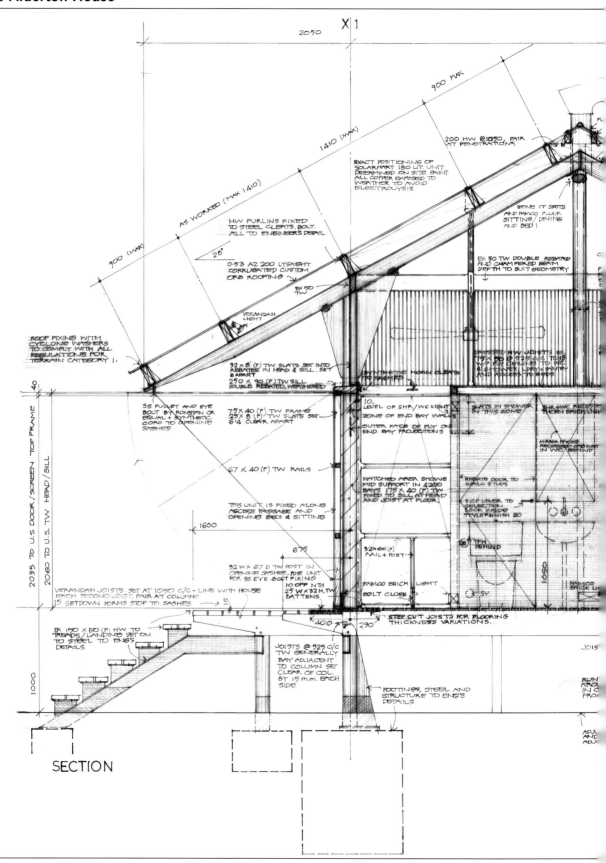

SECTION

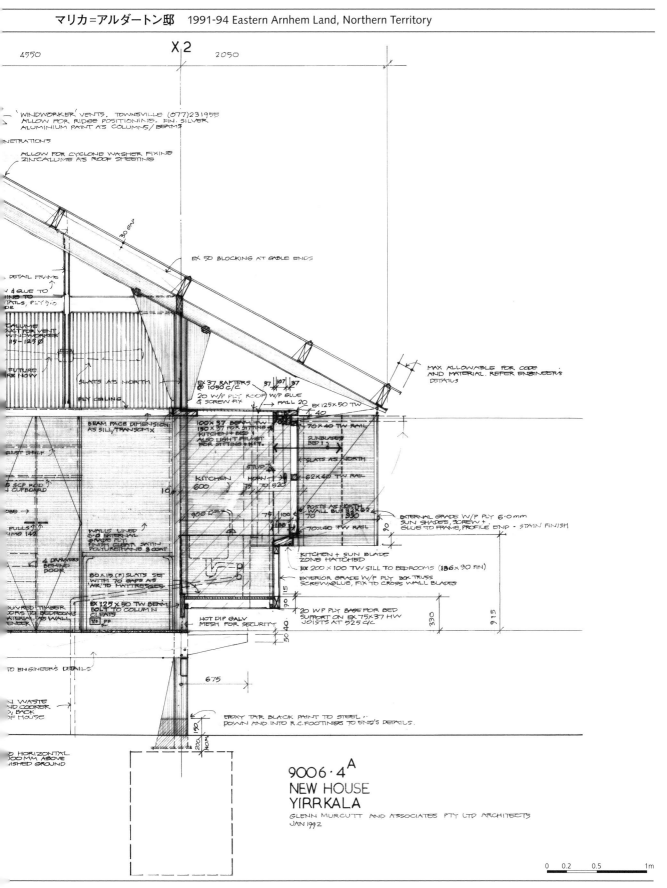

X 2

4550　　　　2050

'WINDWORKER' VENTS. TOWNSVILLE (077)231955
ALLOW FOR RIDGE POSITIONING. FIN. SILVER
ALUMINIUM PAINT AS COLUMNS/BEAMS
PENETRATIONS

ALLOW FOR CYCLONE WASHER FIXING
ZINCALUME AS ROOF SHEETING

EX 50 BLOCKING AT GABLE ENDS

DETAIL FRAME
& GLUE TO
TAILS, PLY 9·10
DE

CALUME
DUCT VENT
WINDWORKER
115-125 Ø

FUTURE
E NOW

SLATS AS NORTH

PLY CEILING

MAX ALLOWABLE FOR CODE
AND MATERIAL. REFER ENGINEERS
DETAILS

EX 37 RAFTERS　37 107 37
@ 1050 C/C
20 W/P PLY ROOF W/P GLUE
& SCREW FIX　←　FALL 20

EX 125 x 50 TW
40

BEAM FACE DIMENSION
AS SILL/TRANSOM X

100 x 37 BEAM W
150 x 37 FOR SITTING
KITCHEN & BED
ALSO LIGHT PELMET
FOR SITTING + KIT.

70 x 40 TW RAIL

SUNBLADES
BED 1

SLATS AS NORTH

DUST SHELF

STUD

KITCHEN
600　HORN　75　70 520

62 x 40 TW RAIL

5 SCP ROD
CUPBOARD

16

OBE →

900

75　100

PULLS
AND 142

WALLS LINED
6·0 EXTERNAL
GRADE PLY
FINISH CLEAR SATIN
POLYURETHANE 3 COAT

188

POSTS AS NORTH
WALL BUT 35 x 62
70　　350

90

70 x 40 TW RAIL

EXTERNAL GRADE W/P PLY 6·0 mm
SUN SHADES. SCREW +
GLUE TO FRAME, PROFILE END - STAIN FINISH

4 DRAWERS
BEHIND
DOOR

80 x 15 (F) SLATS SET
WITH 70 GAPS AS
'AIR' TO MATTRESSES

KITCHEN + SUN BLADE
ZONE HATCHED

EX 200 x 100 TW SILL TO BEDROOMS (186 x 90 FIN)

EXTERIOR GRADE W/P PLY BOX TRUSS
SCREW & GLUE, FIX TO CROSS WALL BLADES

LOUVRED TIMBER
ORS TO BEDROOMS
ATERIAL AS WALL
ENDER

EX 125 x 50 TW BEAM
BOLT TO COLUMN
CLEATS

90　115

90　40

20 WP PLY BASE FOR BED
SUPPORT ON EX 75 x 37 HW
JOISTS AT 525 C/C

330

915

HOT DIP GALV
MESH FOR SECURITY

50　40

TO ENGINEER'S DETAILS

675

WASTE
ND COOKER
, BACK
OF HOUSE

EPOXY TAR BLACK PAINT TO STEEL
DOWN AND INTO R.C. FOOTINGS TO ENG'S DETAILS.

150

200

HORIZONTAL
00 MM ABOVE
ISHED GROUND

9006·4 A
NEW HOUSE
YIRRKALA
GLENN MURCUTT AND ASSOCIATES PTY LTD ARCHITECTS
JAN 1992

0　0.2　0.5　1m

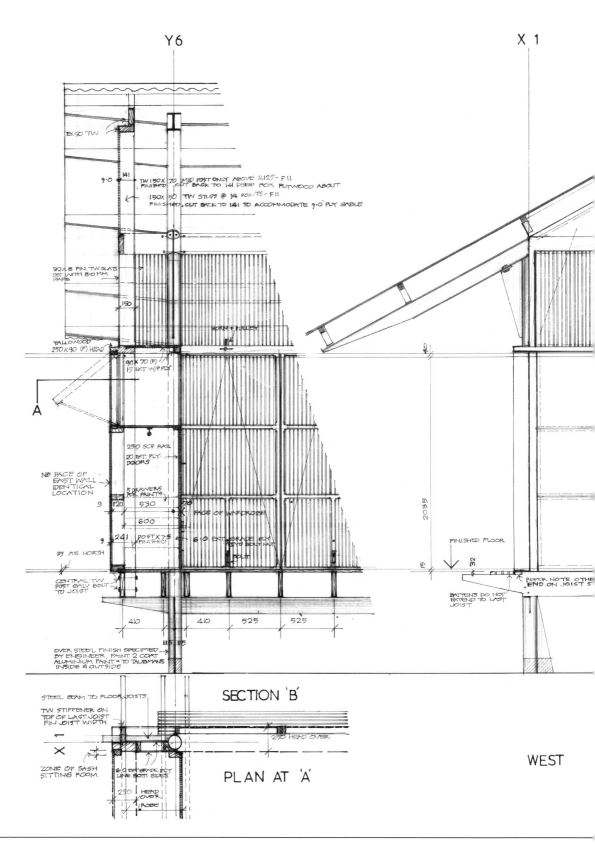

Y6

X 1

EX 50 TW

TW 150 X 70 MID POST ONLY ABOVE 2125 - F 11
FINISHED, CUT BACK TO 141 DEEP FOR PLYWOOD ABOUT
150 X 50 TW STUDS @ 1/4 POINTS - F 11
FINISHED, CUT BACK TO 141 TO ACCOMMODATE 9.0 PLY GABLE

9.0

141

32 X 8 FIN. TW SLATS
SET WITH 8.0 MM
GAPS

150

TALLOWOOD
250 X 90 (F) HEAD

90 X 70 (F)
15 EXT W/P PLY

HORN + PULLEY

A

250 SCP RAIL
20 EXT PLY
DOORS

NO FACE OF
EAST WALL
IDENTICAL
LOCATION

5 DRAWERS
FOR PRINTS

FACE OF WARDROBE

9   120   530   70

600

9   241   POST X 75   6.0 EXT GRADE PLY
FINISHED

15 AS NORTH

CENTRAL TW
POST GALV BOLT
TO JOIST

410   410   525   525

FINISHED FLOOR

2035

15   32

REFER NOTE OTHE
END ON JOIST S

BATTENS DO NOT
EXTEND TO LAST
JOIST

OVER STEEL FINISH SPECIFIED
BY ENGINEER, PAINT 2 COAT
ALUMINIUM PAINT = TO TAUBMANS
INSIDE & OUTSIDE

115 115

STEEL BEAM TO FLOOR JOISTS

TW STIFFENER ON
TOP OF LAST JOIST
FIN JOIST WIDTH

1

X

ZONE OF SASH
SITTING ROOM

6.0 EXT GRADE PLY
LINE BOTH SIDES

250 HEAD
OVER
ROBE

250 HEAD OVER

SECTION 'B'

PLAN AT 'A'

WEST

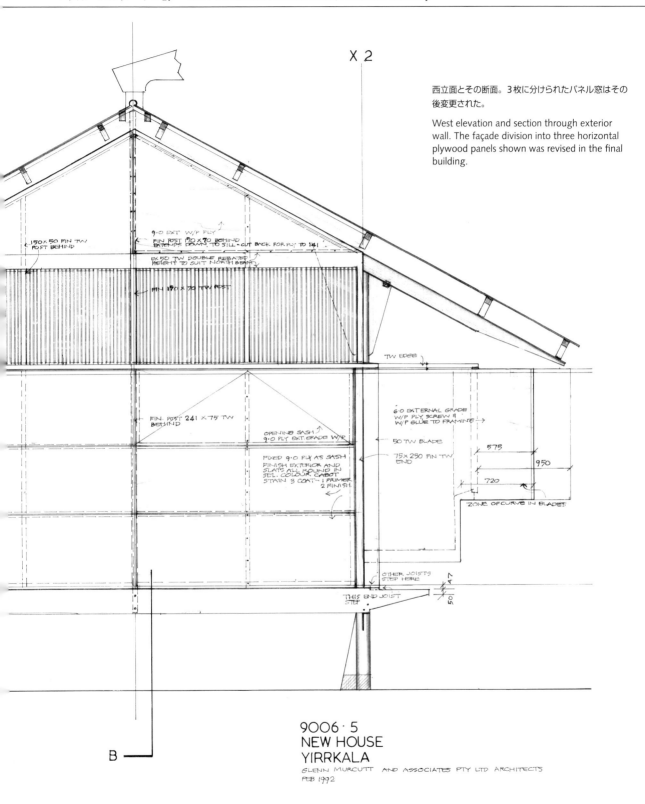

X 2

西立面とその断面。3枚に分けられたパネル窓はその後変更された。

West elevation and section through exterior wall. The façade division into three horizontal plywood panels shown was revised in the final building.

150 X 50 FIN TW POST BEHIND

9·0 EXT W/P PLY BEHIND
FIN POST 150 X 70 BEHIND
EXTENDS DOWN TO SILL - CUT BACK FOR PLY TO 141

8X 50 TW DOUBLE REBATED
HEIGHT TO SUIT NORTH BEAM

FIN 150 X 70 TW POST

TW EDGE

FIN POST 241 X 75 TW BEHIND

6·0 EXTERNAL GRADE
W/P PLY SCREW &
W/P GLUE TO FRAMING

OPENING SASH
9·0 PLY EXT. GRADE W/R

50 TW BLADE

75 X 250 FIN TW END

575

950

FIXED 9·0 PLY AS SASH
FINISH EXTERIOR AND
SLATS ALL ROUND IN
SEL. COLOUR CABOT
STAIN 3 COAT - 1 PRIMER
2 FINISH

720

ZONE OF CURVE IN BLADES

OTHER JOISTS
STEP HERE

50 147

THIS END JOIST
STEP

B

9006 · 5
NEW HOUSE
YIRRKALA
GLENN MURCUTT AND ASSOCIATES PTY LTD ARCHITECTS
FEB 1992

0   0.2   0.5   1m

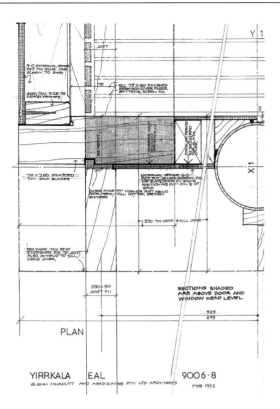

PLAN

YIRRKALA EAL 9006·8
GLENN MURCUTT AND ASSOCIATES PTY LTD ARCHITECTS FEB 1992

入口鎧戸の平面詳細図。突き上げの戸をドアとしても開けられる
ように考えられたスケッチ。

Detailed plan at screen door. The doors were designed to
push up and stay, and also partly enable to open as
a side-hinged door.

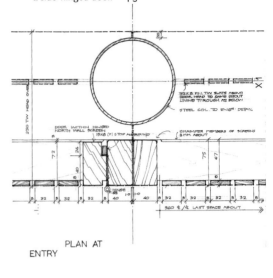

PLAN AT
ENTRY

YIRRKALA EAL 9006·6
GLENN MURCUTT AND ASSOCIATES PTY LTD ARCHITECTS FEB 1992

北東出隅部分の平面詳細図。
Detailed plan of north-east corner.

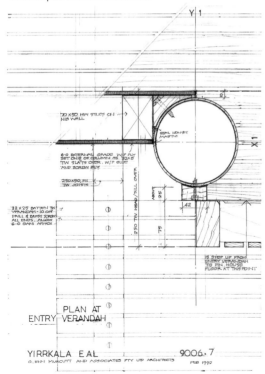

PLAN AT
ENTRY VERANDAH

YIRRKALA EAL 9006·7
GLENN MURCUTT AND ASSOCIATES PTY LTD ARCHITECTS FEB 1992

実現されなかった入口のベランダデッキの平面詳細図。
Detailed plan of unrealized entrance deck.

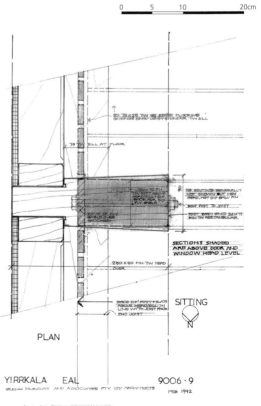

SITTING

PLAN

YIRRKALA EAL 9006·9
GLENN MURCUTT AND ASSOCIATES PTY LTD ARCHITECTS FEB 1992

突き上げ戸の平面詳細図。
Detailed plan of top-hinged panel windows.

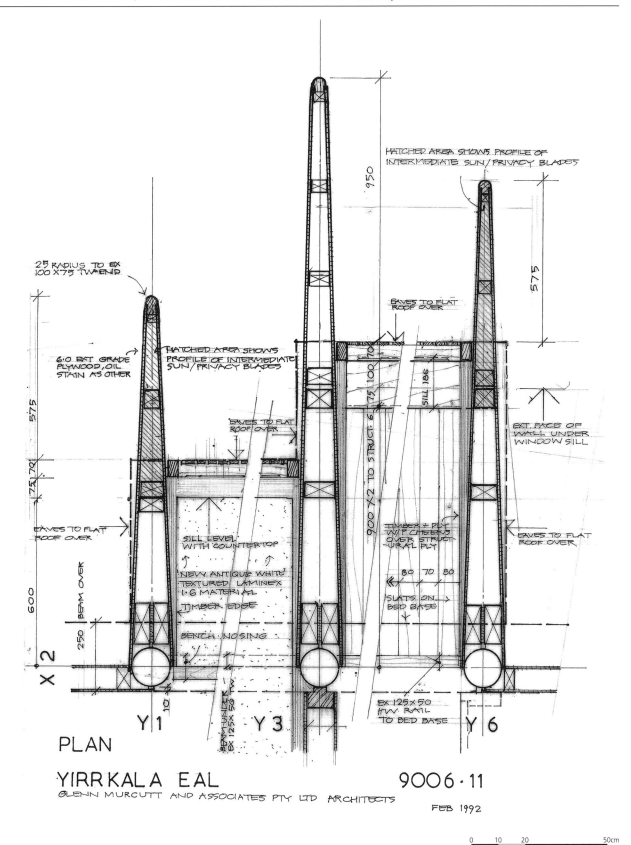

25 RADIUS TO EX
100 X75 TW+END

6.0 EXT GRADE
PLYWOOD,OIL
STAIN AS OTHER

HATCHED AREA SHOWS
PROFILE OF INTERMEDIATE
SUN/PRIVACY BLADES

575

75.70

EAVES TO FLAT
ROOF OVER

600

250 BEAM OVER

SILL LEVEL
WITH COUNTERTOP

NEW ANTIQUE WHITE
TEXTURED LAMINEX
1.6 MATERIAL

TIMBER EDGE

BENCH NOSING

BEAM UNDER
EX 125 X 50 TW

10

Y 1

PLAN

YIRRKALA EAL

GLENN MURCUTT AND ASSOCIATES PTY LTD ARCHITECTS

EAVES TO FLAT
ROOF OVER

Y 3

HATCHED AREA SHOWS PROFILE OF
INTERMEDIATE SUN/PRIVACY BLADES

950

EAVES TO FLAT
ROOF OVER

575

175 100 70

SILL 186

900 X2 TO STRUCT 6

EXT. FACE OF
WALL UNDER
WINDOW SILL

TIMBER + PLY
W/F CHEEKS
OVER STRUCT
-URAL PLY

80 70 80

SLATS ON
BED BASE

EX 125 X 50
H/W RAIL
TO BED BASE

EAVES TO FLAT
ROOF OVER

Y 6

9006·11

FEB 1992

0   10   20   50cm

Murcutt Guest Studio

1992 Kempsey, New South Wales

海抜14m。温暖気候でも暑い地域、亜熱帯に近い。多雨。
夏の気温は26度前後で、北東の風により涼しさがもたらされる。
冬の気温は18度前後。水はけの悪い粘土層に建つ。

Altitude: 14m above sea level. Warm-temperate/sub-tropical climate. High rainfall. Summer, circa 26 deg C cooled by north-east winds. Winter circa 18 deg C. Clay soils with poor drainage.

ゲストルームと、増築されたバスルームの断面詳細図。実現され
たものは、両端のガラスを既存の木の壁にし、上部の三角形の
ガラスも考え直されている。

Section drawing through studio and new bathroom.
The glazing shown either side of the central windows
was revised and the built version has timber walls in this
location. The high triangular glass was also reconfigured.

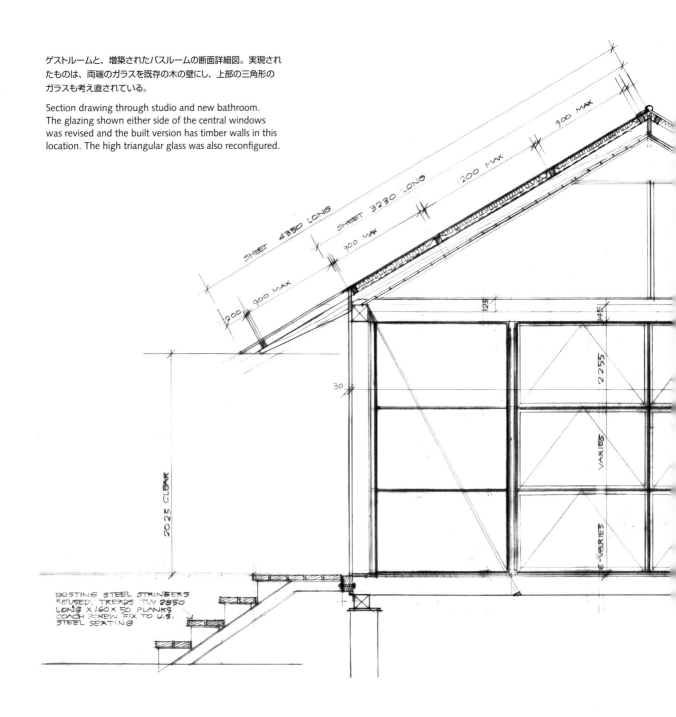

SECTION

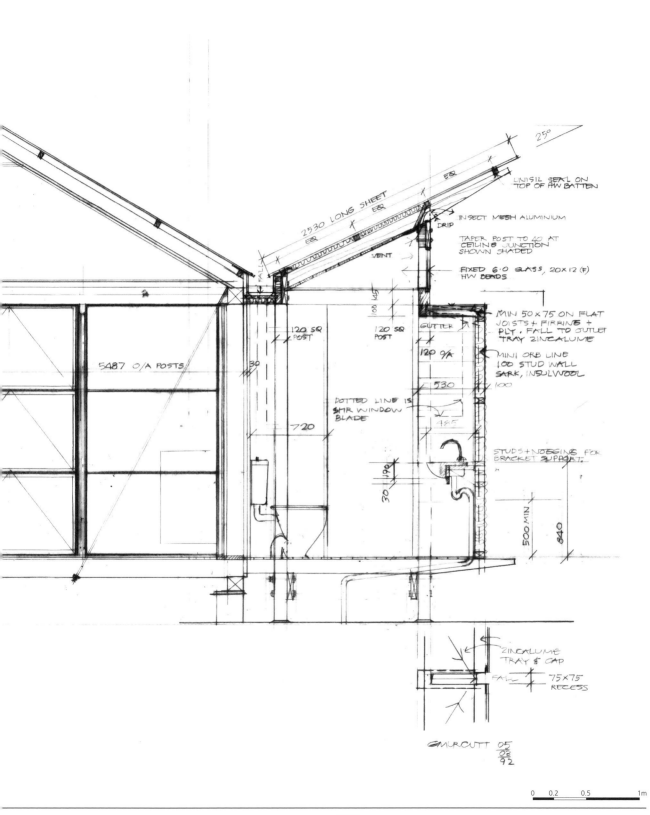

25°

UNISIL SEAL ON
TOP OF HW BATTEN

2530 LONG SHEET

EQ

EQ

EQ

INSECT MESH ALUMINIUM

DRIP

TAPER POST TO 40 AT
CEILING JUNCTION
SHOWN SHADED

VENT

FIXED 6·0 GLASS, 20×12 (F)
HW BEADS

FALL

100

145

120 SQ
POST

120 SQ
POST

GUTTER

MIN 50×75 ON FLAT
JOISTS + FIRRING +
PLY. FALL TO OUTLET
TRAY ZINCALUME

5487 O/A POSTS

30

120 %A

MINI ORB LINE
100 STUD WALL
SARK, INSULWOOL

100

720

530

DOTTED LINE IS
SHR WINDOW
BLADE

485

STUDS + NOGGINS FOR
BRACKET SUPPORT.

30 |190

500 MIN

840

ZINCALUME
TRAY & CAP

FALL

75×75
RECESS

GMURCUTT 05
08
92

0   0.2   0.5   1m

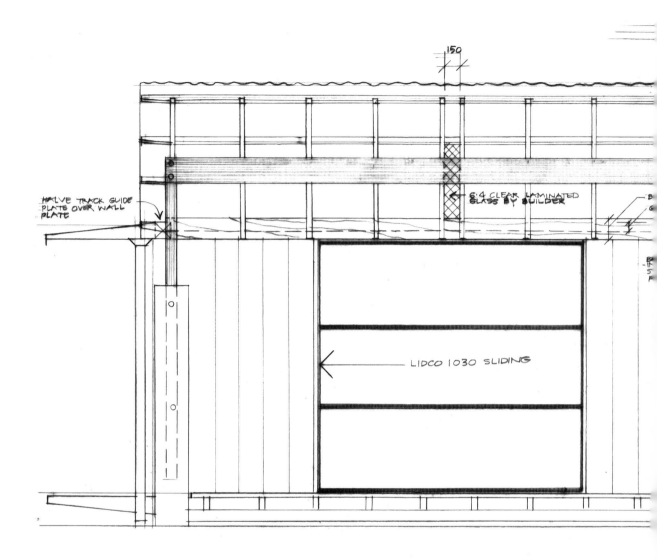

150

HALVE TRACK GUIDE
PLATE OVER WALL
PLATE

6·4 CLEAR LAMINATED
GLASS BY BUILDER

LIDCO 1030 SLIDING

ELEVATION

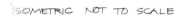

ISOMETRIC NOT TO SCALE

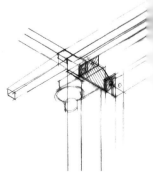

北立面図、部分平面図、エントランスポーチの断面図。

Northern elevation, part plan and detailed short
section through entry porch.

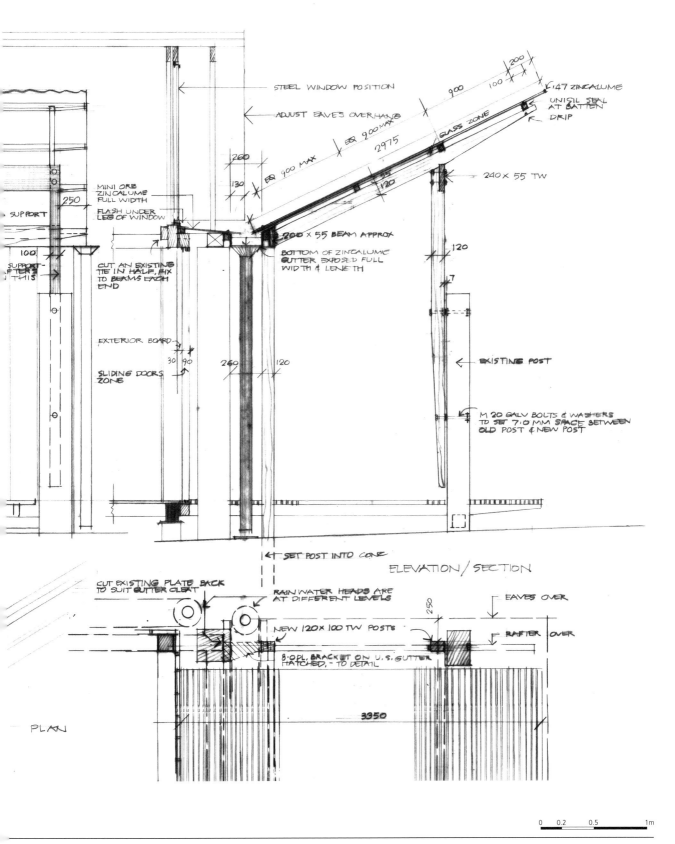

STEEL WINDOW POSITION

ADJUST EAVES OVERHANG

200

900   100

.47 ZINCALUME

UNISIL SEAL
AT BATTEN

DRIP

EQ 900 MAX   GLASS ZONE

2975

EQ 900 MAX

260

130

55

120

240 × 55 TW

SUPPORT

250

MINI ORB
ZINCALUME
FULL WIDTH

FLASH UNDER
LEG OF WINDOW

200 × 55 BEAM APPROX

BOTTOM OF ZINCALUME
GUTTER EXPOSED FULL
WIDTH & LENGTH

120

100

SUPPORT
AFTER
THIS

CUT AN EXISTING
TIE IN HALF, FIX
TO BEAMS EACH
END

7

EXTERIOR BOARD

30 90

260   120

EXISTING POST

SLIDING DOORS
ZONE

M 20 GALV BOLTS & WASHERS
TO SET 7·0 MM SPACE BETWEEN
OLD POST & NEW POST

SET POST INTO CONC

ELEVATION / SECTION

CUT EXISTING PLATE BACK
TO SUIT GUTTER CLEAT

RAIN WATER HEADS ARE
AT DIFFERENT LEVELS

250

EAVES OVER

NEW 120 × 100 TW POSTS

RAFTER OVER

8·0 PL. BRACKET ON U.S. GUTTER
HATCHED, — TO DETAIL

3350

PLAN

0   0.2   0.5   1m

Fletcher-Page House

1996-98 Kangaroo Valley, New South Wales

海抜200m。北東方向からの陸をわたる涼しい海風の、多少の影響がある温暖気候。良好な雨量。熱帯雨林に近接する。夏の気温は26度、冬の気温は23度前後だが、最低気温は5度まで下がる。火山灰土壌、砂岩地質で水はけは良い。

Altitude: 200m above sea level. Temperate climate with some influence from cooling north-east on-shore winds. Good rainfall. At edge of rainforest. Summer, circa 26 deg C. Winter, circa 23 deg C with lows of 5 deg C. Volcanic and sandstone soils with good drainage.

Darwin

Northern Territory

Queensland

Western Australia

South Australia

New South Wales

Adelaide

○ Brisbane

○ Sydney

Victoria

Melbourne

Kangaroo Valley

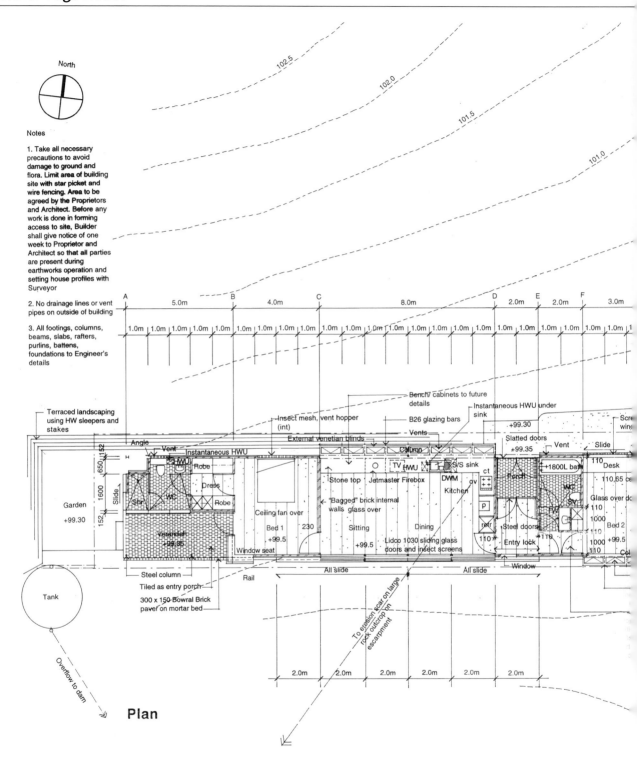

Plan

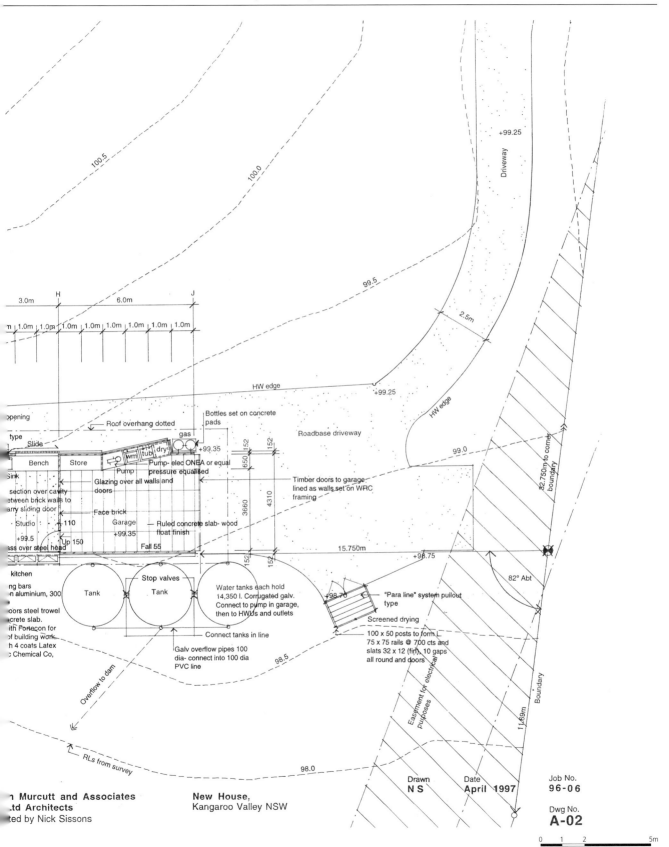

+99.25

Driveway

100.5

100.0

99.5

2.5m

99.5

HW edge

+99.25

HW edge

32.750m to corner boundary

99.0

3.0m H 6.0m J

1.0m 1.0m 1.0m 1.0m 1.0m 1.0m 1.0m 1.0m

opening

Roof overhang dotted

type

Slide

Bench Store

Sink

section over cavity
between brick walls to
carry sliding door

Studio 110

+99.5

Up 150

ass over steel head

kitchen

ng bars
n aluminium, 300

oors steel trowel
crete slab.

ith Fortecon for
f building work
h 4 coats Latex
c Chemical Co,

Bottles set on concrete
pads

gas

wm tub dry +99.35

Pump

Pump- elec ONEA or equal
pressure equalised

Glazing over all walls and
doors

Face brick
Garage
+99.35

Ruled concrete slab- wood
float finish

Fall 55

Roadbase driveway

152 152

650 152

3660 4310

Timber doors to garage
lined as walls set on WRC
framing

15.750m

+98.75

152 152

+98.70

82° Abt

Tank Tank Stop valves

Water tanks each hold
14,350 l. Corrugated galv.
Connect to pump in garage,
then to HWUs and outlets

Connect tanks in line

Galv overflow pipes 100
dia- connect into 100 dia
PVC line

98.5

"Para line" system pullout
type

Screened drying

100 x 50 posts to form L.
75 x 75 rails @ 700 cts and
slats 32 x 12 (fin), 10 gaps
all round and doors

Overflow to dam

RLs from survey

98.0

Easement for electrical
purposes

Boundary

11.69m

n Murcutt and Associates
td Architects
ed by Nick Sissons

New House,
Kangaroo Valley NSW

Drawn	Date	Job No.
N S	April 1997	96-06

Dwg No.
A-02

0 1 2 5m

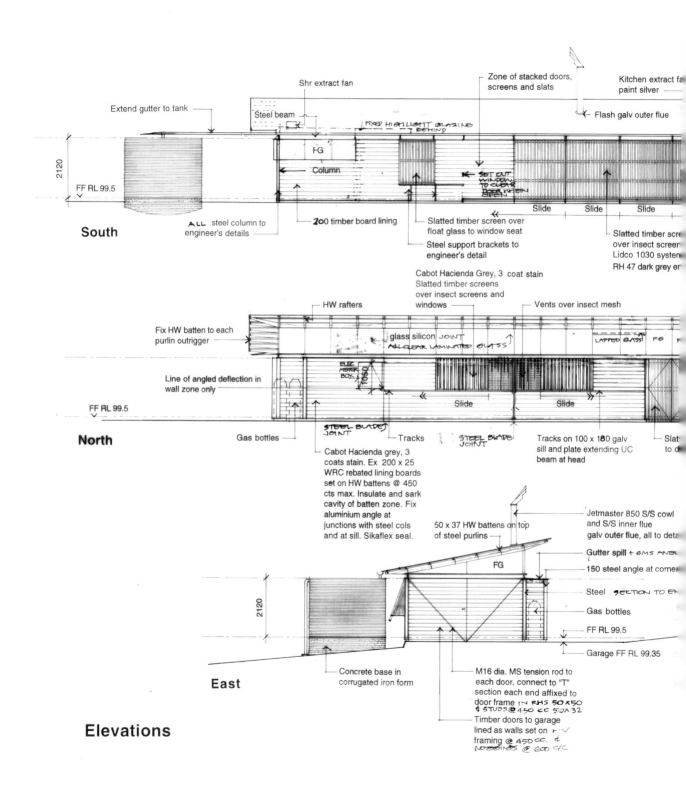

South

Extend gutter to tank

2120

FF RL 99.5

Shr extract fan

Steel beam

FIXED HIGHLIGHT GLAZING BEHIND

FG

Column

ALL steel column to engineer's details

200 timber board lining

Zone of stacked doors, screens and slats

Kitchen extract fan paint silver

Flash galv outer flue

SET OUT WINDOW TO CLEAR DOOR WHEN OPEN

Slide   Slide   Slide

Slatted timber screen over float glass to window seat

Steel support brackets to engineer's detail

Slatted timber scre over insect screen Lidco 1030 system RH 47 dark grey er

Cabot Hacienda Grey, 3 coat stain Slatted timber screens over insect screens and windows

North

HW rafters

Vents over insect mesh

Fix HW batten to each purlin outrigger

glass silicon JOINT
ALL CLEAR LAMINATED GLASS

LAPPED GLASS   FG

Line of angled deflection in wall zone only

ELEC METER BOX

FF RL 99.5

Slide   Slide

Gas bottles

STEEL BLADE JOINT

Tracks

STEEL BLADE JOINT

Tracks on 100 x 180 galv sill and plate extending UC beam at head

Slat to d

Cabot Hacienda grey, 3 coats stain. Ex 200 x 25 WRC rebated lining boards set on HW battens @ 450 cts max. Insulate and sark cavity of batten zone. Fix aluminium angle at junctions with steel cols and at sill. Sikaflex seal.

50 x 37 HW battens on top of steel purlins

Jetmaster 850 S/S cowl and S/S inner flue galv outer flue, all to deta

Gutter spill + 6MS ANGL

150 steel angle at corner

Steel SECTION TO EN

Gas bottles

FF RL 99.5

Garage FF RL 99.35

East

2120

FG

Concrete base in corrugated iron form

M16 dia. MS tension rod to each door, connect to "T" section each end affixed to door frame IN RHS 50 x 50 & STUDS @ 450 CC 50 x 32

Timber doors to garage lined as walls set on HW framing @ 450 CC & NOGGINGS @ 600 C/C

Elevations

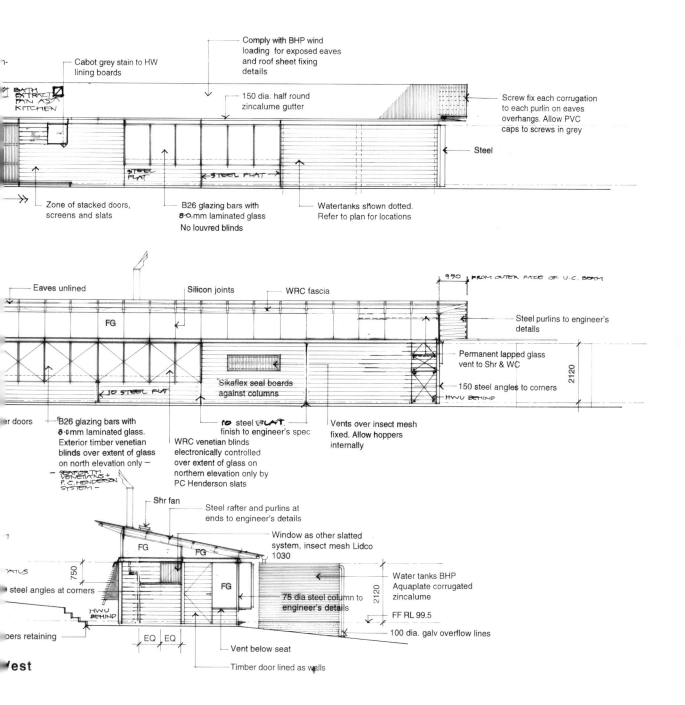

Comply with BHP wind loading for exposed eaves and roof sheet fixing details

Cabot grey stain to HW lining boards

150 dia. half round zincalume gutter

Screw fix each corrugation to each purlin on eaves overhangs. Allow PVC caps to screws in grey

BATH EXTRACT FAN AS KITCHEN

Steel

STEEL FLAT

STEEL FLAT

Zone of stacked doors, screens and slats

B26 glazing bars with 8·0 mm laminated glass No louvred blinds

Watertanks shown dotted. Refer to plan for locations

Eaves unlined

Silicon joints

WRC fascia

950 FROM OUTER FACE OF U.C. BEAM

FG

Steel purlins to engineer's details

Permanent lapped glass vent to Shr & WC

2120

TO STEEL FLAT

Sikaflex seal boards against columns

150 steel angles to corners

HWU BEHIND

er doors

B26 glazing bars with 8·0 mm laminated glass. Exterior timber venetian blinds over extent of glass on north elevation only —

SEATORTH VENETIANS + P.C. HENDERSON SYSTEM —

TO steel FLAT finish to engineer's spec

WRC venetian blinds electronically controlled over extent of glass on northern elevation only by PC Henderson slats

Vents over insect mesh fixed. Allow hoppers internally

Shr fan

Steel rafter and purlins at ends to engineer's details

Window as other slatted system, insect mesh Lidco 1030

FG

FG

750

FG

Water tanks BHP Aquaplate corrugated zincalume

75 dia steel column to engineer's details

2120

FF RL 99.5

steel angles at corners

HWU BEHIND

100 dia. galv overflow lines

oers retaining

EQ EQ

Vent below seat

Timber door lined as walls

est

0 1 2   5m

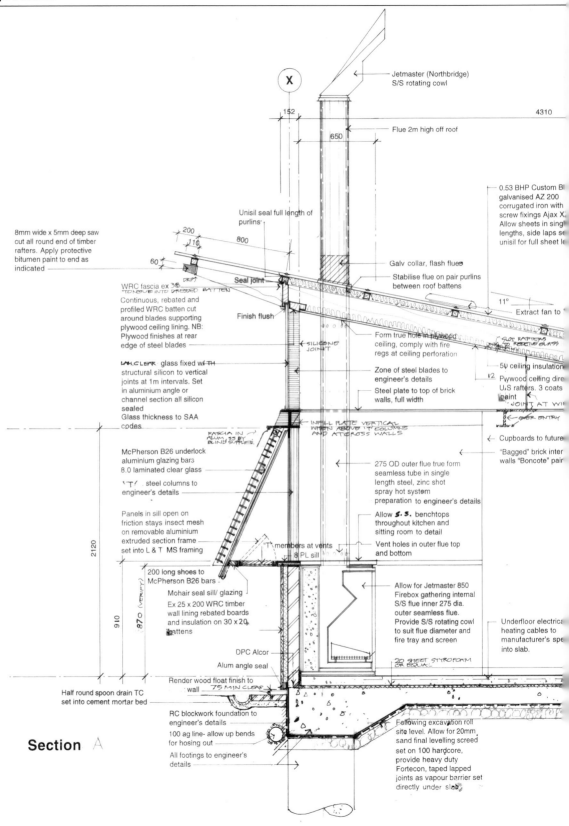

X

Jetmaster (Northbridge)
S/S rotating cowl

152

4310

650

Flue 2m high off roof

0.53 BHP Custom Bl
galvanised AZ 200
corrugated iron with
screw fixings Ajax X.
Allow sheets in singl
lengths, side laps se
unisil for full sheet le

8mm wide x 5mm deep saw
cut all round end of timber
rafters. Apply protective
bitumen paint to end as
indicated

200

110

800

60

Unisil seal full length of
purlins

Galv collar, flash flues

Stabilise flue on pair purlins
between roof battens

WRC fascia ex 38
TONGUE INTO DRESSED BATTEN
Continuous, rebated and
profiled WRC batten cut
around blades supporting
plywood ceiling lining. NB:
Plywood finishes at rear
edge of steel blades

Seal joint

Finish flush

11°

Extract fan to

LAM.CLEAR glass fixed WITH
structural silicon to vertical
joints at 1m intervals. Set
in aluminium angle or
channel section all silicon
sealed
Glass thickness to SAA
codes

SILICONE
JOINT

Form true hole in plywood
ceiling, comply with fire
regs at ceiling perforation

SLOT RAFTERS
RECEIVE GLASS

Zone of steel blades to
engineer's details

50 ceiling insulation

12 Plywood ceiling dire
U.S rafters. 3 coats
paint

Steel plate to top of brick
walls, full width

JOINT AT WI

INFILL PLATE VERTICAL
WHEN ABOVE 'T' COLUMNS
AND ATCROSS WALLS

OVER ENTRY

FASCIA IN
ALUM 35 BY
BLIND SUPPLIER

Cupboards to future

McPherson B26 underlock
aluminium glazing bars
8.0 laminated clear glass

"Bagged" brick inter
walls "Boncote" pair

275 OD outer flue true form
seamless tube in single
length steel, zinc shot
spray hot system
preparation to engineer's details

'T' steel columns to
engineer's details

Panels in sill open on
friction stays insect mesh
on removable aluminium
extruded section frame
set into L & T MS framing

'T' members at vents

8 PL sill

Allow S.S. benchtops
throughout kitchen and
sitting room to detail

Vent holes in outer flue top
and bottom

2120

200 long shoes to
McPherson B26 bars

Mohair seal sill/ glazing

Ex 25 x 200 WRC timber
wall lining rebated boards
and insulation on 30 x 20
battens

Allow for Jetmaster 850
Firebox gathering internal
S/S flue inner 275 dia.
outer seamless flue.
Provide S/S rotating cowl
to suit flue diameter and
fire tray and screen

Underfloor electrica
heating cables to
manufacturer's spe
into slab.

910

870 (VERIFY)

DPC Alcor

Alum angle seal

Render wood float finish to
wall

75 MIN CLEAR

20 SHEET STYROFOAM
OR EQUAL

Half round spoon drain TC
set into cement mortar bed

RC blockwork foundation to
engineer's details

100 ag line- allow up bends
for hosing out

All footings to engineer's
details

Following excavation roll
site level. Allow for 20mm
sand final levelling screed
set on 100 hardcore,
provide heavy duty
Fortecon, taped lapped
joints as vapour barrier set
directly under slab.

Section A

ダイニングルーム断面詳細図。
Detailed section of dining room.

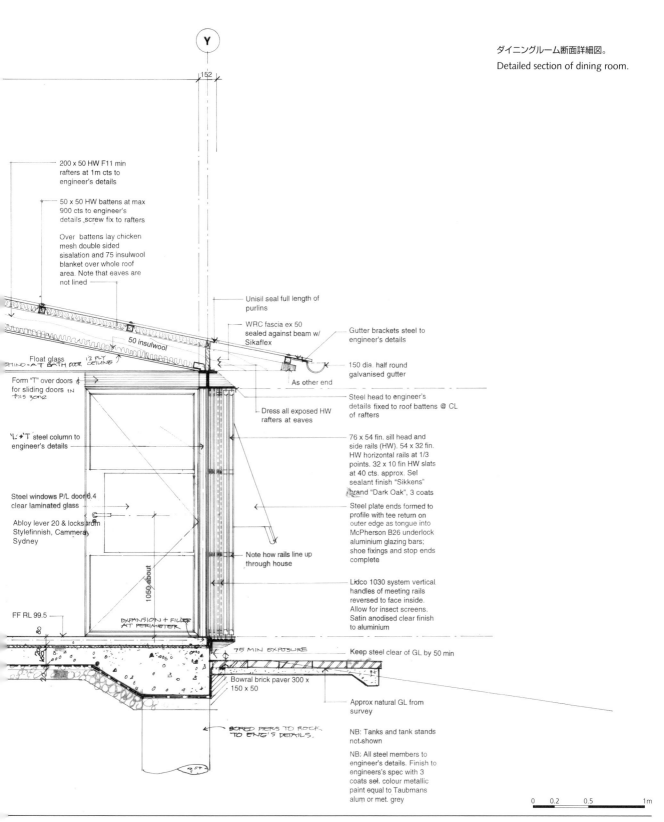

200 x 50 HW F11 min rafters at 1m cts to engineer's details

50 x 50 HW battens at max 900 cts to engineer's details .screw fix to rafters

Over battens lay chicken mesh double sided sisalation and 75 insulwool blanket over whole roof area. Note that eaves are not lined

50 insulwool

Float glass BEHIND AT BATH DOOR

12 PLY CEILING

Form "T" over doors & for sliding doors IN this zone

L # T steel column to engineer's details

Steel windows P/L door 6.4 clear laminated glass

Abloy lever 20 & locks from Stylefinnish, Cammeray Sydney

1050 about

FF RL 99.5

80

EXPANSION + FILLER AT PERIMETER

BORED PIERS TO ROCK TO ENG'S DETAILS.

Unisil seal full length of purlins

WRC fascia ex 50 sealed against beam w/ Sikaflex

As other end

Dress all exposed HW rafters at eaves

Note how rails line up through house

75 MIN EXPOSURE

Bowral brick paver 300 x 150 x 50

Gutter brackets steel to engineer's details

150 dia. half round galvanised gutter

Steel head to engineer's details fixed to roof battens @ CL of rafters

76 x 54 fin. sill head and side rails (HW). 54 x 32 fin. HW horizontal rails at 1/3 points. 32 x 10 fin HW slats at 40 cts. approx. Sel sealant finish "Sikkens" brand "Dark Oak", 3 coats

Steel plate ends formed to profile with tee return on outer edge as tongue into McPherson B26 underlock aluminium glazing bars; shoe fixings and stop ends complete

Lidco 1030 system vertical handles of meeting rails reversed to face inside. Allow for insect screens. Satin anodised clear finish to aluminium

Keep steel clear of GL by 50 min

Approx natural GL from survey

NB: Tanks and tank stands not shown

NB: All steel members to engineer's details. Finish to engineers's spec with 3 coats sel. colour metallic paint equal to Taubmans alum or met. grey

0   0.2   0.5   1m

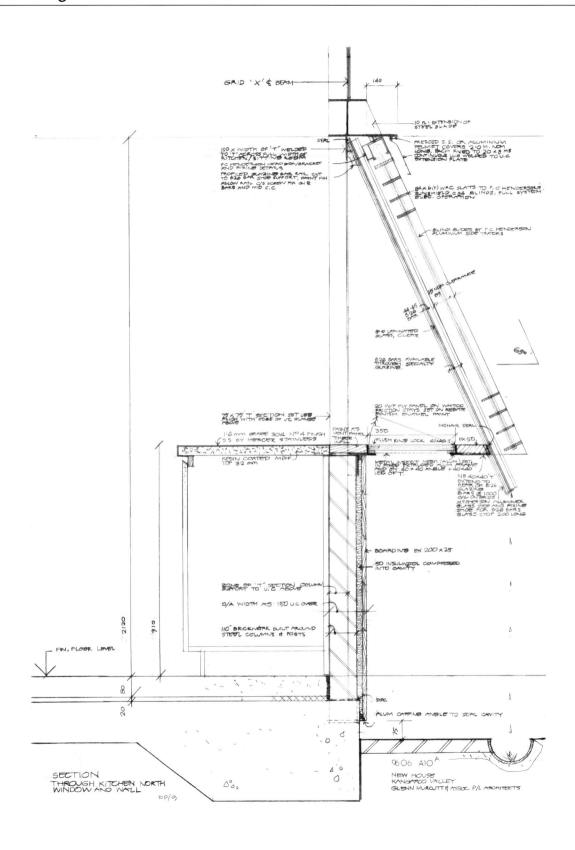

SECTION
THROUGH KITCHEN NORTH
WINDOW AND WALL

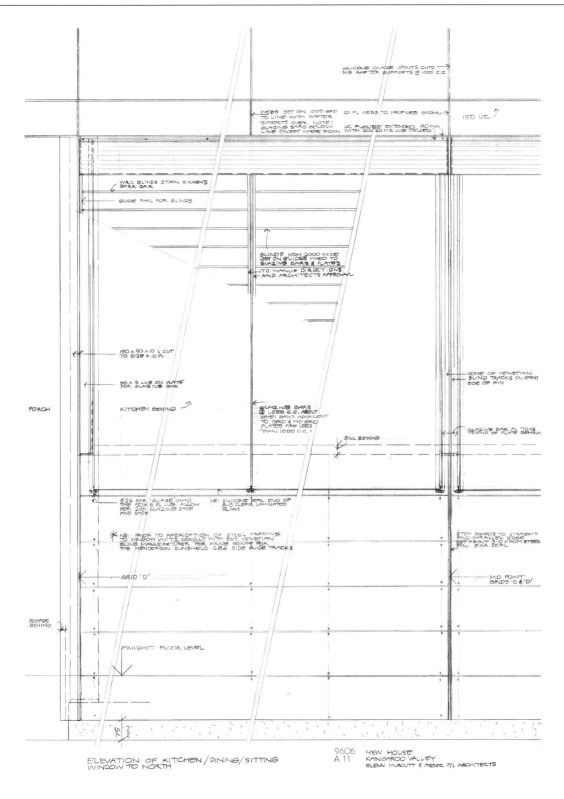

ELEVATION OF KITCHEN/DINING/SITTING
WINDOW TO NORTH

9606
A 11

NEW HOUSE
KANGAROO VALLEY
GLENN MURCUTT & ASSOC P/L ARCHITECTS

0　10　20　　　　　50cm

フレッチャー=ペイジ邸　1996-98 Kangaroo Valley, New South Wales

断面詳細図：鎧戸、網戸、ガラス戸が３連に鉄のプレート枠に納められた。

Detailed section through the windows showing 'tri-partite' layers of shutters, insect screens and glass doors framed in steel plate.

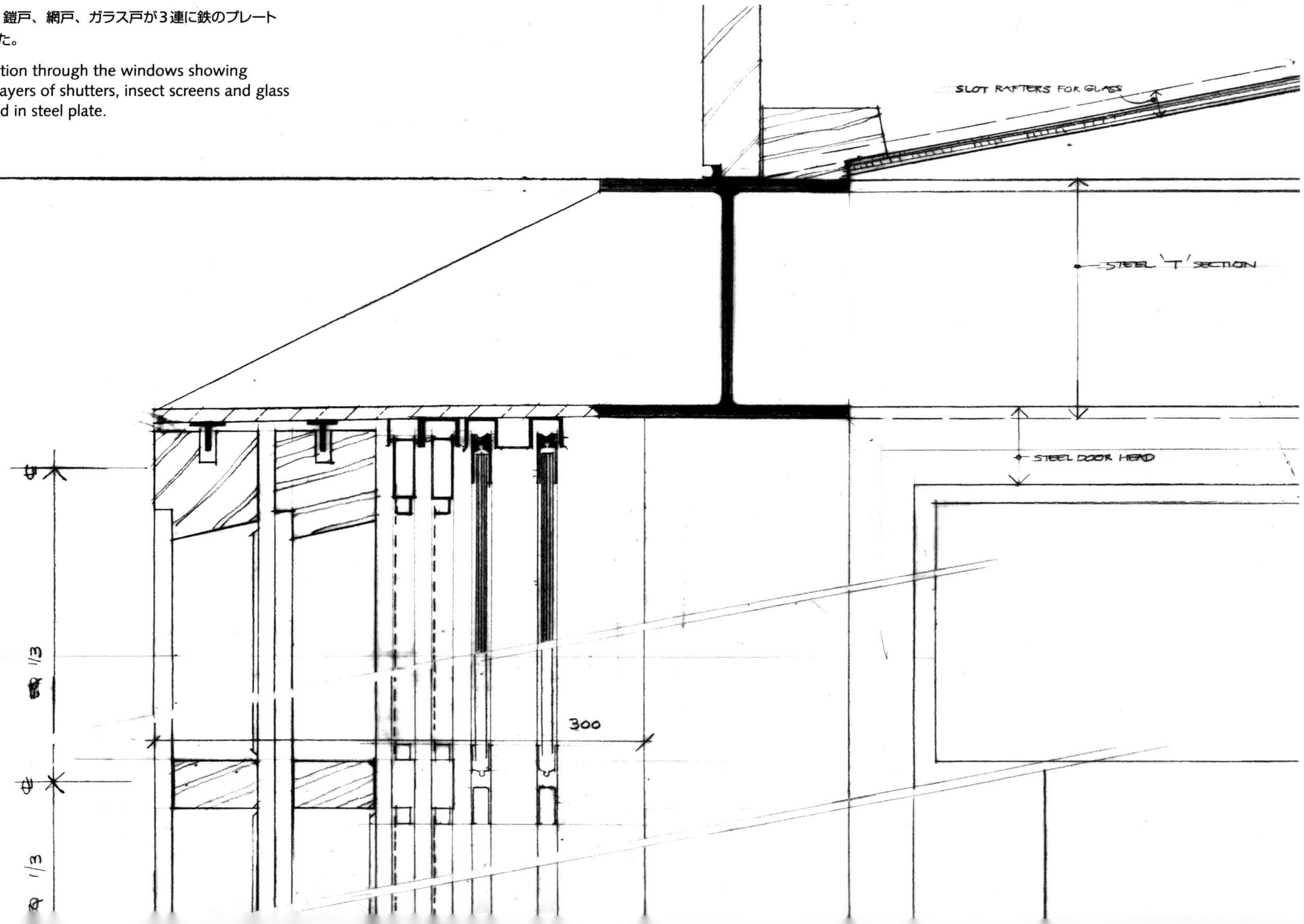

SLOT RAFTERS FOR GLASS

STEEL 'T' SECTION

STEEL DOOR HEAD

300

∅ 1/3

∅ 1/3

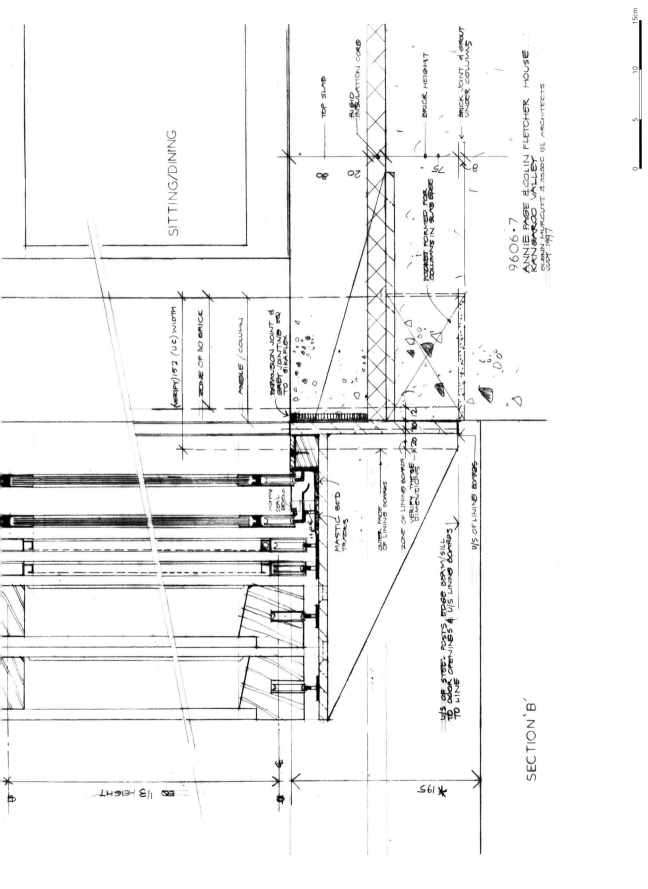

SITTING/DINING

SECTION 'B'

9606·7
ANNIE PAGE & COLIN FLETCHER HOUSE
KANGAROO VALLEY
GLENN MURCUTT & ASSOC P/L ARCHITECTS
JULY 1997

TOP SLAB

RIGID INSULATION CORE

BRICK HEIGHT

BRICK JOINT & GROUT
UNDER COLUMNS

POCKET FORMED FOR
COLUMNS IN SLAB EDGE

(VERIFY) 152 (U.C) WIDTH
ZONE OF 110 BRICK
ANGLE / COLUMN
EXPANSION JOINT &
GREY JOINTING EQ
TO SIKAFLEX

MOHAIR
SEAL
BOARD

MASTIC BED
TRACKS

OUTER FACE
OF LINING BOARDS
ZONE OF LINING BOARDS
VERIFY THESE
DIMENSIONS

U/S OF LINING BOARDS

U/S OF STEEL POSTS & EDGE BEAM/SILL
TO DOOR OPENINGS & U/S LINING BOARDS
TO LINE

1/3 HEIGHT

195

15cm
10
5
0

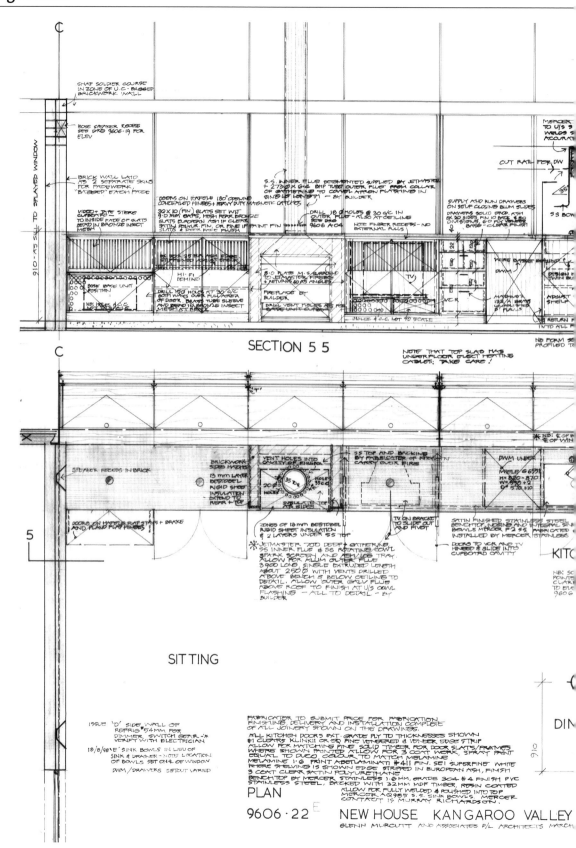

SECTION 5 5

SITTING

PLAN

9606·22 E   NEW HOUSE KANGAROO VALLEY

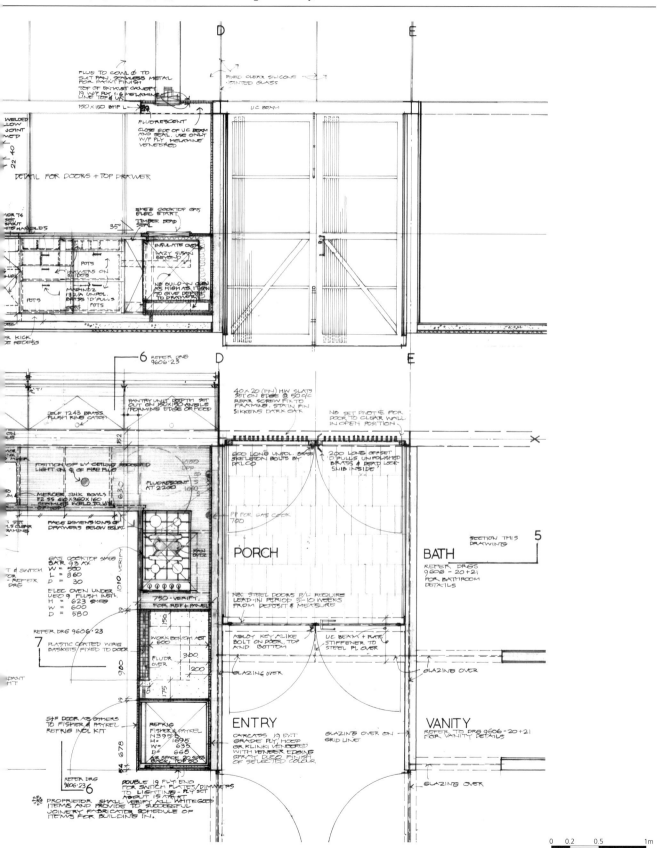

PORCH

BATH

ENTRY

VANITY

0   0.2   0.5   1m

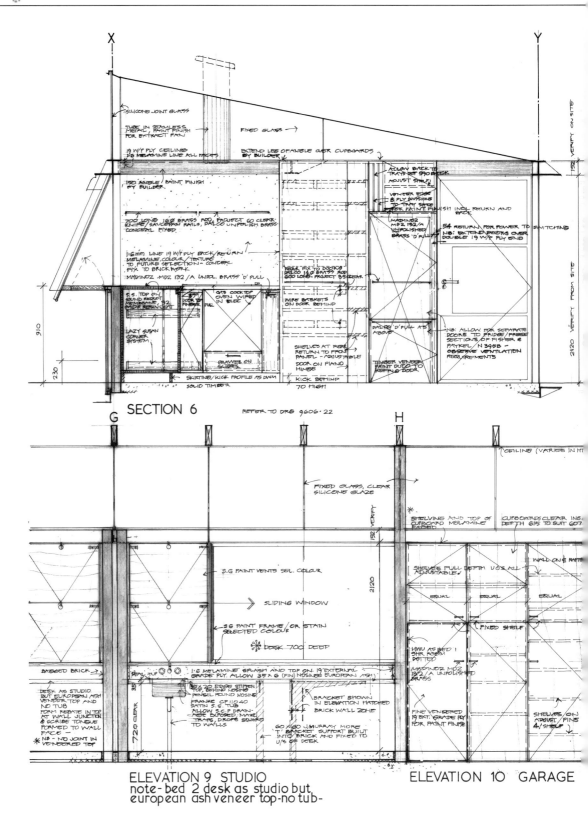

SECTION 6

REFER TO DRG 9606·22

ELEVATION 9 STUDIO
note- bed 2 desk as studio but
european ash veneer top-no tub-

ELEVATION 10 GARAGE

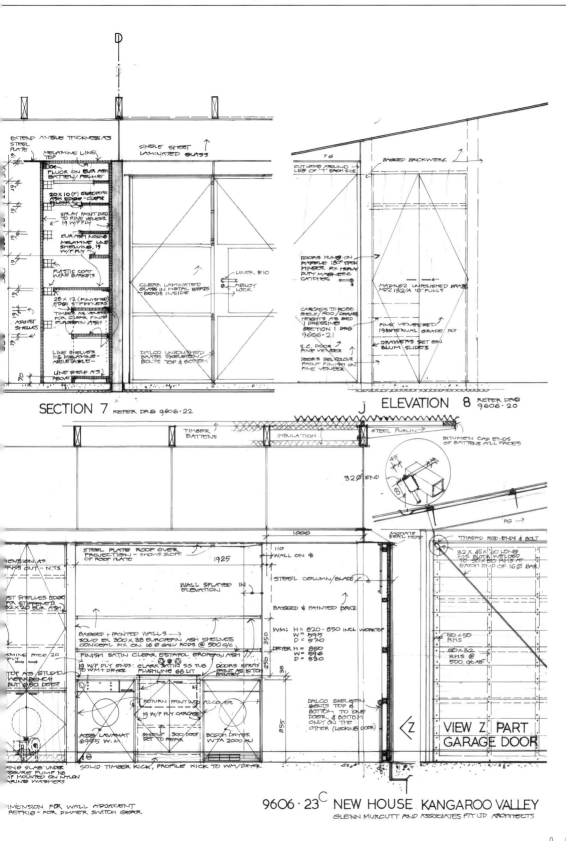

SECTION 7　REFER DRG 9606·22

ELEVATION　8　REFER DRG 9606·20

VIEW Z PART GARAGE DOOR

9606·23C NEW HOUSE KANGAROO VALLEY
GLENN MURCUTT AND ASSOCIATES PTY LTD ARCHITECTS

0　0.2　0.5　1m

Arthur and Yvonne Boyd Art Centre

1996-99 Riversdale, West Cambewarra, New South Wales
Collaborating architects: Reg Lark and Wendy Lewin

海抜20m。温暖気候。年間雨量約1,500mm。ユーカリ林と、手入れされた農場の境界に建つ。コジオスコ山の冷たい風を遮る山の裏にある。夏は、気温は24度、稀に40度となるが、北東と南東からの涼しい海風が吹く。冬は20度前後、最低気温12度だが、時折5度まで下がる。砂岩と頁岩の粒状ローム層。

Altitude: 20m above sea level. Temperate climate. Rainfall circa 1,500mm per year. Sited between eucalypt forest and cultivated farming land, in the lee of a hill which protects it from cold winds off Mount Kosciusko. Summer, circa 24 deg C, infrequently up to 40 deg C with some influence from cooling north-east and south-east on-shore winds. Winter, circa 20 deg C with lows of circa 12 deg C occasionally down to 5 deg C. Granular loam soil of sandstone and shale.

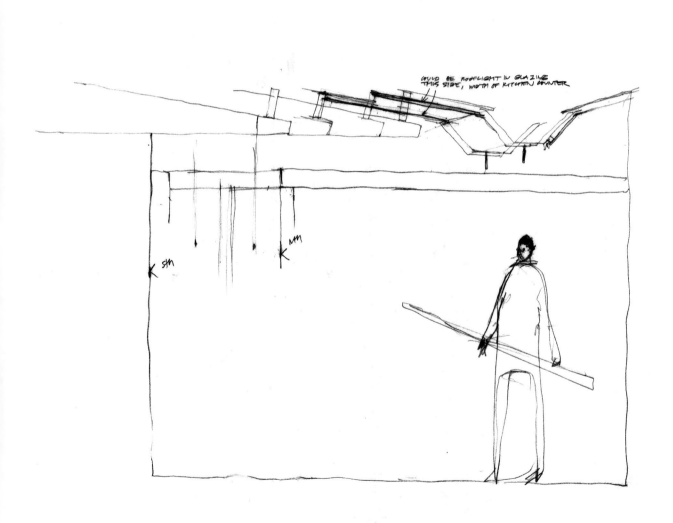

ダイニングホールとサービス部分を分ける断面と樋のスケッチ。

Sketch variations for the internal gutter between the dining hall and the service wing.

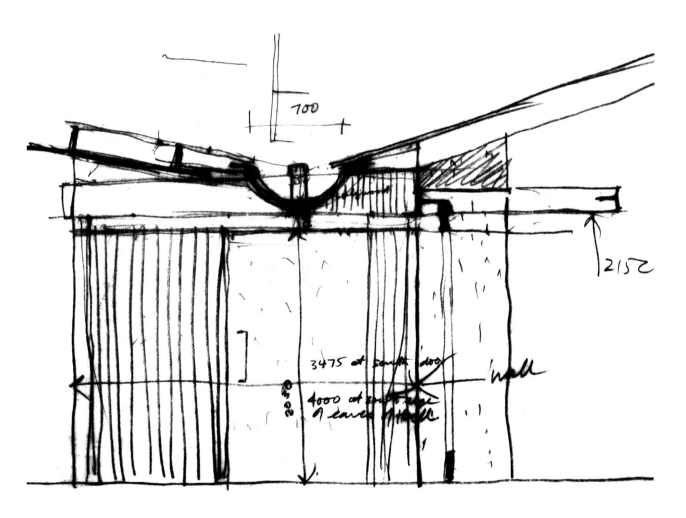

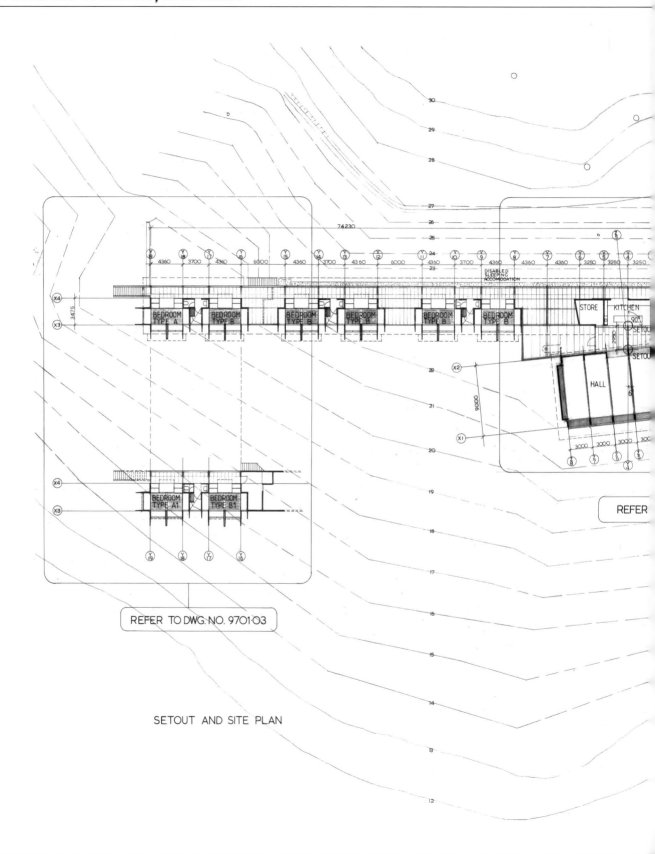

REFER TO DWG. NO. 9701·03

SETOUT AND SITE PLAN

敷地全体配置図。小さな駐車場から既存の3棟のコテージを抜ける、新しい建物へのアプローチが示されている。大きな広場へ辿り着くと川への眺めとともにセンターの正面が明らかになる。屋外ひな段座席（アンフィシアター）は実現されていない。

Site layout plan of the entire complex showing the relationship of the new structures to three existing cottages which frame an entrance sequence from a small car park. The new buildings are visible on arrival at a large open platform with views of the river. The amphitheatre shown has not yet been realised.

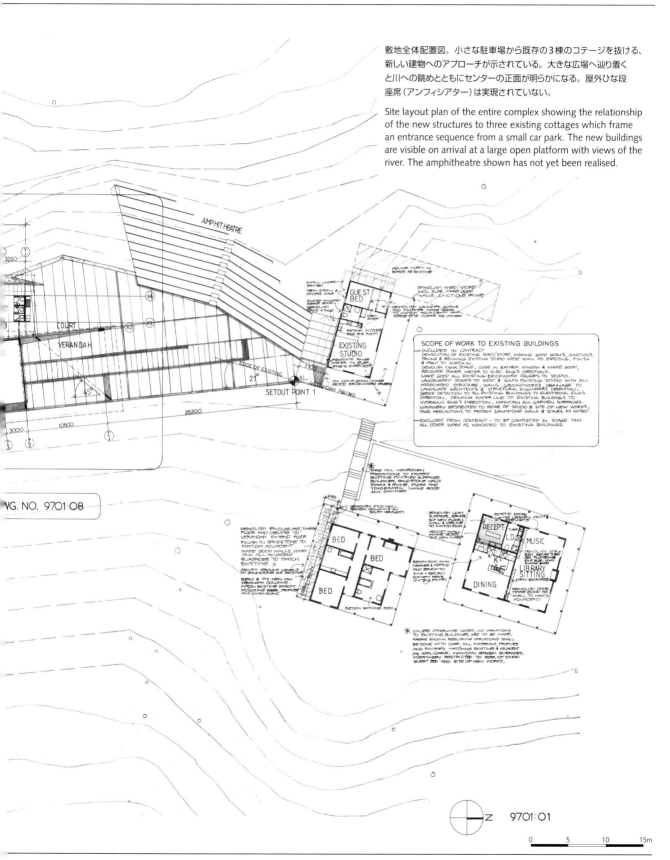

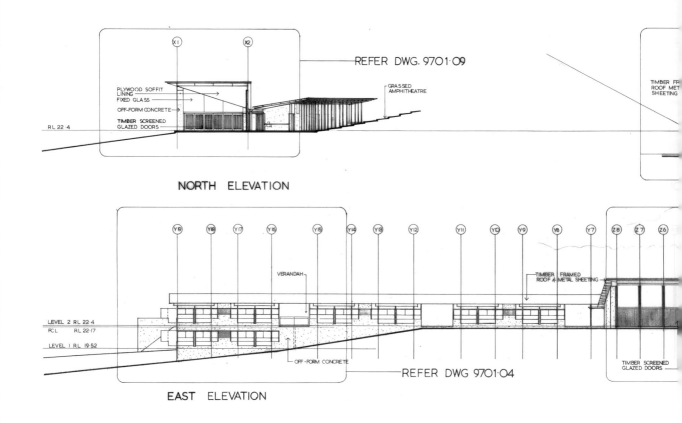

REFER DWG. 9701·09

PLYWOOD SOFFIT LINING
FIXED GLASS
OFF-FORM CONCRETE
TIMBER SCREENED GLAZED DOORS

GRASSED AMPHITHEATRE

RL 22·4

TIMBER FR
ROOF MET
SHEETING

NORTH ELEVATION

VERANDAH

TIMBER FRAMED
ROOF + METAL SHEETING

LEVEL 2 RL 22·4
FCL   RL 22·17
LEVEL 1 RL 19·52

OFF-FORM CONCRETE

REFER DWG 9701·04

TIMBER SCREENED
GLAZED DOORS

EAST ELEVATION

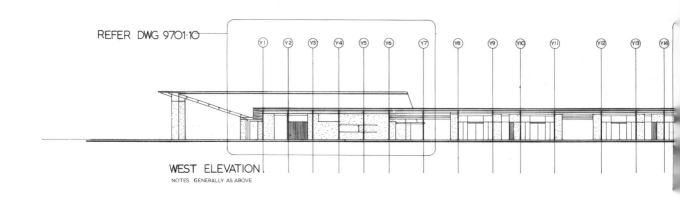

REFER DWG 9701·10

WEST ELEVATION
NOTES GENERALLY AS ABOVE

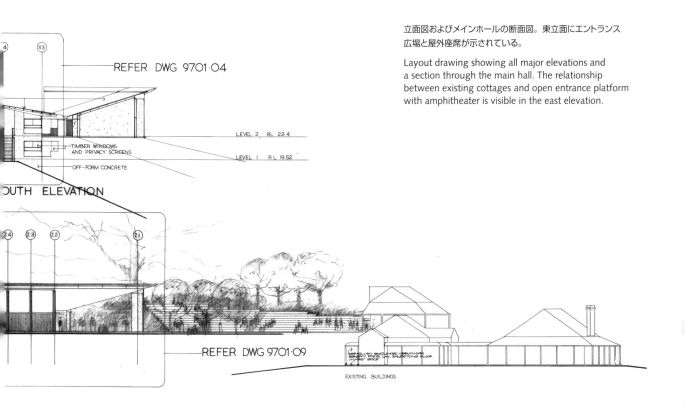

立面図およびメインホールの断面図。東立面にエントランス
広場と屋外座席が示されている。

Layout drawing showing all major elevations and
a section through the main hall. The relationship
between existing cottages and open entrance platform
with amphitheater is visible in the east elevation.

REFER DWG 9701·04

LEVEL 2 RL 22·4

LEVEL 1 RL 19·52

TIMBER WINDOWS
AND PRIVACY SCREENS

OFF-FORM CONCRETE

OUTH ELEVATION

REFER DWG 9701·09

EXISTING BUILDINGS

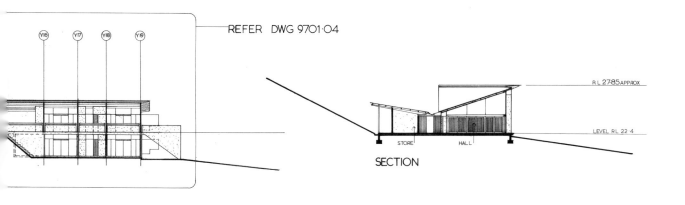

REFER DWG 9701·04

RL 27·85 APPROX

LEVEL RL 22·4

STORE   HALL

SECTION

0   5   10   15m

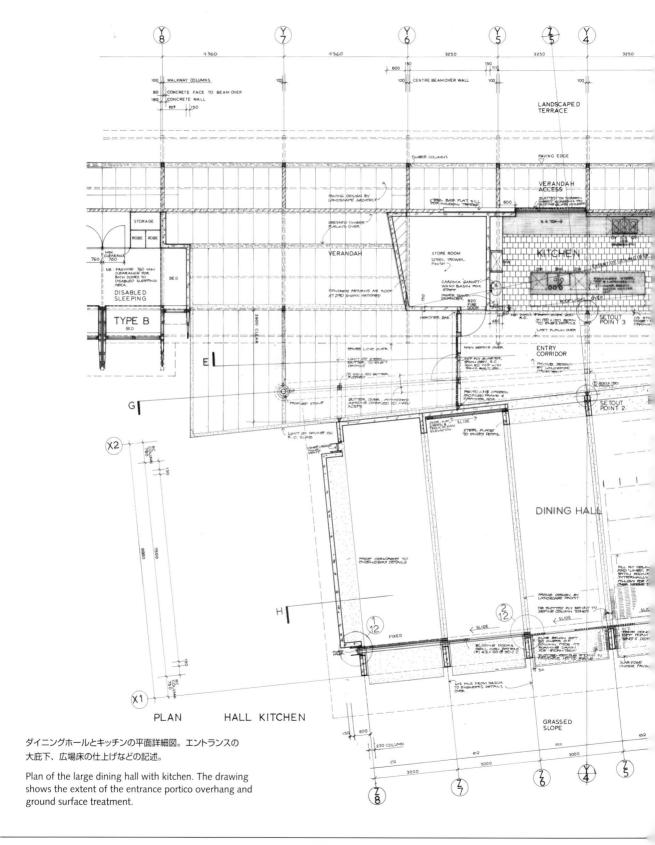

PLAN   HALL   KITCHEN

ダイニングホールとキッチンの平面詳細図。エントランスの
大庇下、広場床の仕上げなどの記述。

Plan of the large dining hall with kitchen. The drawing
shows the extent of the entrance portico overhang and
ground surface treatment.

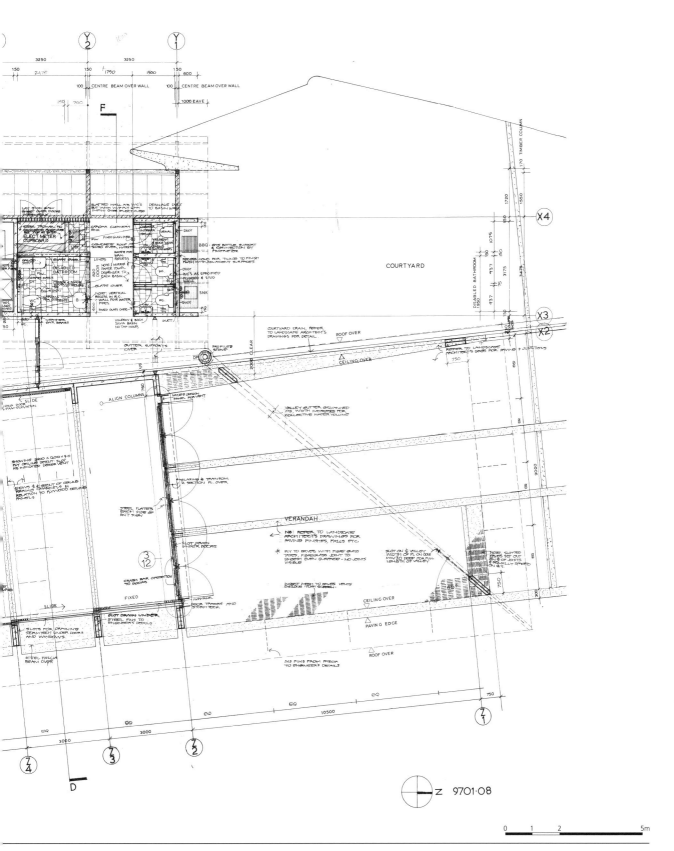

0   1   2   5m

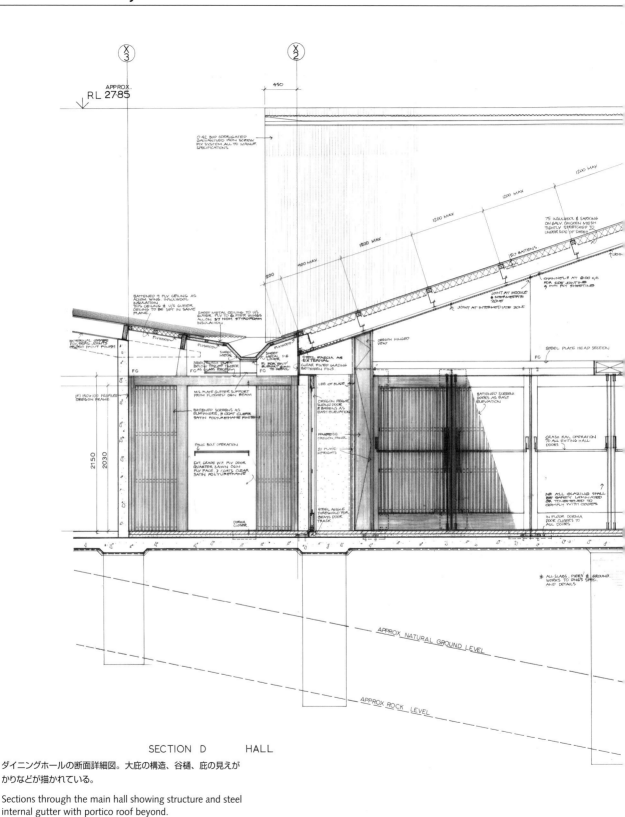

SECTION D HALL

ダイニングホールの断面詳細図。大庇の構造、谷樋、庇の見えがかりなどが描かれている。

Sections through the main hall showing structure and steel internal gutter with portico roof beyond.

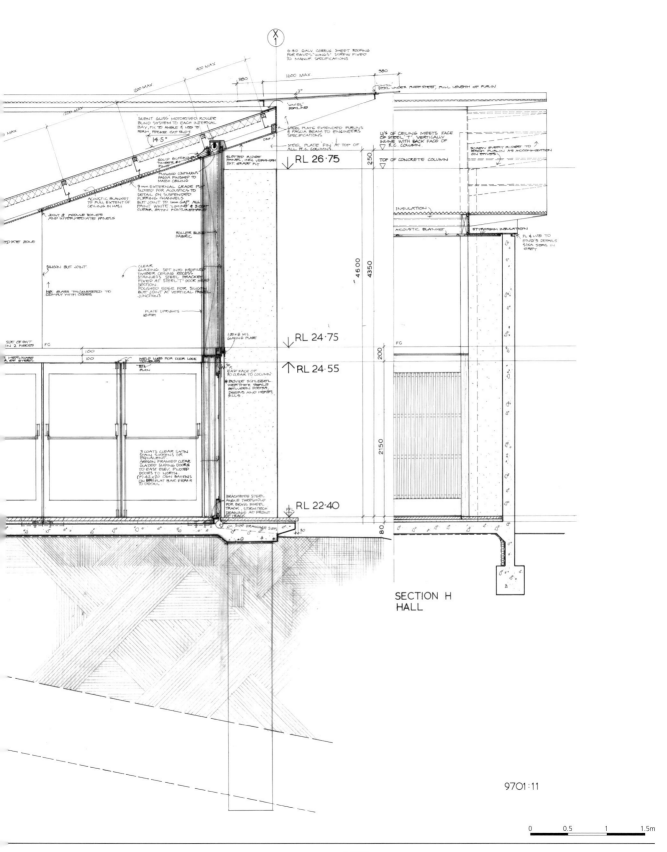

SECTION H
HALL

9701:11

0   0.5   1   1.5m

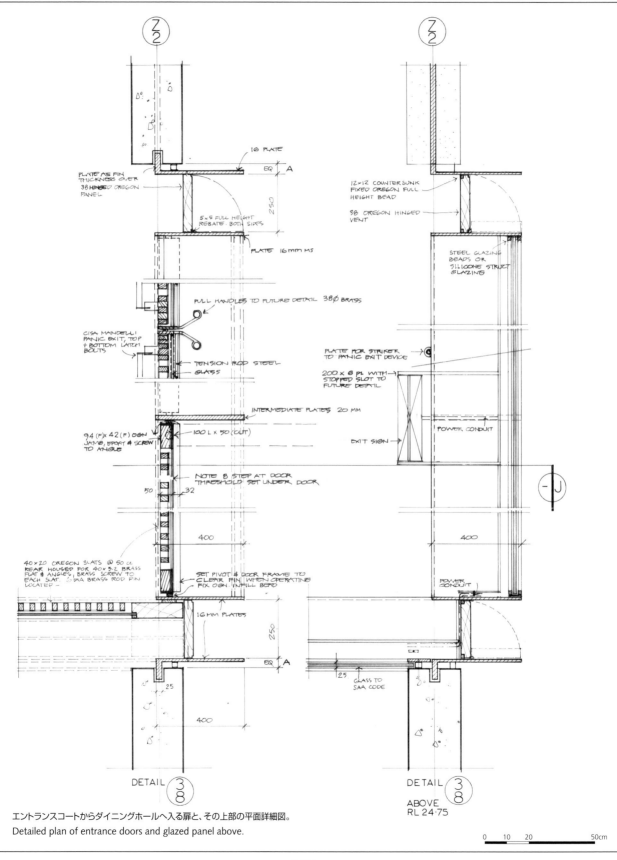

PLATE AS FIN THICKNESS OVER 38 HINGED OREGON PANEL

16 PLATE

EQ A

250

5 x 5 FULL HEIGHT REBATE. BOTH SIDES

PLATE 16mm MS

PULL HANDLES TO FUTURE DETAIL 38Ø BRASS

CISA MANDELLI PANIC EXIT, TOP + BOTTOM LATCH BOLTS

TENSION ROD STEEL GLASS

INTERMEDIATE PLATES 20 MM

94 (M) x 42 (F) OGN JAMB, EPOXY & SCREW TO ANGLE

100 L x 50 (CUT)

NOTE 8 STEP AT DOOR THRESHOLD SET UNDER DOOR

50 32

400

40 x 20 OREGON SLATS @ 50 cc REAR HOUSED FOR 40 x 3.2 BRASS FLAT & ANGLES, BRASS SCREW TO EACH SLAT - 5 DIA BRASS ROD FIN LOCATED -

SET PIVOT & DOOR FRAME TO CLEAR FIN WHEN OPERATING FIX OGN. INFILL BEAD

16 MM PLATES

250

EQ A

25

400

DETAIL 3/8

12 x 12 COUNTER SUNK FIXED OREGON FULL HEIGHT BEAD

38 OREGON HINGED VENT

STEEL GLAZING BEADS OR SILICONE STRUCT GLAZING

PLATE FOR STRIKER TO PANIC EXIT DEVICE

200 x 6 PL WITH STOPPED SLOT TO FUTURE DETAIL

POWER CONDUIT

EXIT SIGN

400

POWER CONDUIT

25 GLASS TO SAA CODE

DETAIL 3/8

ABOVE RL 24.75

エントランスコートからダイニングホールへ入る扉と、その上部の平面詳細図。
Detailed plan of entrance doors and glazed panel above.

0   10   20   50cm

ダイニングホール鎧戸の立面／断面詳細図。
Elevation and section of dining hall shutter windows.

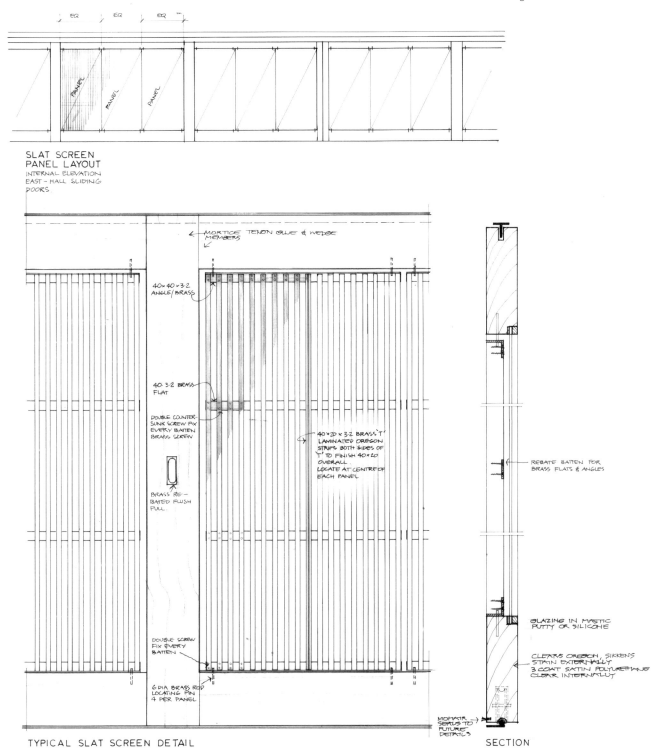

SLAT SCREEN
PANEL LAYOUT
INTERNAL ELEVATION
EAST – HALL SLIDING
DOORS.

TYPICAL SLAT SCREEN DETAIL

SECTION

宿泊棟平面詳細図（上階）。各部屋4人が泊まれる部屋が
2組ずつバスルームを挟んで構成され、このユニットはベ
ランダを介して独立している。部屋の内部寸法はベッドの
長さで決められ、1部屋をさらに2分割できるように中心に
引戸が仕込まれた。

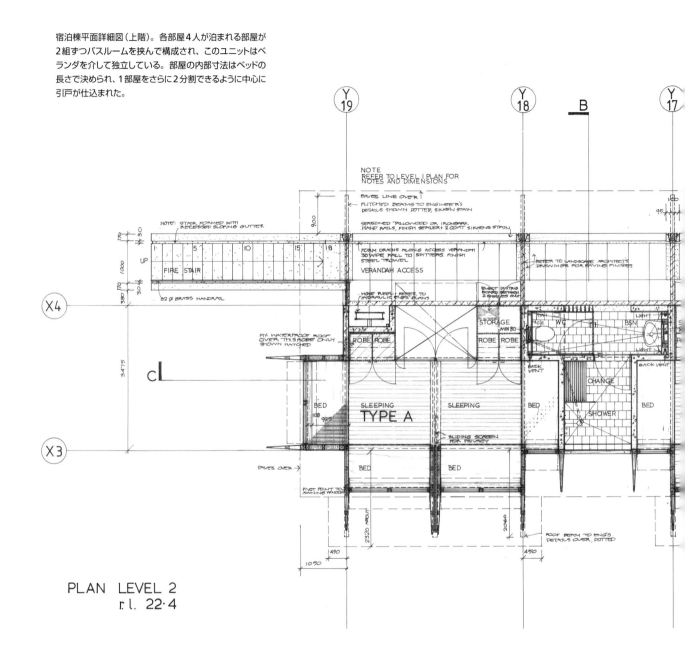

PLAN LEVEL 2
r. l. 22·4

Plan of the upper level dormitory accommodation. The layout shows a typical bedroom cluster of two rooms each with four beds grouped around a shared bathroom and separated from the next group by an open breezeway. The room size is determined in relation to the specific dimensions of the beds with a sliding internal door allowing for the division of each room into two.

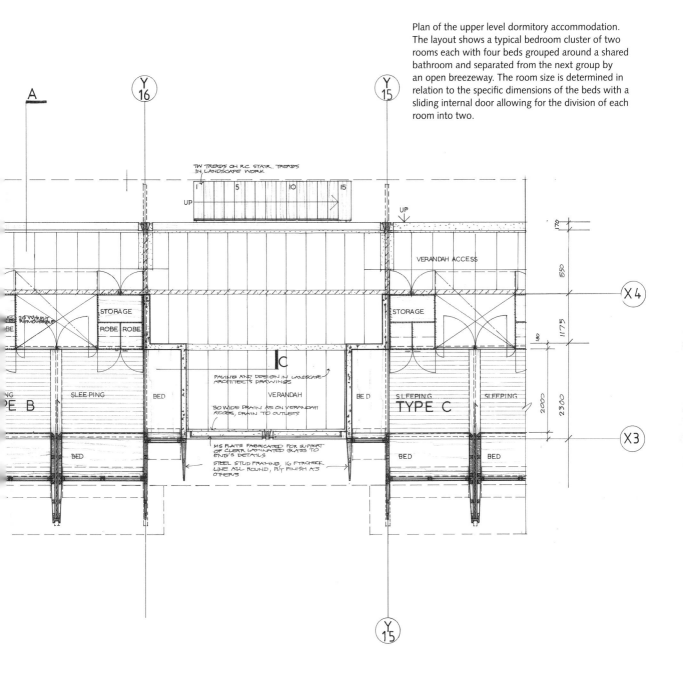

0   1   2   3m

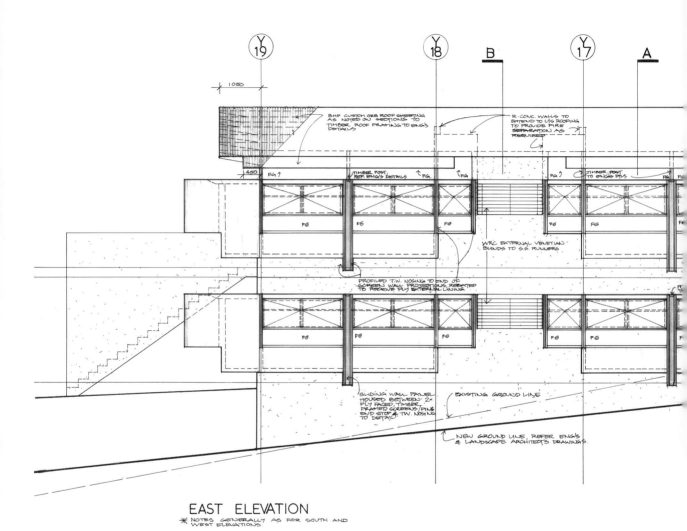

EAST ELEVATION
✳ NOTES GENERALLY AS FOR SOUTH AND WEST ELEVATIONS.

宿泊棟東立面図。各寝床は独立した窓をもつ。バス
ルームは窓がなく、ブラインドが固定された。

East elevation of the dormitory accommodation.
The drawing shows the individual windows for
each bed, framing personal views of the landscape.
The openings to the shared bathrooms have
external blinds with no glazing.

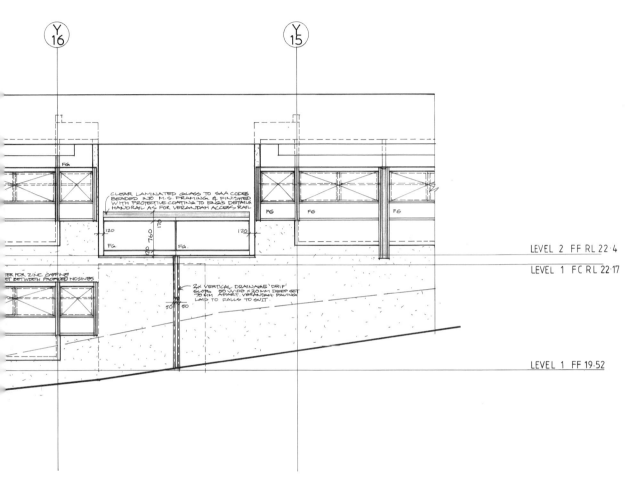

LEVEL 2 FF RL 22·4

LEVEL 1 FC RL 22·17

LEVEL 1 FF 19·52

NOTE: FOR DETAILED REFERENCES AND DIMENSIONS
REFER TO SECTIONS A, B AND C

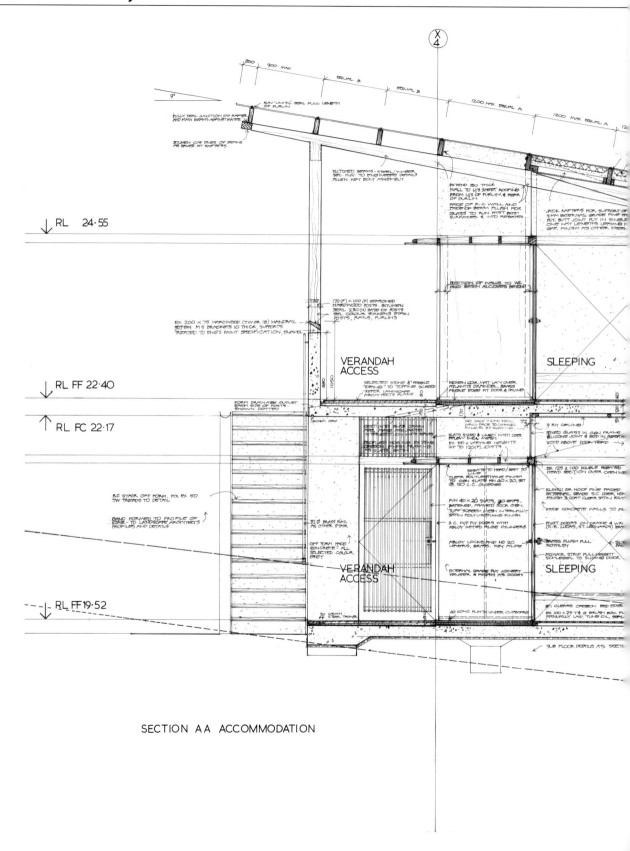

SECTION A·A ACCOMMODATION

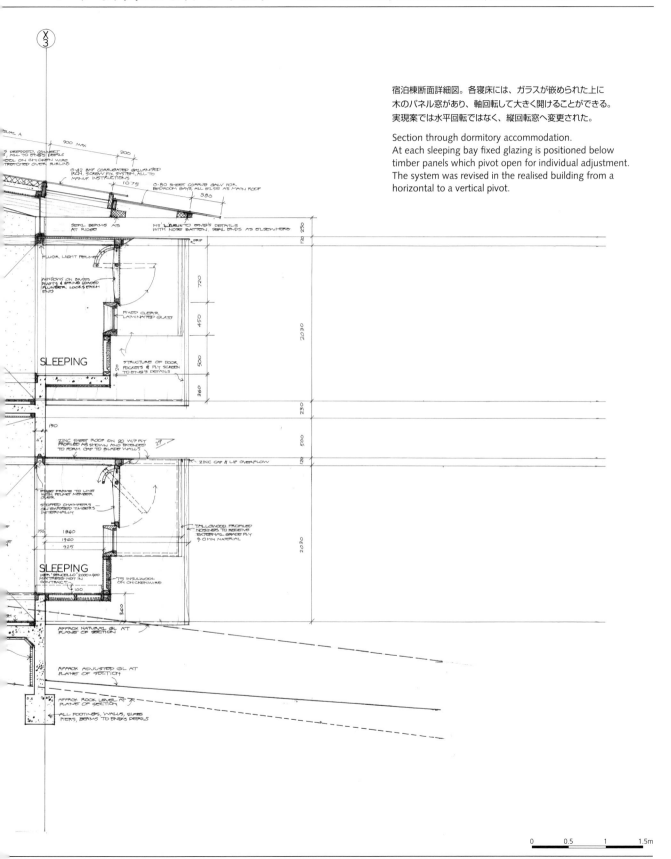

宿泊棟断面詳細図。各寝床には、ガラスが嵌められた上に
木のパネル窓があり、軸回転して大きく開けることができる。
実現案では水平回転ではなく、縦回転窓へ変更された。

Section through dormitory accommodation.
At each sleeping bay fixed glazing is positioned below
timber panels which pivot open for individual adjustment.
The system was revised in the realised building from a
horizontal to a vertical pivot.

SLEEPING

SLEEPING

0   0.5   1   1.5m

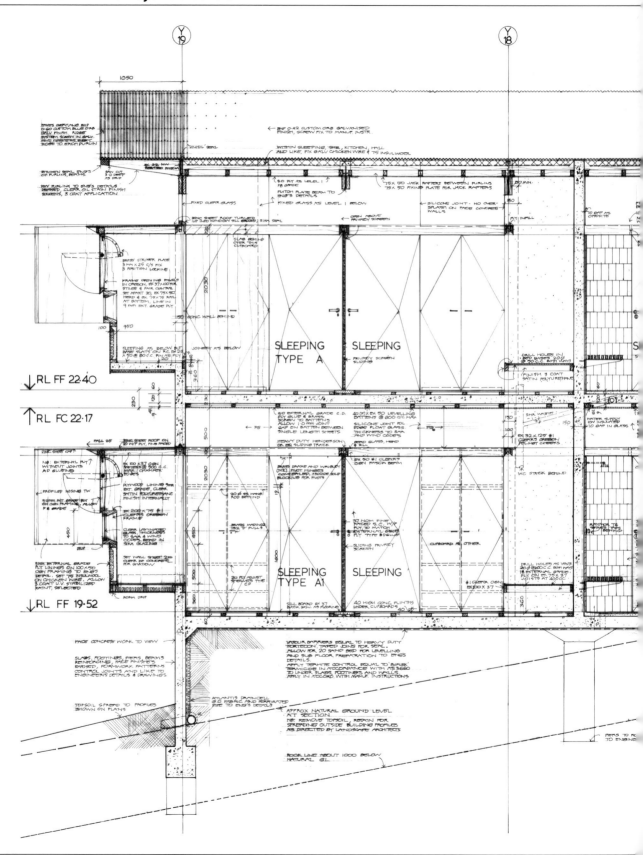

SLEEPING
TYPE A

SLEEPING

SLEEPING
TYPE A1

SLEEPING

↓ RL FF 22·40

↑ RL FC 22·17

↓ RL FF 19·52

宿泊棟断面詳細図。

Long section through dormitory
accommodation and shared bathrooms.

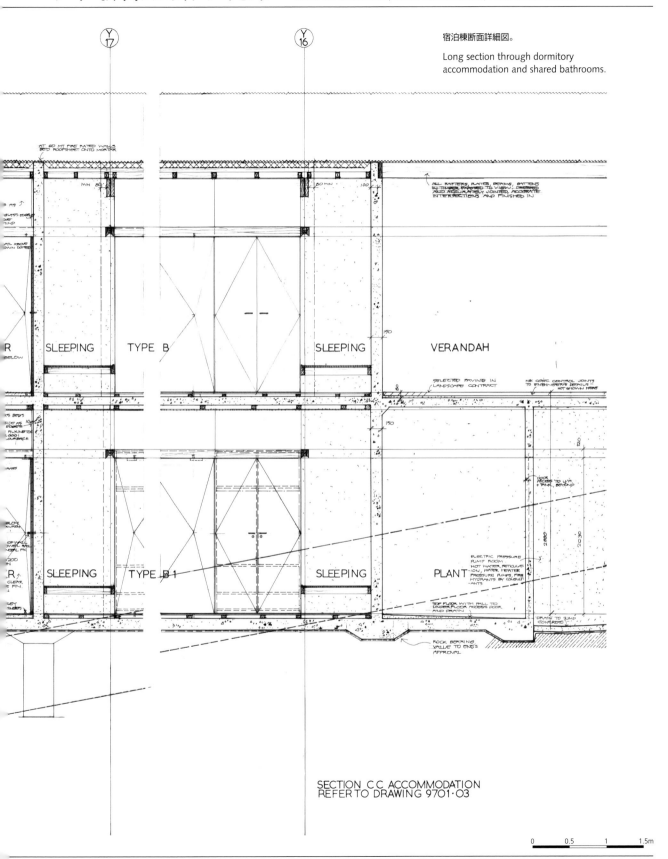

SLEEPING　　TYPE B

SLEEPING

VERANDAH

SLEEPING　　TYPE B1

SLEEPING

PLANT

SECTION CC ACCOMMODATION
REFER TO DRAWING 9701·03

0　　0.5　　1　　1.5m

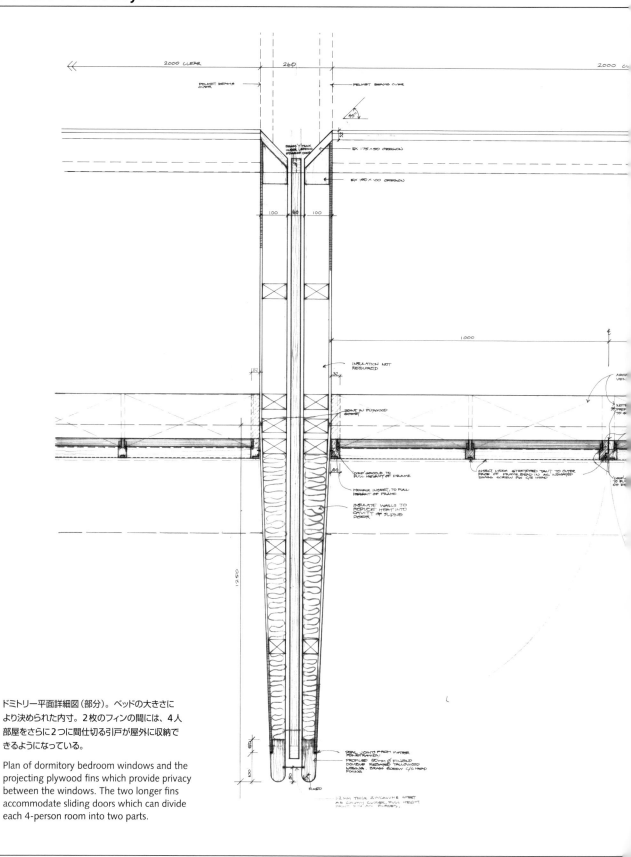

ドミトリー平面詳細図（部分）。ベッドの大きさに
より決められた内寸。2枚のフィンの間には、4人
部屋をさらに2つに間仕切る引戸が屋外に収納で
きるようになっている。

Plan of dormitory bedroom windows and the
projecting plywood fins which provide privacy
between the windows. The two longer fins
accommodate sliding doors which can divide
each 4-person room into two parts.

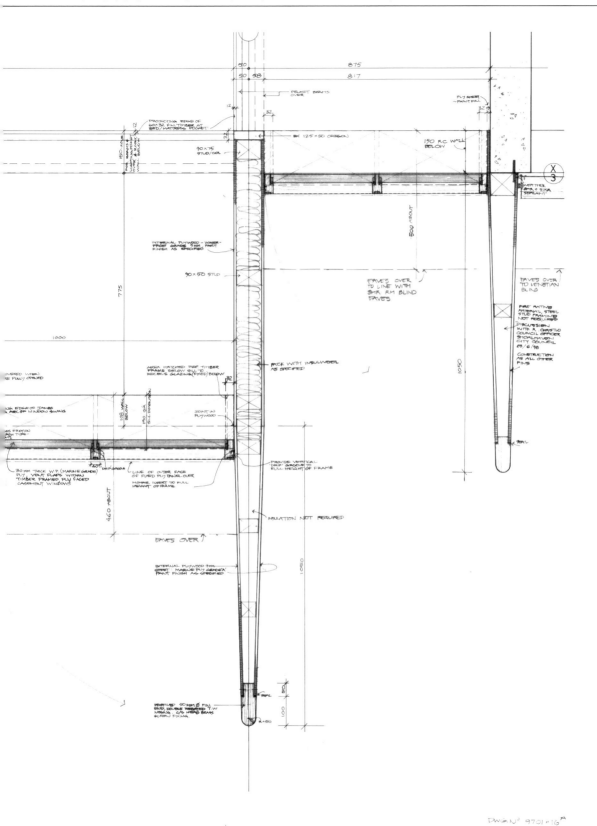

PLAN OF BEDROOM WINDOWS, SLIDING DOOR/WALL PANEL & PROJECTING FINS.

DWG N° 9701-16ᴬ

0　　10　　20　　　　　　50cm

House in the Southern Highlands

1997-2001 Kangaloon, New South Wales

海抜900m。温暖気候でも寒い地域。
夏の気温は25度、冬は18度前後だが、南西のクジオスコ山
からの冷たい強風が、気温をマイナス3度まで下げる。
花崗岩が混在する火山灰土壌。水はけは良い。

Altitude: 900m above sea level. Temperate/cool-temperate
climate. Summer, circa 25 deg C. Winter, circa 18 deg C
with high-velocity, extremely cold winds from south-west off
Mt. Kosciusko bringing lows of -3 deg C. Volcanic soils
interspersed with granite. Good drainage.

Darwin

Northern
Territory

Western Australia

Queensland

South Australia

o Brisbane

New South Wales

Adelaide

o Sydney

Victoria

Kangaloon

Melbourne

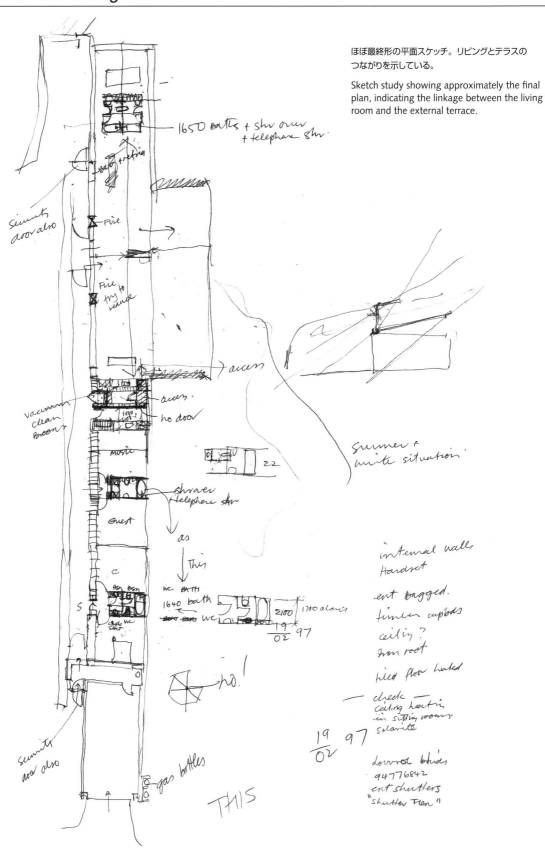

ほぼ最終形の平面スケッチ。リビングとテラスの
つながりを示している。

Sketch study showing approximately the final
plan, indicating the linkage between the living
room and the external terrace.

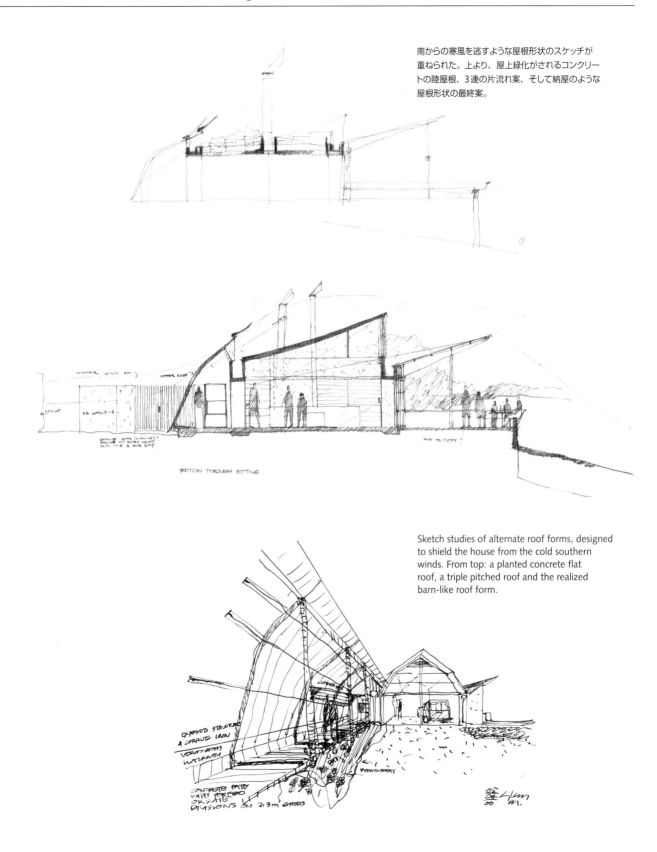

南からの寒風を逃すような屋根形状のスケッチが重ねられた。上より、屋上緑化がされるコンクリートの陸屋根、3連の片流れ案、そして納屋のような屋根形状の最終案。

Sketch studies of alternate roof forms, designed to shield the house from the cold southern winds. From top: a planted concrete flat roof, a triple pitched roof and the realized barn-like roof form.

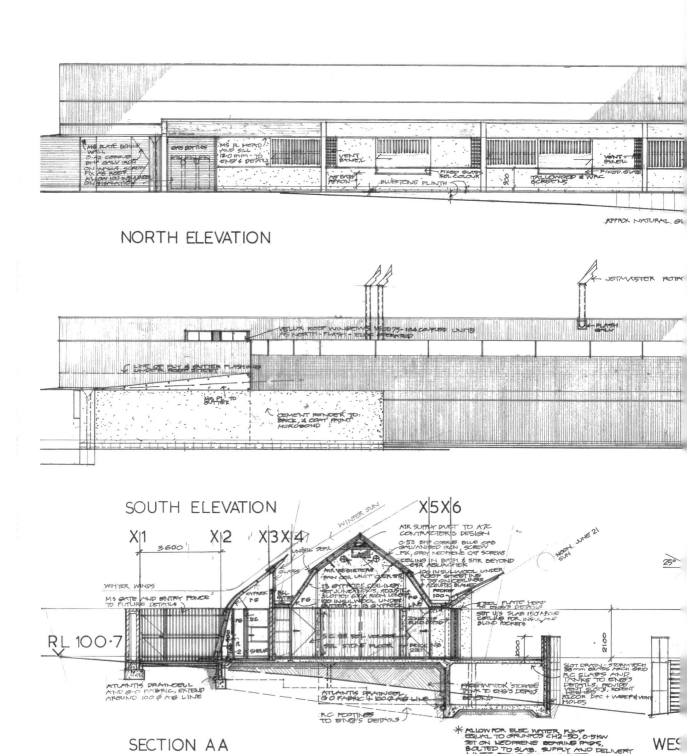

NORTH ELEVATION

SOUTH ELEVATION

SECTION AA

RL 100·7

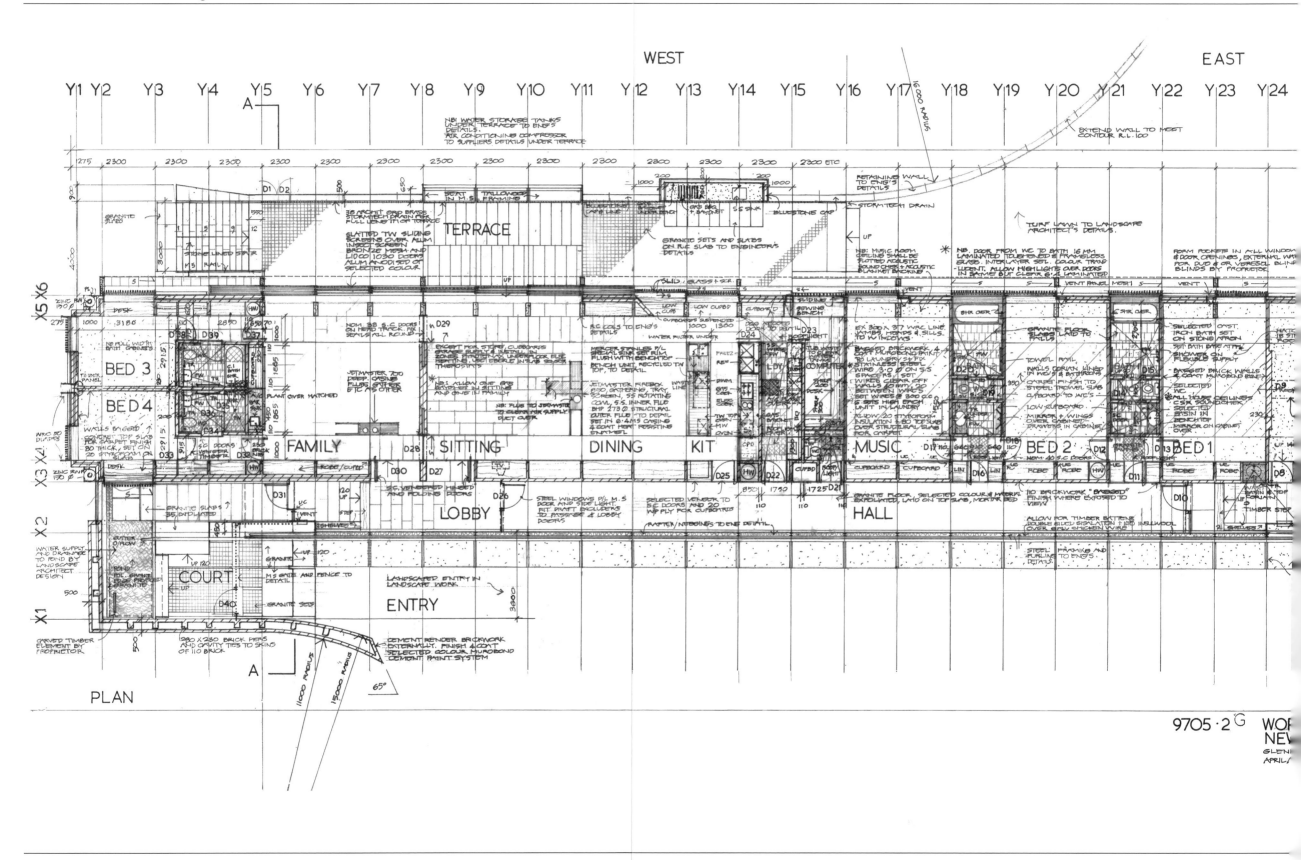

WEST

EAST

Y1 Y2 Y3 Y4 Y5 Y6 Y7 Y8 Y9 Y10 Y11 Y12 Y13 Y14 Y15 Y16 Y17 Y18 Y19 Y20 Y21 Y22 Y23 Y24

TERRACE

BED 3

BED 4

FAMILY

SITTING

DINING

KIT

MUSIC

BED 2

BED 1

LOBBY

HALL

COURT

ENTRY

PLAN

A

65°

9705·2 G

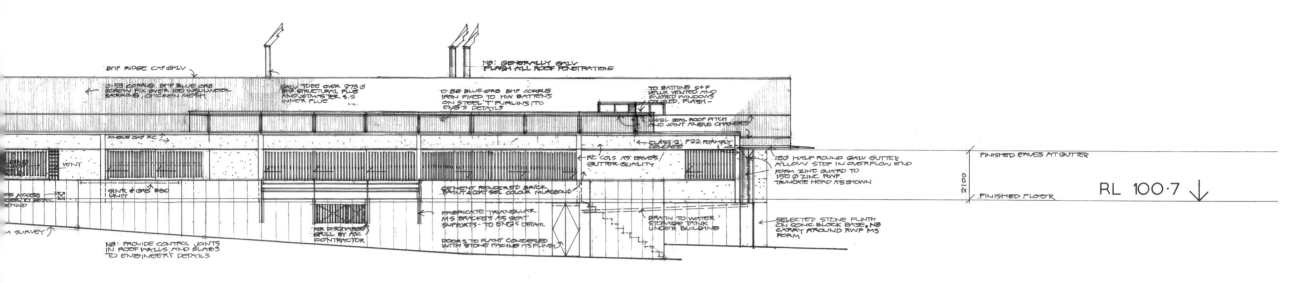

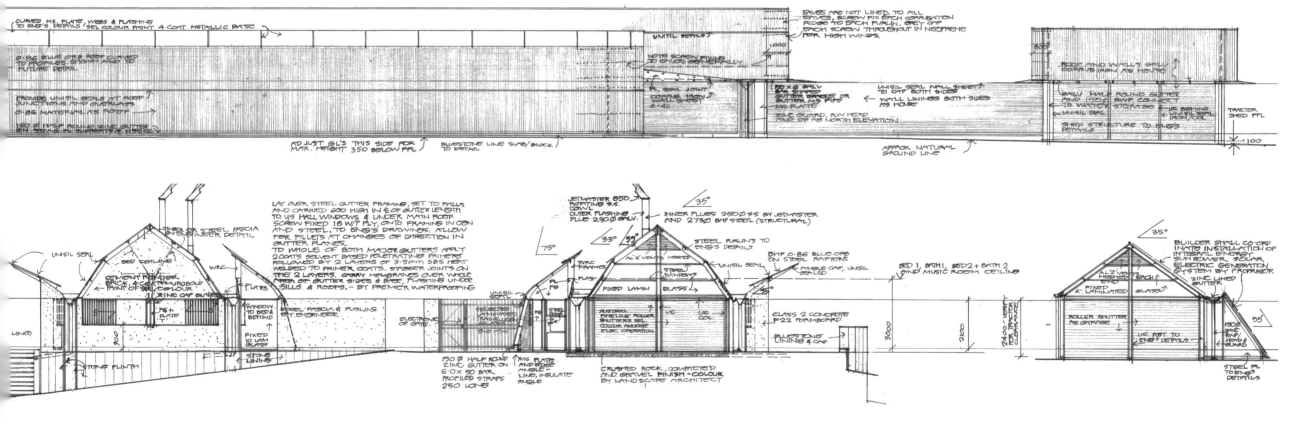

EAST

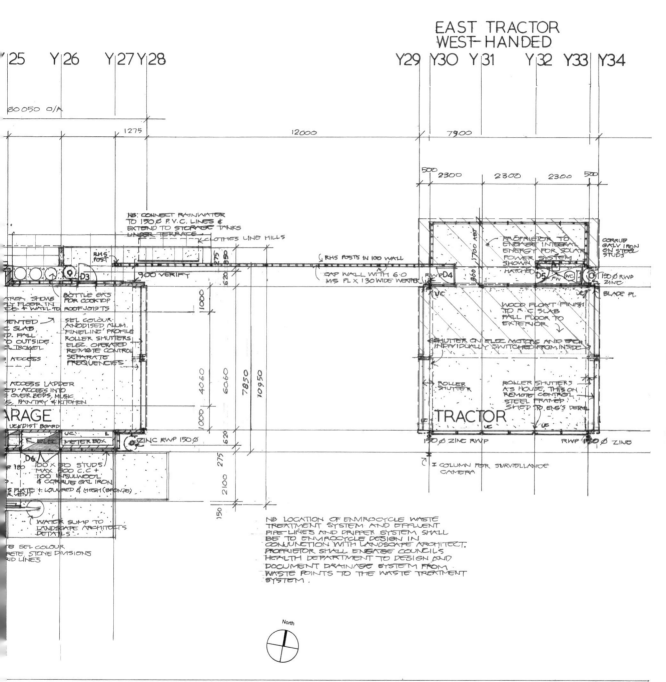

EAST TRACTOR
WEST-HANDED

Y25　Y26　Y27 Y28　　　　Y29 Y30　Y31　Y32 Y33 Y34

60.050 O/A

1275　　　12000　　　7900

500　2300　　2300　　2300　500

NB: CONNECT RAINWATER
TO 150∅ P.V.C. LINES &
EXTEND TO STORAGE TANKS
UNDER TERRACE
CLOTHES LINE HILLS

RHS POSTS IN 100 WALL
CAP WALL WITH 6.0
M.S. PL x 130 WIDE WEATHER

RHS POST

D3

900 VERIFY

RWP D4

D5

150∅ RWP ZINC

PROPRIETOR TO
ENGAGE INTERNAL
ENERGY FOR SOLAR
POWER SYSTEM
SHOWN HATCHED

CORRUG
GALV IRON
ON STEEL
STUDS

BOTTLE GAS
FOR COOKTOP

SET COLOUR
ANODISED ALUM.
FINELINE PROFILE
ROLLER SHUTTERS
ELEC. OPERATED
REMOTE CONTROL
SEPARATE
FREQUENCIES

WC

BLADE PL

WOOD FLOAT FINISH
TO R.C. SLAB
FALL FLOOR TO
EXTERIOR

SHUTTER ON ELEC MOTORS AND EACH
INDIVIDUALLY SWITCHED FROM INSIDE

ACCESS LADDER
ACCESS INTO
OVER BEDS, MUSIC
PANTRY & KITCHEN

ROLLER
SHUTTER

ROLLER SHUTTERS
AS HOUSE, THIS ON
REMOTE CONTROL
STEEL FRAMED
SHED TO ENG'S DETAIL

GARAGE

TRACTOR

ELEC METER BOX

D6

ZINC RWP 150∅

150∅ ZINC RWP

RWP 150∅ ZINC

100 x 50 STUDS
MAX 600 C.C. +
100 INSULWOOL
& CORRUG GAL IRON

PLATE + LOUVRE & MESH (BRONZE)
VENT

COLUMN FOR SURVEILLANCE
CAMERA

WATER SUMP TO
LANDSCAPE ARCHITECTS
DETAILS

SET COLOUR
STONE DIVISIONS
LINES

NB LOCATION OF ENVIROCYCLE WASTE
TREATMENT SYSTEM AND EFFLUENT
PIPE LINES AND DRIPPER SYSTEM SHALL
BE TO ENVIROCYCLE DESIGN IN
CONJUNCTION WITH LANDSCAPE ARCHITECT.
PROPRIETOR SHALL ENGAGE COUNCIL'S
HEALTH DEPARTMENT TO DESIGN AND
DOCUMENT DRAINAGE SYSTEM FROM
WASTE POINTS TO THE WASTE TREATMENT
SYSTEM.

North

ING DRAWING
OUSE KANGALOON
RCUTT AND ASSOCIATES PTY LTD ARCHITECTS
98

0　1　2　　　5m

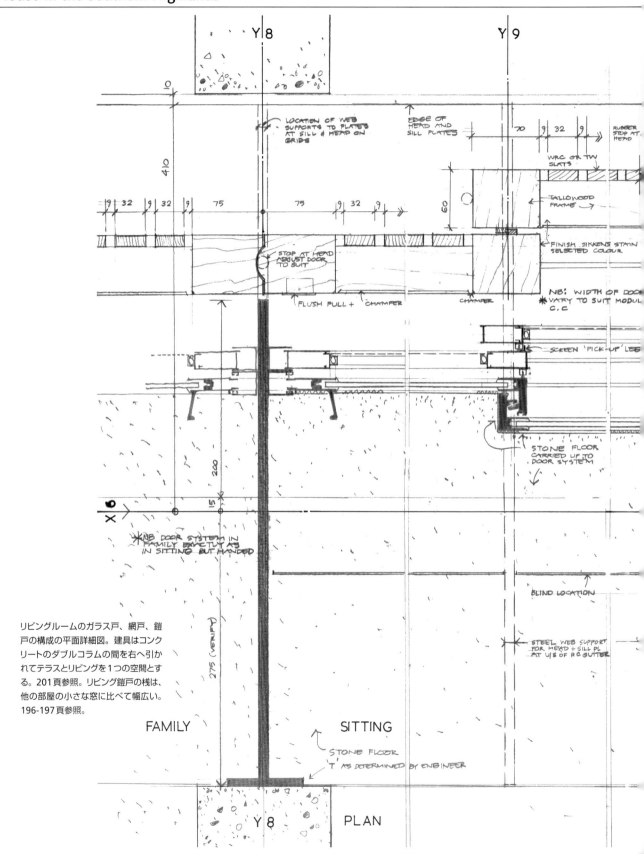

Y 8   Y 9

LOCATION OF WEB
SUPPORTS TO PLATES
AT SILL & HEAD ON
GRIDS

EDGE OF
HEAD AND
SILL PLATES

70   9 32   9

RUBBER
STOP AT
HEAD

WRC OR TW
SLATS

TALLOWOOD
FRAME

FINISH SIKKENS STAIN
SELECTED COLOUR

STOP AT HEAD
ADJUST DOOR
TO SUIT

NB: WIDTH OF DOOR
VARY TO SUIT MODUL
C.C

FLUSH PULL + CHAMFER

CHAMFER

SCREEN 'PICK-UP' LEG

STONE FLOOR
CARRIED UP TO
DOOR SYSTEM

NB DOOR SYSTEM IN
FAMILY EXACTLY AS
IN SITTING BUT HANDED

BLIND LOCATION

STEEL WEB SUPPORT
FOR HEAD + SILL PL
AT U/S OF RC GUTTER

リビングルームのガラス戸、網戸、鎧
戸の構成の平面詳細図。建具はコンク
リートのダブルコラムの間を右へ引か
れてテラスとリビングを1つの空間とす
る。201頁参照。リビング鎧戸の桟は、
他の部屋の小さな窓に比べて幅広い。
196-197頁参照。

FAMILY   SITTING

STONE FLOOR
T' AS DETERMINED BY ENGINEER

Y 8   PLAN

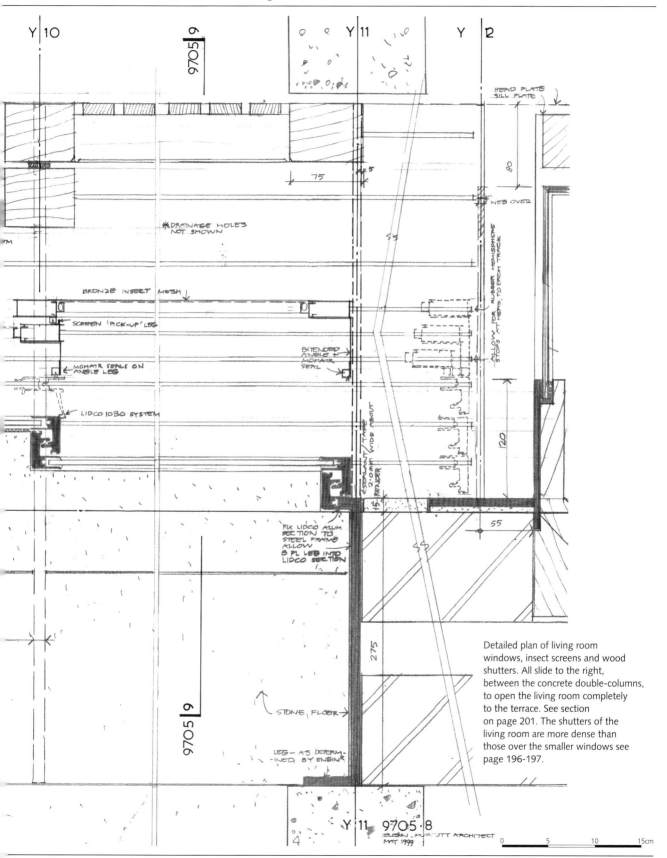

Y 10

9705 9

Y 11

Y 12

HEAD PLATE
SILL PLATE

80

WEB OVER

75

5

55

ALLOW FOR RUBBER HEMISPHERE
STOP'S AT HEAD, TO EACH TRACK

*DRAINAGE HOLES
NOT SHOWN

BRONZE INSECT MESH

SCREEN 'PICK-UP' LEG

EXTENDED
ANGLE +
MOHAIR
SEAL

120

MOHAIR SEALS ON
ANGLE LEG

LIDCO 1030 SYSTEM

SEALANT TAPE
20 MM WIDE ABOUT

15

READER

55

FIX LIDCO ALUM
SECTION TO
STEEL FRAME
ALLOW

8 PL LEG INTO
LIDCO SECTION

9705 9

275

Detailed plan of living room
windows, insect screens and wood
shutters. All slide to the right,
between the concrete double-columns,
to open the living room completely
to the terrace. See section
on page 201. The shutters of the
living room are more dense than
those over the smaller windows see
page 196-197.

STONE FLOOR →

LEG - AS DETERM-
INED BY ENGIN.

Y 11 9705·8
GLENN MURCUTT ARCHITECT
MAY 1999

4

0   5   10   15cm

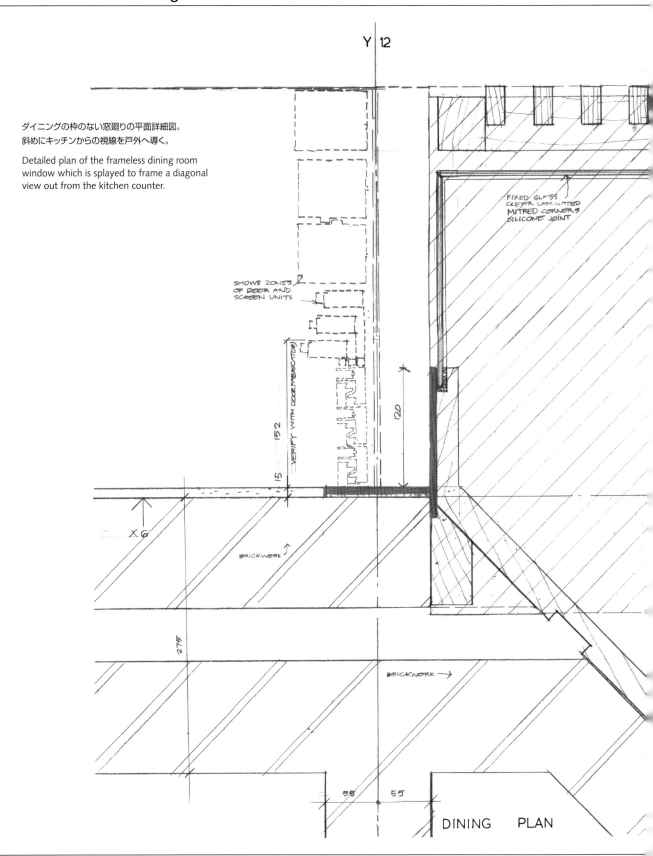

Y 12

ダイニングの枠のない窓廻りの平面詳細図。
斜めにキッチンからの視線を戸外へ導く。

Detailed plan of the frameless dining room
window which is splayed to frame a diagonal
view out from the kitchen counter.

FIXED GLASS
CLEAR LAMINATED
MITRED CORNERS
SILICONE JOINT

SHOWS ZONES
OF DOOR AND
SCREEN UNITS

VERIFY WITH DOOR FABRICATOR

152

15

120

X 6

BRICKWORK

275

BRICKWORK

55   55

DINING   PLAN

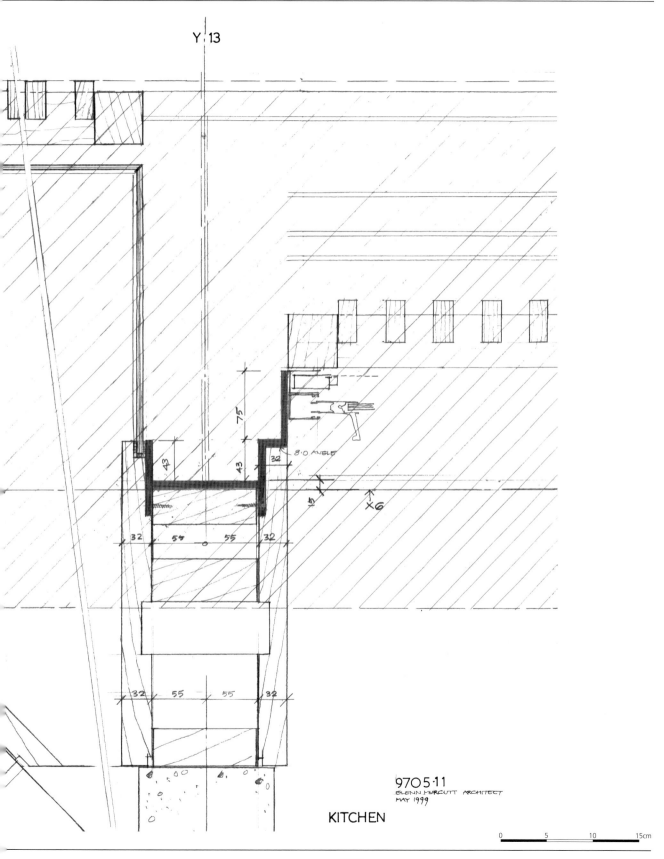

KITCHEN

9705·11
GLENN MURCUTT ARCHITECT
MAY 1999

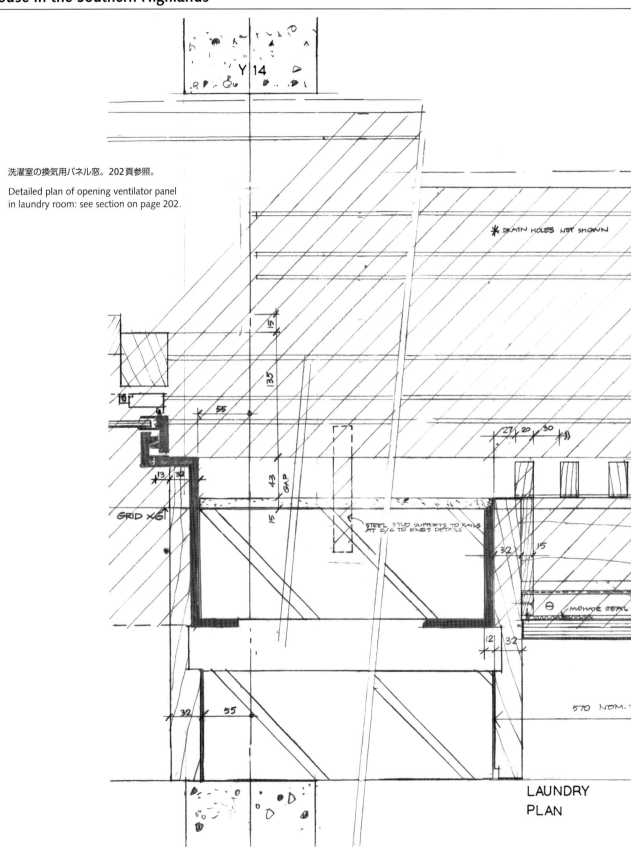

洗濯室の換気用パネル窓。202頁参照。

Detailed plan of opening ventilator panel
in laundry room: see section on page 202.

Y 14

＊ DRAIN HOLES NOT SHOWN

15

13.5

55

10

43 GAP

15

13 32

GRID X6

27 20 30

STEEL STUD SUPPORTS TO RAILS
AT C/C TO ENES DETAILS

32 15

MOHAIR SEAL

12 32

570 NOM.

32 55

LAUNDRY
PLAN

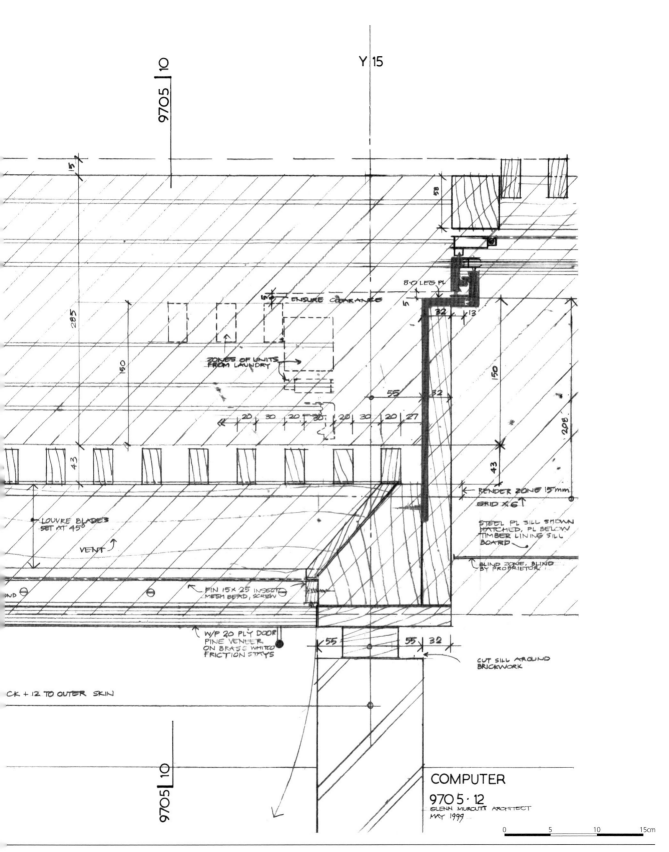

9705 10

Y 15

15

58

285

8·0 LEG PL

5

32   13

ENSURE CLEARANCE

ZONES OF UNITS
FROM LAUNDRY

150

150

32

55   32

208

20 30 20 30 20 30 20 27

43

RENDER ZONE 15mm
GRID x6

43

LOUVRE BLADES
SET AT 45°

STEEL PL SILL SHOWN
HATCHED, PL BELOW
TIMBER LINING SILL
BOARD

VENT

BLIND ZONE, BLIND
BY PROPRIETOR

FIN 15 x 25 INSECT
MESH BEAD, SCREW

W/P 20 PLY DOOR
PINE VENEER
ON BRASS WHITCO
FRICTION STAYS

55

55   32

CUT SILL AROUND
BRICKWORK

CK + 12 TO OUTER SKIN

9705 10

COMPUTER

9705 · 12
GLENN MURCUTT ARCHITECT
MAY 1999

0   5   10   15cm

書斎と音楽室の窓と換気パネルの平面詳細図。
Detailed plan of music room window and ventilator panel.

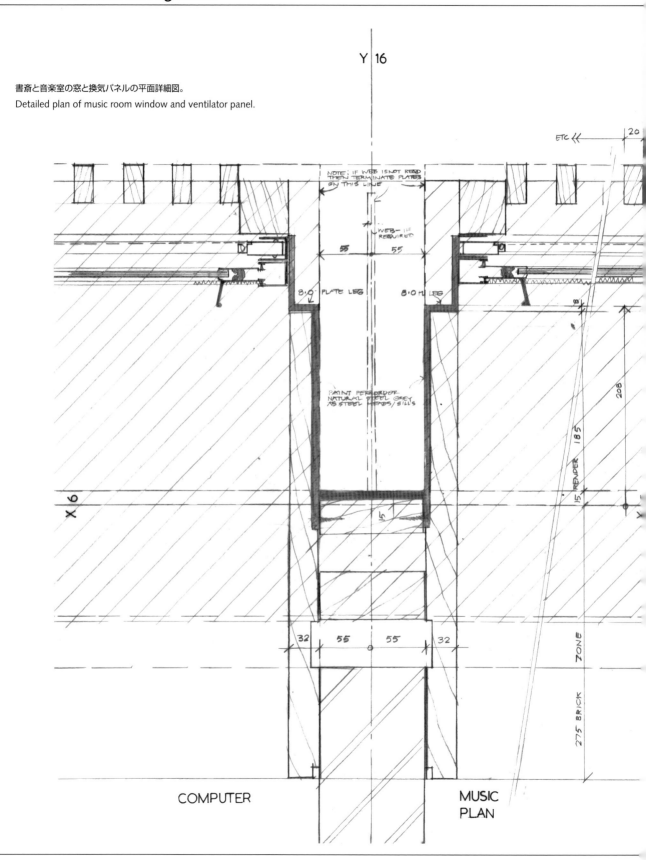

Y 16

ETC ‹‹   20

NOTE: IF WEB IS NOT READ
THEN TERMINATE PLATES
ON THIS LINE

WEB - IF
REQUIRED

55   55

8.0 PLATE LEG   8.0 M LEG

PAINT FERRODOR
NATURAL STEEL GREY
AS STEEL HEADS/SILLS

X 6

X 6

15 RENDER   185   208

18

32   55   55   32

275 BRICK   ZONE

COMPUTER

MUSIC
PLAN

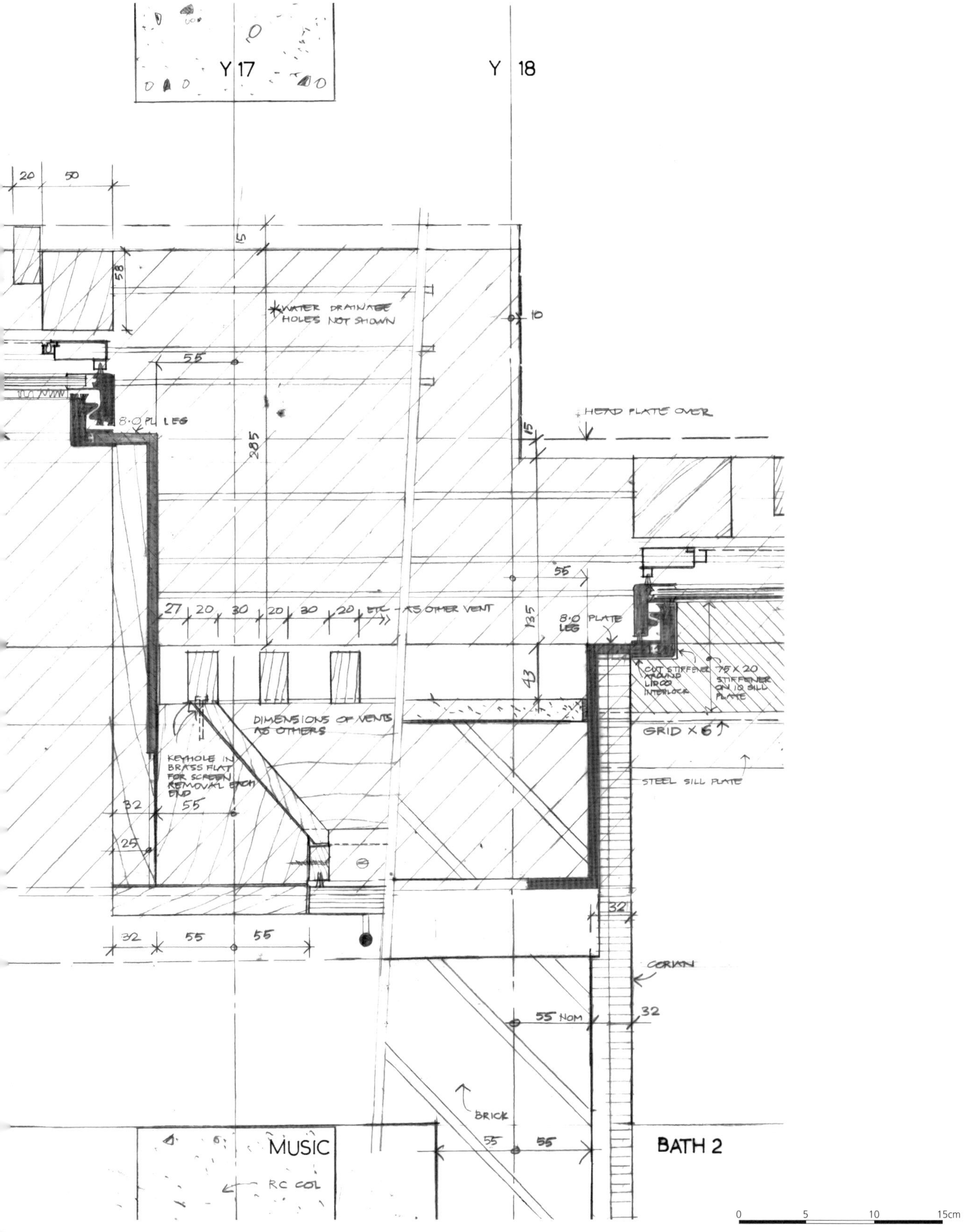

Y 17

Y 18

20 50

15

58

* WATER DRAINAGE
HOLES NOT SHOWN

10

55

HEAD PLATE OVER

15

8·0 PL LEG

285

55

8·0 PLATE
LEG

27 20 30 20 30 20 ETC AS OTHER VENT

135

CUT STIFFENER 78 × 20
AROUND
LIPGO
INTERLOCK

STIFFENER
ON 10 SILL
PLATE

43

DIMENSIONS OF VENTS
AS OTHERS

GRID × 6

KEYHOLE IN
BRASS FLAT
FOR SCREEN
REMOVAL EACH
END

STEEL SILL PLATE

32 55

25

32 55 55

32

CORIAN

55 NOM

32

BRICK

55 55

MUSIC

BATH 2

RC COL

0   5   10   15cm

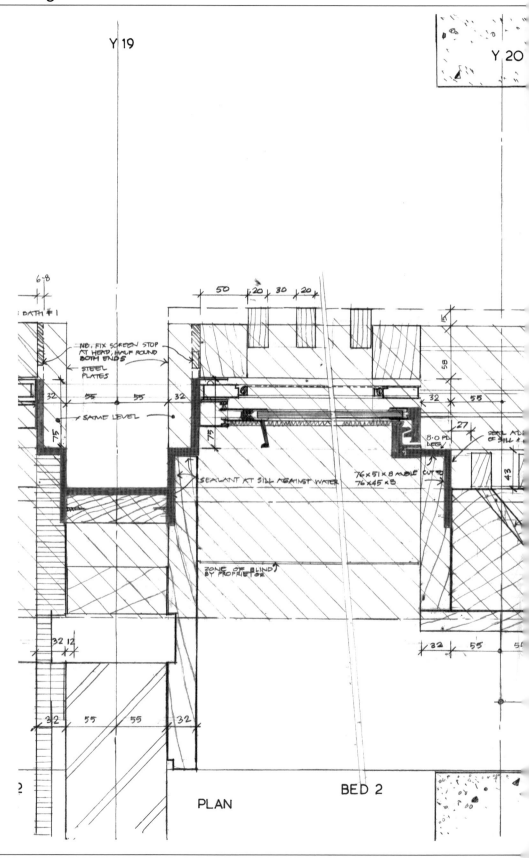

寝室の窓と換気用パネルの平面詳細図。
Detailed plan of bedroom window and ventilator panel.

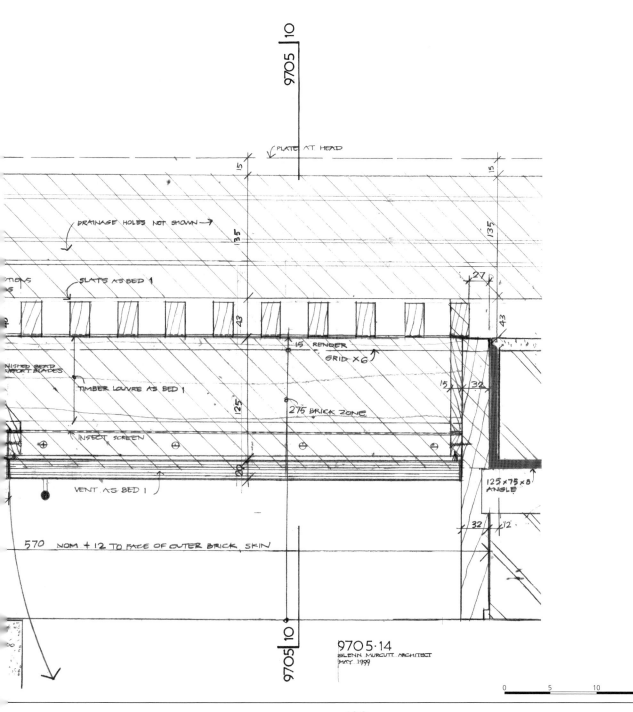

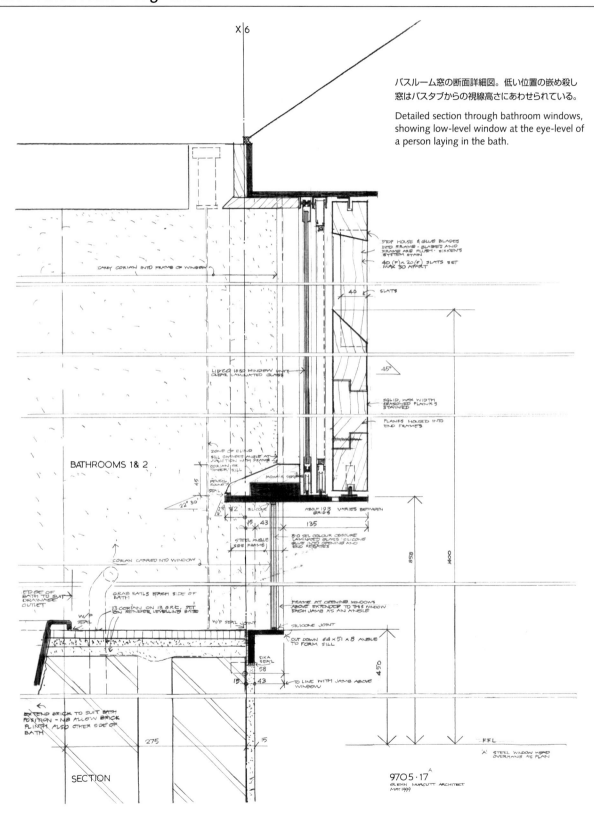

バスルーム窓の断面詳細図。低い位置の嵌め殺し窓はバスタブからの視線高さにあわせられている。

Detailed section through bathroom windows, showing low-level window at the eye-level of a person laying in the bath.

BATHROOMS 1 & 2

SECTION

9705·17
GLENN MURCUTT ARCHITECT
MAY 1999

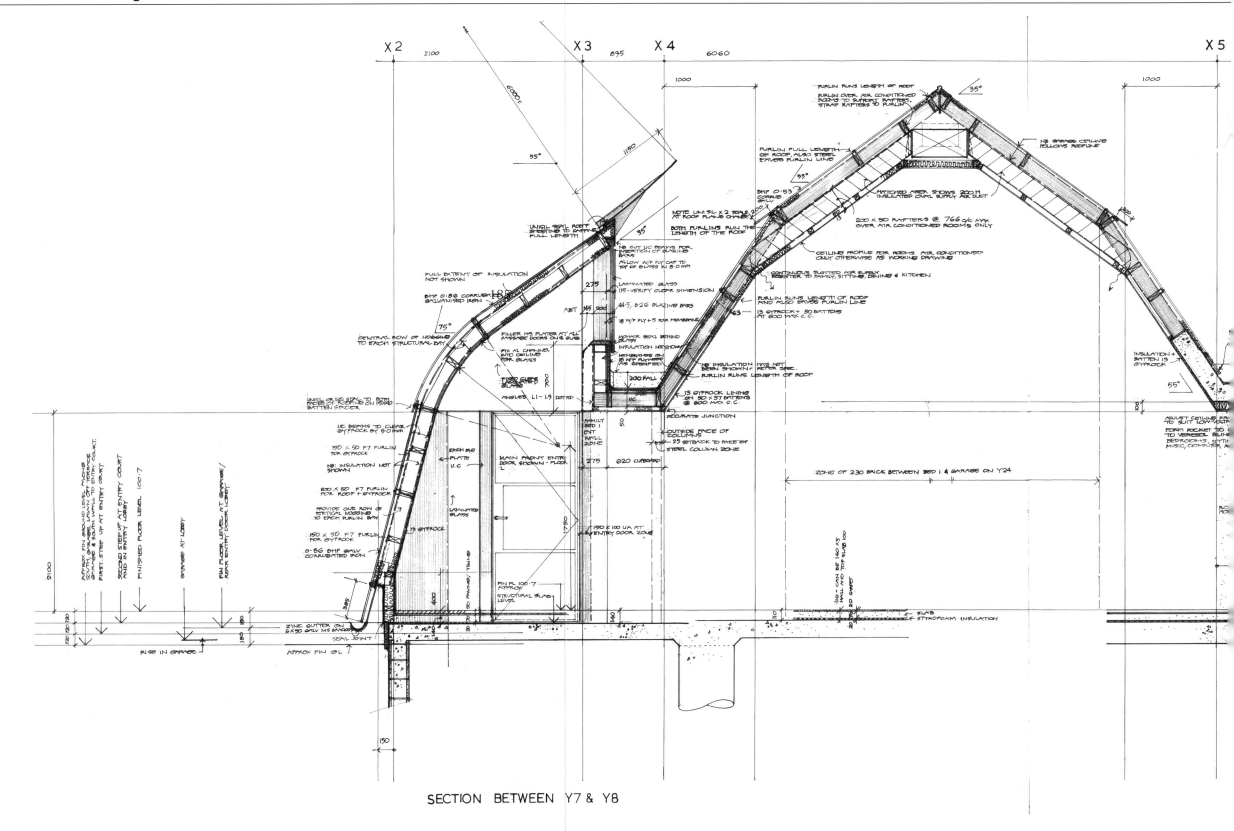

SECTION BETWEEN Y7 & Y8

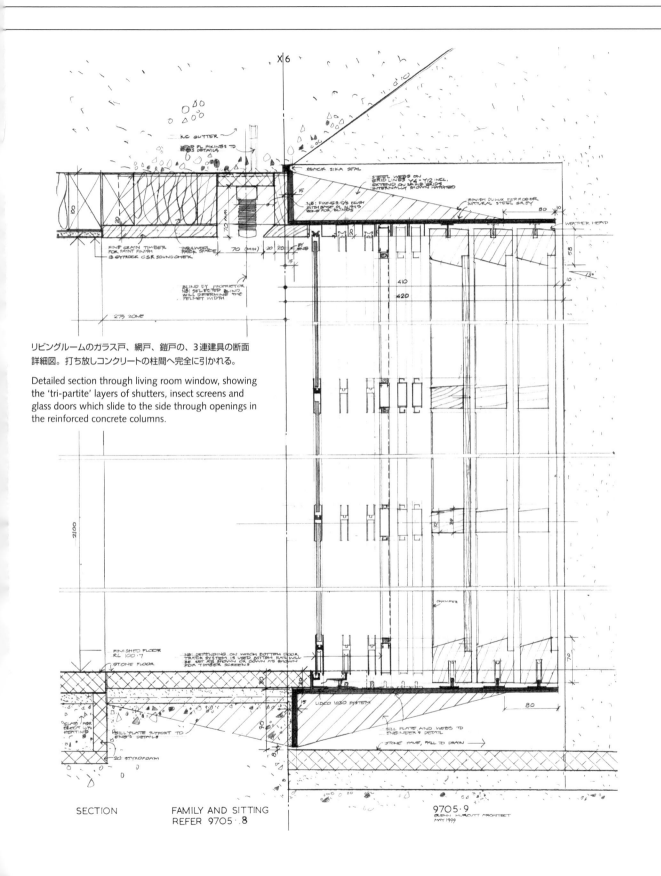

リビングルームのガラス戸、網戸、鎧戸の、3連建具の断面
詳細図。打ち放しコンクリートの柱間へ完全に引かれる。

Detailed section through living room window, showing
the 'tri-partite' layers of shutters, insect screens and
glass doors which slide to the side through openings in
the reinforced concrete columns.

SECTION　　FAMILY AND SITTING
REFER 9705 · 8

9705·9

換気用パネルの断面詳細図。

Detailed section through opening
ventilator panel.

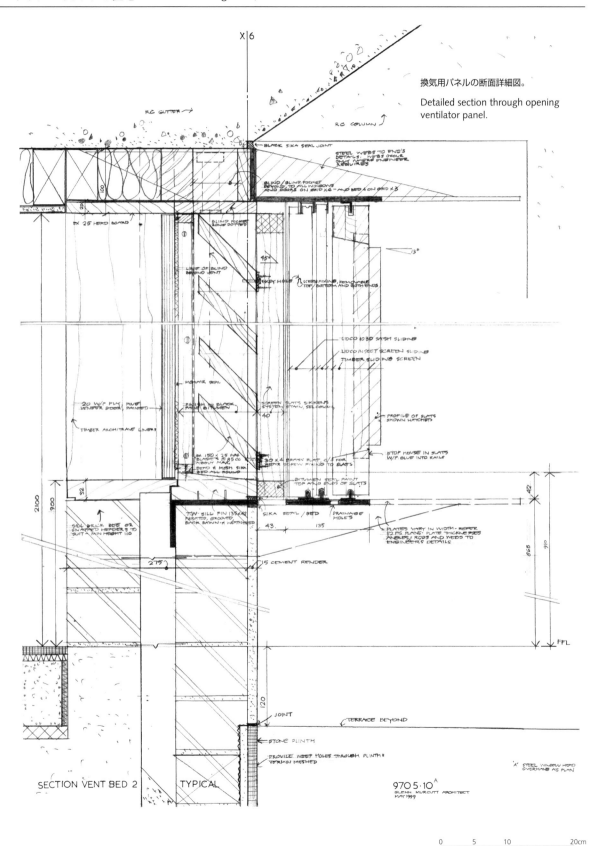

SECTION VENT BED 2　　TYPICAL

9705·10

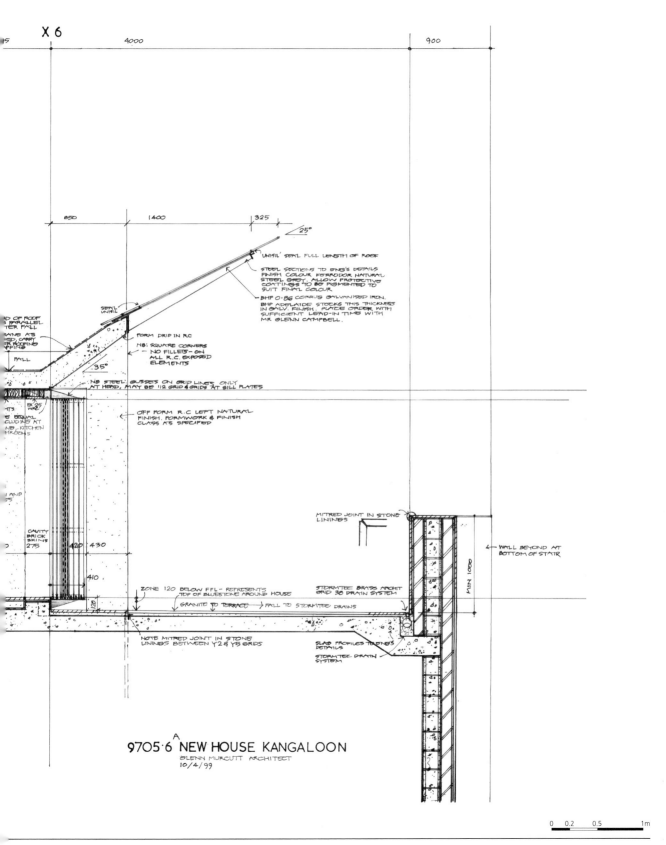

X 6

4000

900

850　　　1400　　325

25°

'UNISIL' SEAL FULL LENGTH OF ROOF

STEEL SECTIONS TO ENG'S DETAILS
FINISH COLOUR FERRODOR NATURAL
STEEL GREY. ALLOW PROTECTIVE
COATINGS TO BE PIGMENTED TO
SUIT FINAL COLOUR

BHP 0·86 CORRUG GALVANISED IRON.
BHP ADELAIDE STOCKS THIS THICKNESS
IN GALV. FINISH. PLACE ORDER WITH
SUFFICIENT LEAD-IN TIME WITH
MR GLENN CAMPBELL.

SEAL
UNISIL

FORM DRIP IN RC

NB: SQUARE CORNERS
– NO FILLETS – ON
ALL R.C. EXPOSED
ELEMENTS

35°

NB STEEL GUSSETS ON GRID LINES ONLY
AT HEAD, MAY BE 112 GRID & GRIDS AT SILL PLATES

OFF FORM R.C LEFT NATURAL
FINISH. FORMWORK & FINISH
CLASS A5 SPECIFIED

MITRED JOINT IN STONE
LININGS

WALL BEYOND AT
BOTTOM OF STAIR

CAVITY
BRICK
SKINS
275

420　430

MIN 1000

410

120

ZONE 120 BELOW FFL – REPRESENTS
TOP OF BLUESTONE AROUND HOUSE

STORMTEC BRASS ARCHIT
GRID 38 DRAIN SYSTEM

GRANITE TO TERRACE　FALL TO STORMTEC DRAINS

NOTE MITRED JOINT IN STONE
LININGS BETWEEN Y2 & Y5 GRIDS

SLAB PROFILES TO ENG'S
DETAILS

STORMTEC DRAIN
SYSTEM

9705·6 NEW HOUSE KANGALOON
GLENN MURCUTT ARCHITECT
10/4/99

0　0.2　0.5　　1m

Murcutt-Lewin House and Studio

2000-03 Mosman, Sydney, New South Wales
Collaborating architect: Wendy Lewin

海抜150m。温暖な気候。夏は平均気温25度、稀に40度まで
上がるが、北東、南東からの涼風がある。
冬は18度前後、時折、西南西の冷たい風が10度まで下げる。
有機質、砂岩の混合分解地質。

Altitude: 150m above sea level. Temperate climate.
Summer, circa 25 deg C, infrequently up to 40 deg C with
north-east/south-east cooling winds. Winter, circa 18 deg C,
occasionally with cold west-south-west winds off
Mt. Kosciusko bringing lows of 10 deg C. Decomposed
sandstone soils and organic matter.

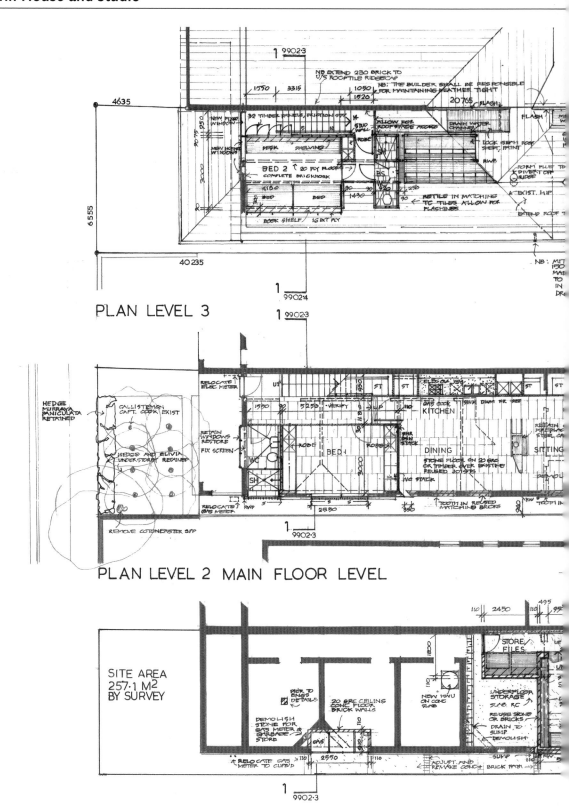

PLAN LEVEL 3

PLAN LEVEL 2 MAIN FLOOR LEVEL

SITE AREA
257·1 M²
BY SURVEY

PLAN LEVEL 1

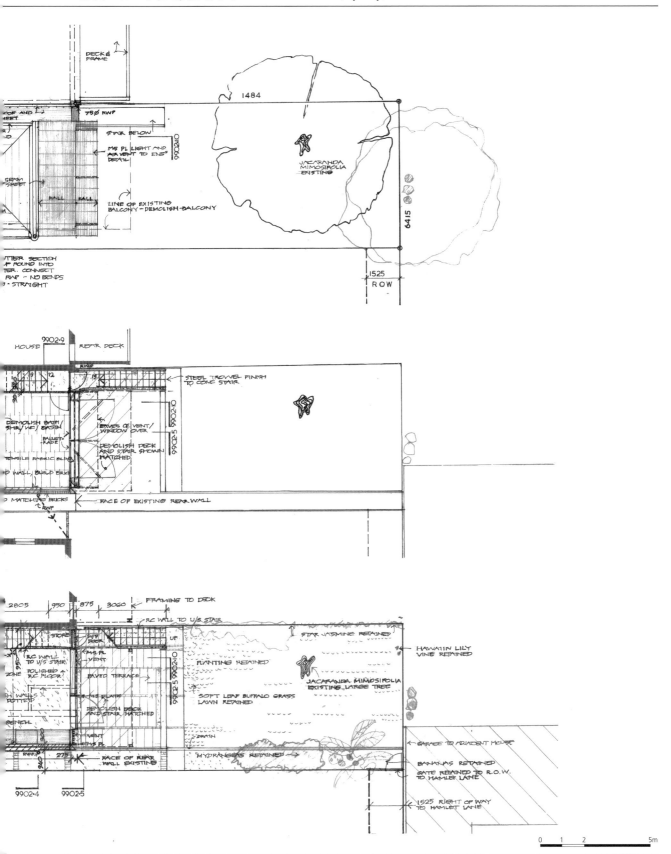

1484

750 RWP

DECK &
FRAME

STAIR BELOW

MS PL LIGHT AND
AIR VENT TO ENS
DETAIL

ROOF AND
SHEET

LINE OF EXISTING
BALCONY - DEMOLISH BALCONY

SKIN
SHEET

FALL   FALL

JACARANDA
MIMOSIFOLIA
EXISTING

6415

1525
ROW

UTTER SECTION
F ROUND INTO
TER. CONNECT
RAP - NO BENDS
- STRAIGHT

HOUSE   9902·9   REAR DECK

RWP

STEEL TROWEL FINISH
TO CONC STAIR

9902·10

9902·5

10   9   12   13

DEMOLISH BATH
SHR/WC/ BASIN

BALUST
RADE

EAVES OF VENT/
WINDOW OVER

TENSILE FABRIC BLIND

O WALL BUILD BRICK

DEMOLISH DECK
AND STAIR SHOWN
HATCHED

O MATCHING BRICKS
RWP

FACE OF EXISTING REAR WALL

2805   950   875   3060

FRAMING TO DECK

RC WALL TO U/S STAIR

STORE

RC WALL
TO U/S STAIR

MS PL
VENT

UP

STAR JASMINE RETAINED

HAWAIIN LILY
VINE RETAINED

PLANTING RETAINED

9902·10

9902·5

ZONE

POLISHED
RC FLOOR

PAVED TERRACE

H WALLS
ROTTED

MS PLATE

BENCH

DEMOLISH DECK
AND STAIR HATCHED

JACARANDA MIMOSIFOLIA
EXISTING LARGE TREE

SOFT LEAF BUFFALO GRASS
LAWN RETAINED

VENT

MS PL

DRAIN

RWP   940   270

FACE OF REAR
WALL EXISTING

HYDRANGEAS RETAINED

GARAGE TO ADJACENT HOUSE

BANANAS RETAINED
GATE RETAINED TO R.O.W.
TO HAMLET LANE

9902·4   9902·5

1525 RIGHT OF WAY
TO HAMLET LANE

0   1   2   5m

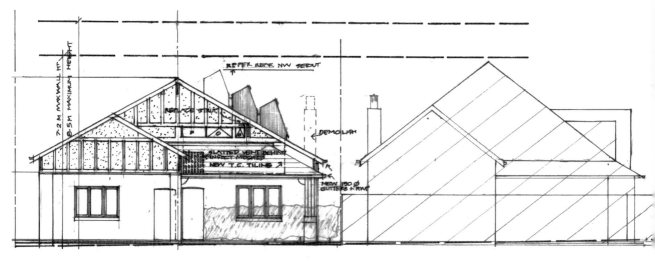

市内の典型的な2戸1棟式家屋の改築。通りから見ると、
既存屋根に取り付けられた天窓のみが改築を示す。

The project involved alterations to a typical small semi-detached
suburban house. From the street, the only indications of the new
work are the partial views of the skylights in the side roof.

SE FRONT

9902·10

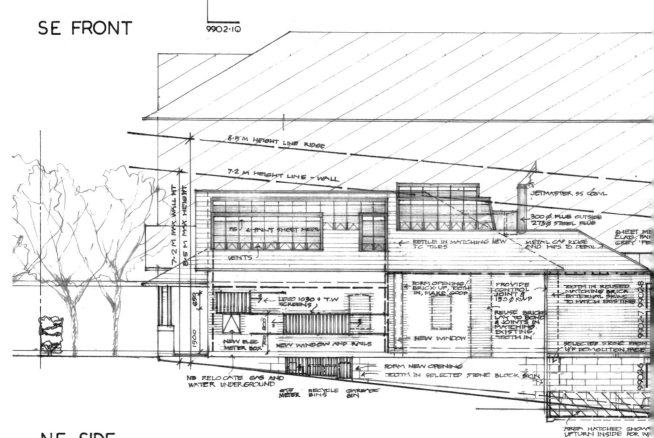

NE SIDE

ELEVATIONS
SECTION

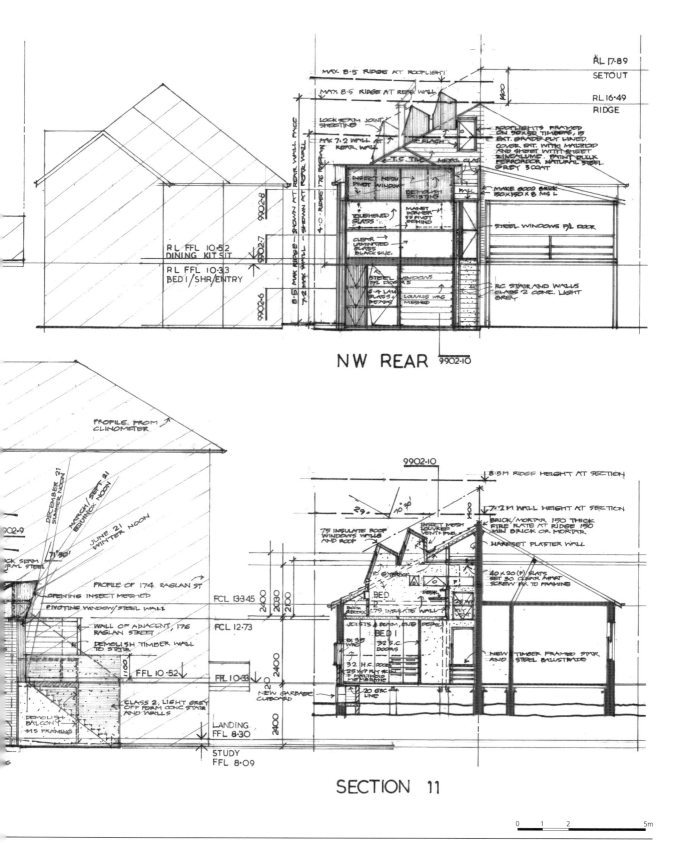

NW REAR

SECTION 11

0　1　2　　　　5m

長手断面図は、既存家屋の輪郭を大きく変えずに、まったく
違う内部空間を構成し直したことを表している。

Long section through the house showing a complete
re-configuration of the interior, achieved with only
minor changes to the exterior form.

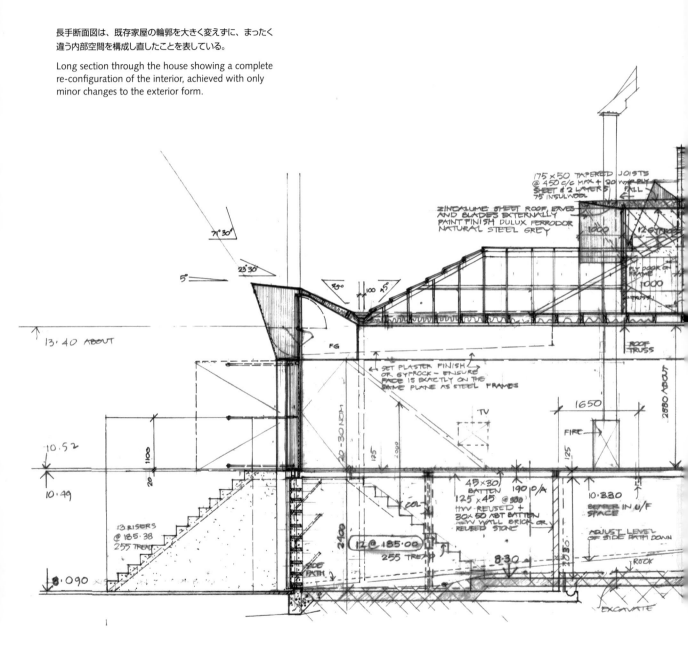

SECTION

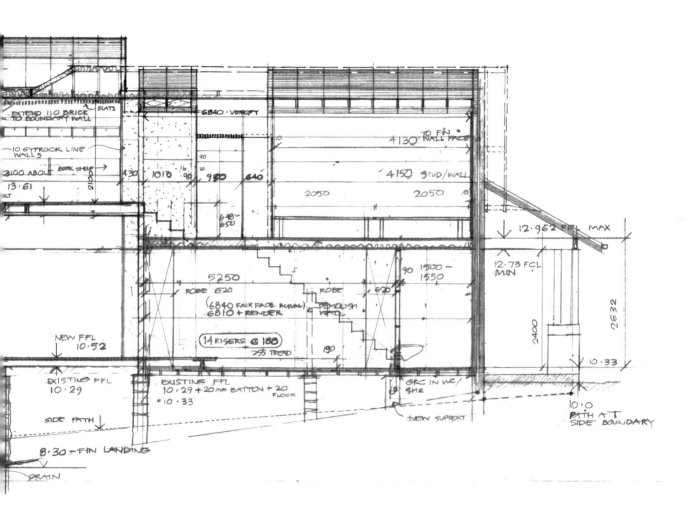

EXTEND 110 BRICK
TO BOUNDARY WALL

SLATS

6840 · VERIFY

TO FIN
WALL FACE
4130

−10 GYPROCK LINE
WALLS

90

3100 ABOUT   BOOK SHELF
13·61
OUT

4130   1010   90   930   640

4150 STUD/WALL

2050   2050

640 −
650

12·962 FFL MAX

5250

12·73 FCL
MIN

ROBE 620

90 1500 −
1550

ROBE   620

(6840 FAIR FACE ACTUAL)
6810 + RENDER

DEMOLISH
WALL

2400

2632

NEW FFL
10·52

14 RISERS @ 188

255 TREAD   190

10·33

EXISTING FFL
10·29

EXISTING FFL
10·29 + 20mm BATTEN + 20
= 10·33   FLOOR

GRC IN WC/
SHR

SIDE PATH

NEW SUPPORT

10·0
PATH AT
SIDE BOUNDARY

8·30 = FIN LANDING

DRAIN

9902·10°

0   1   2   3m

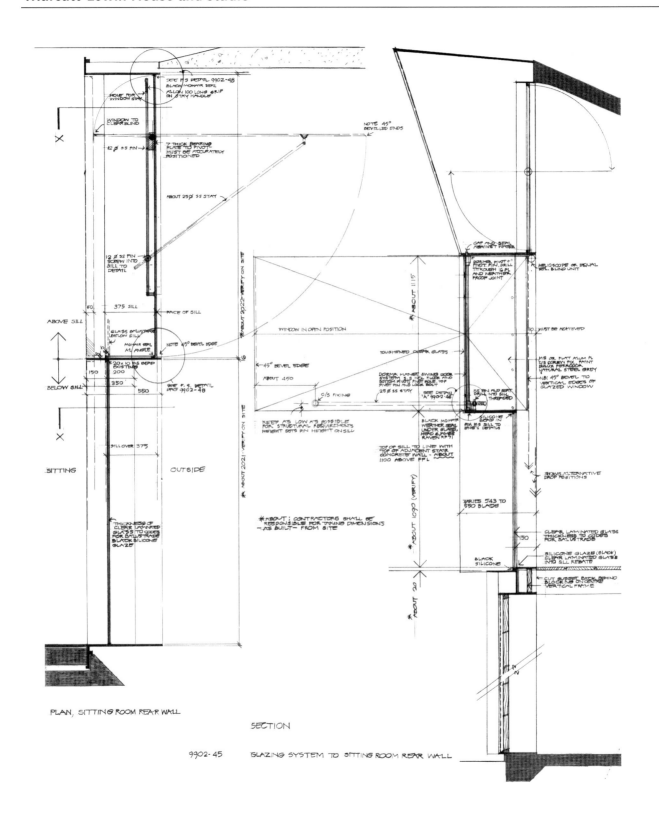

PLAN, SITTING ROOM REAR WALL

SECTION

9902-45   GLAZING SYSTEM TO SITTING ROOM REAR WALL

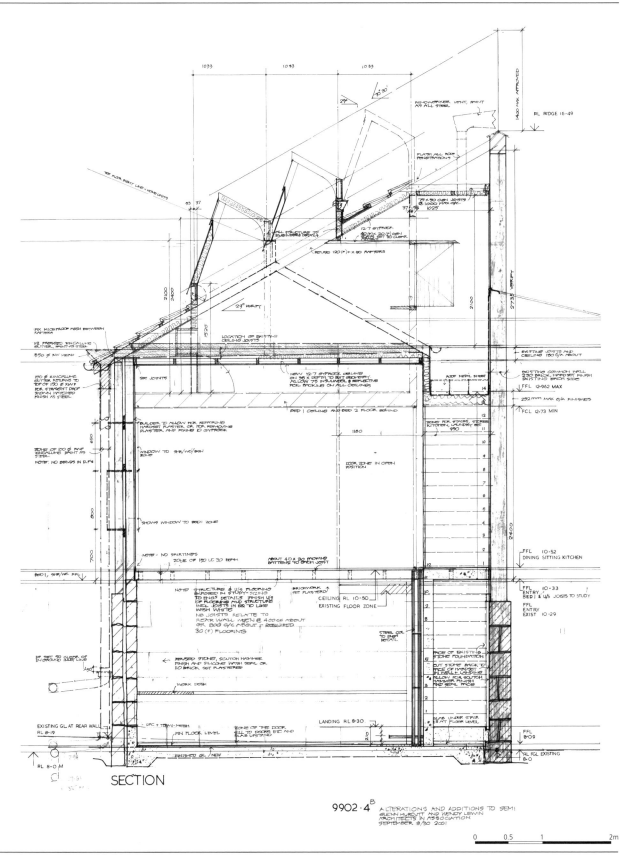

SECTION

9902·4^B ALTERATIONS AND ADDITIONS TO SEMI
GLENN MURCUTT AND WENDY LEWIN
ARCHITECTS IN ASSOCIATION
SEPTEMBER 18/30 2001

0   0.5   1   2m

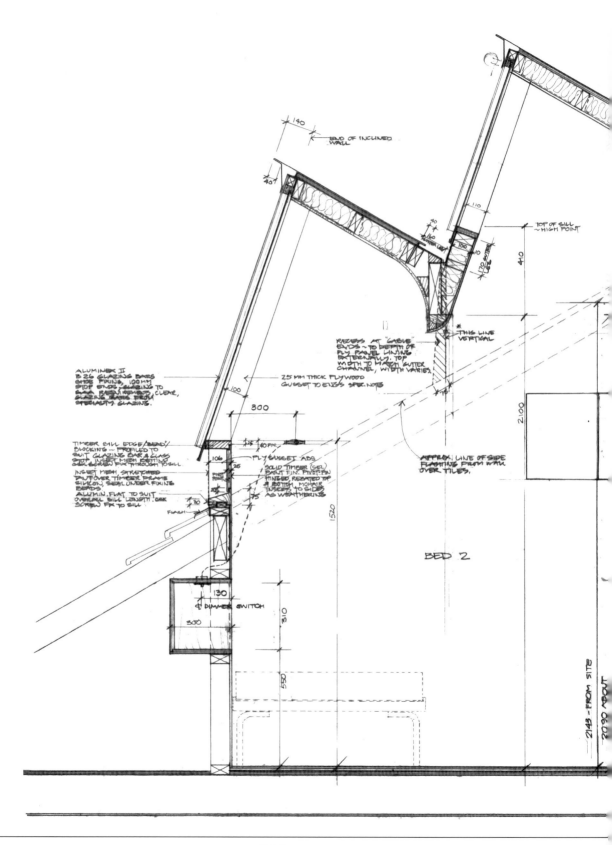

140
END OF INCLINED WALL

40

110

TOP OF SILL ~ HIGH POINT

40
160

100

410

RECESS AT GABLE ENDS ~ TO DEPTH OF FLY PANEL LINING EXTERNALLY. TOP WIDTH TO MATCH GUTTER CHANNEL. WIDTH VARIES.

THIS LINE VERTICAL

ALUMINEX II B26 GLAZING BARS SIDE FIXING, 100MM STOP ENDS. GLAZING TO SUIT. REFER RENDER, CLEAR, SPECIALTY GLAZING.

25 MM THICK PLYWOOD GUSSET TO ENGS SPEC NOTES

100

300

2100

TIMBER SILL EDGE / BEAD / BLOCKING — PROFILED TO SUIT GLAZING BAR & GLASS. INSET LINING FIX THROUGH TO SILL
INSECT MESH, STRETCHED TAUT OVER TIMBER FRAME SILICON, SEAL UNDER FIXING BEADS.
ALUMIN. FLAT TO SUIT OVERALL SILL LENGTH. OAK SCREW FIX TO SILL

125 40 PIN

FLY GUSSET TABS
SOLID TIMBER (SEL) PAINT FIN. PIVOT PIN HINGED, REBATED TOP & BOTTOM, MOHAIR INSERTS TO SIDES AS WEATHERLINE

106

25

PIVOT POINT

30

FLASH

APPROX. LINE OF SIDE FLASHING FROM WALL OVER TILES.

1520

130

¢ DIMMER SWITCH

300

310

550

2145 - FROM SITE

2090 ABOUT

BED 2

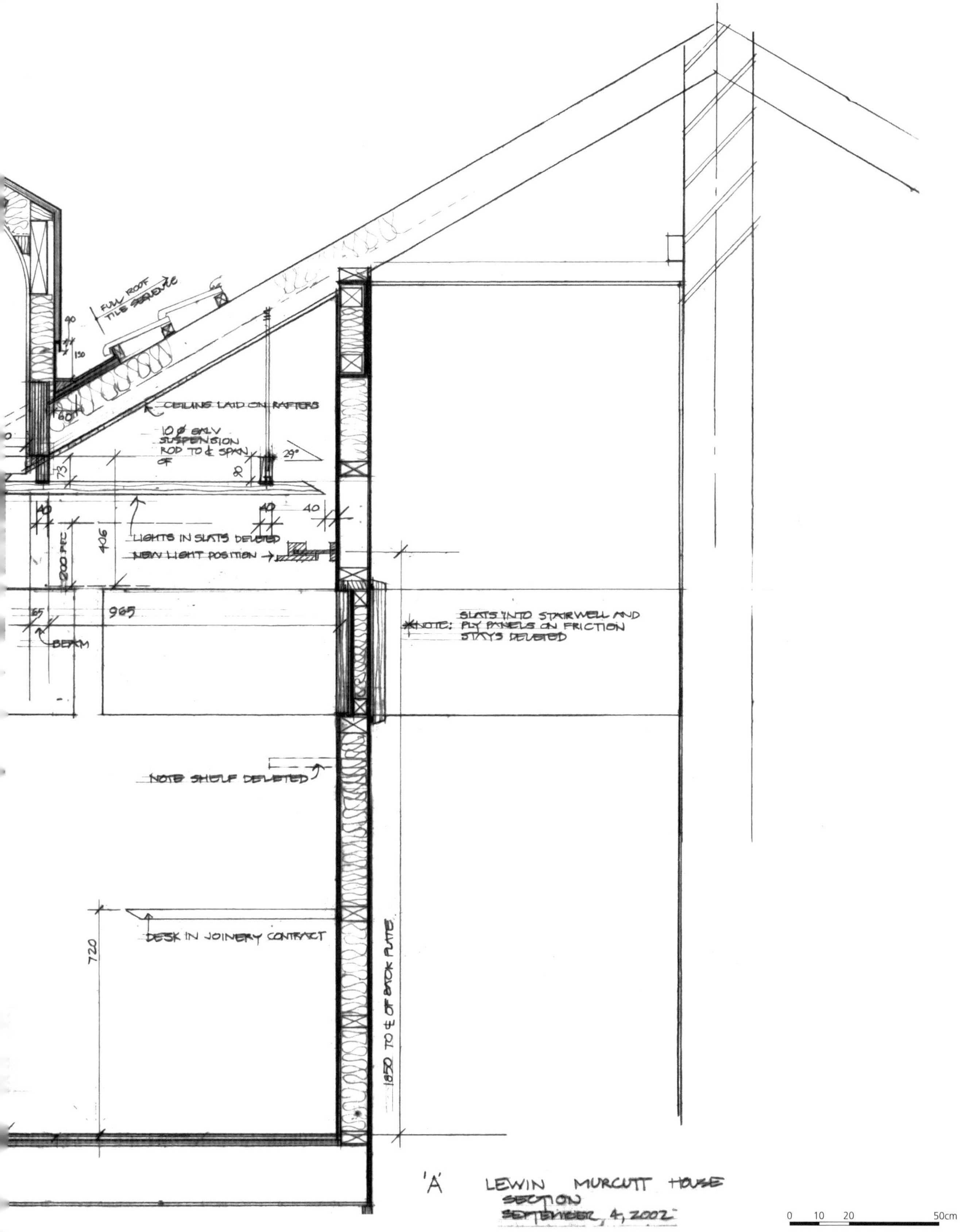

FULL ROOF TILE SCHEDULE

90

150

CEILING LAID ON RAFTERS

10 Ø GALV SUSPENSION ROD TO & SPAN OF

29°

73

LIGHTS IN SLATS DELETED

NEW LIGHT POSITION →

40   40   40

106

200 REG

55   965

BEAM

SLATS INTO STAIRWELL AND
*NOTE: PLY PANELS ON FRICTION
STAYS DELETED

← NOTE SHELF DELETED ↑

720

DESK IN JOINERY CONTRACT

1850 TO ₵ OF BACK PLATE

'A'   LEWIN   MURCUTT HOUSE
SECTION
SEPTEMBER 4, 2002

0   10   20   50cm

Walsh House

2001-05 Kangaroo Valley, New South Wales

海抜100m。温暖な気候。年間降雨量1,500mm。夏の気温は26度。冬の気温は23度前後だが、コジオスコ山からの風で最低気温は5度まで下がる。砂岩と粘土、有機物の混合分解地質。

Altitude: 100m above sea level. Temperate climate. Rainfall circa 1,500mm per year. Summer, circa 26 deg C. Winter, circa 23 deg C with winds off Mt. Kosciusko bringing lows of 5 deg C. Decomposed sandstone soils with organic matter and clay.

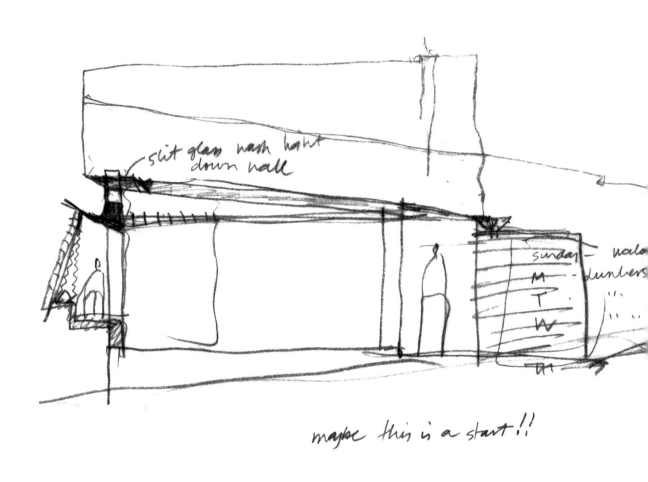

slit glass wash light
down wall

sunday — walo
M — dunkers
T
W

maybe this is a start !!

出窓の形状と使い方の検討。
Studies of the bay windows, and their ways of use.

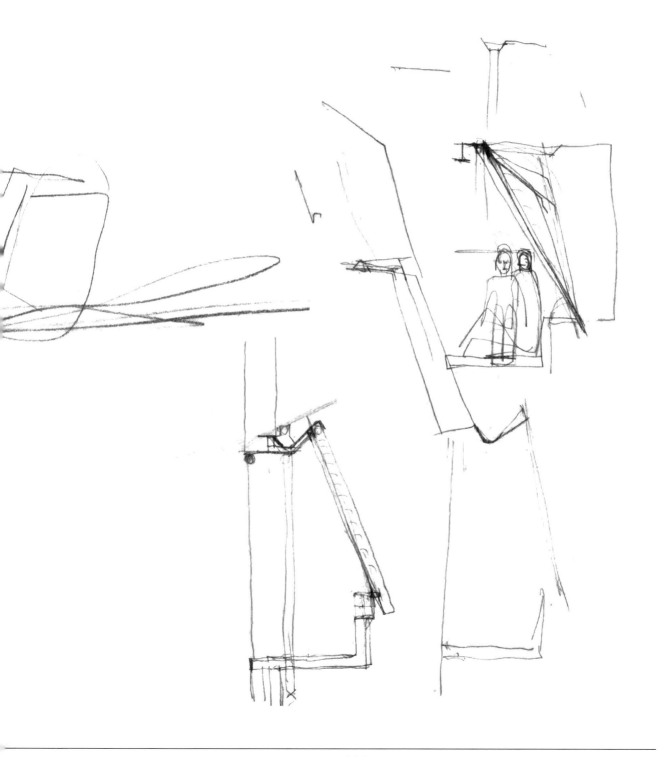

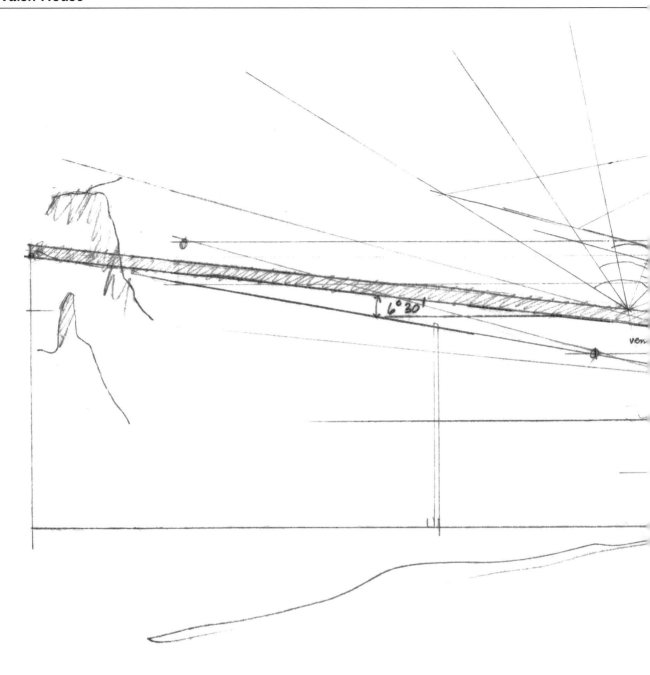

6°30'

ven

敷地周辺の顕著なランドスケープへの眺めを確保する屋根勾配の
検討。夏至、冬至の太陽光線の反射が、丘の上方の農家へまぶしく
ないようにとの配慮もしている。

Study of roof angle to frame views of surrounding landscape
features. The radiating lines indicate the angles of the sun
at mid-summer and mid-winter equinoxes, and its reflection
off the roof—ensuring the reflections do not disturb
neighbouring farm-houses.

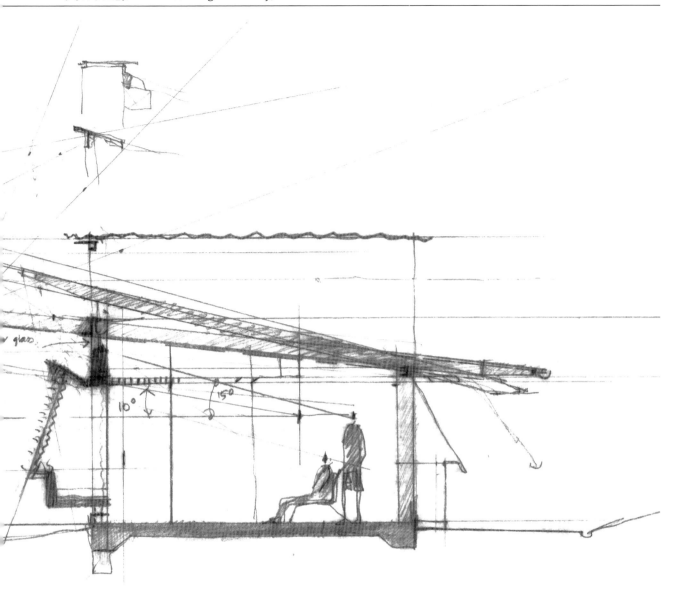

I'M LOOKING AT ANGLE VIEWS OF WEDDING CAKE MOUNTAIN TO THE NORTH AND THE PLUG TO THE EAST ON THE SAME DRAWING, MAKING SURE MY ROOF ANGLE DOES NOT CUT OUT HALF (OR ANY) OF THESE SUPERB LANDSCAPE ELEMENTS —

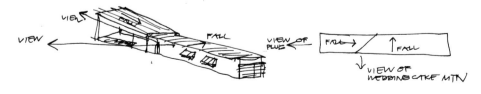

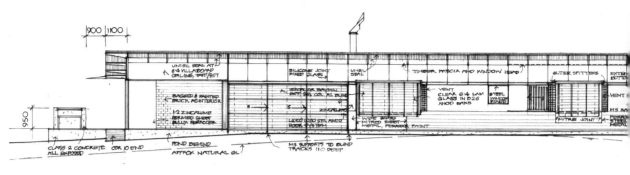

NORTH

SOUTH

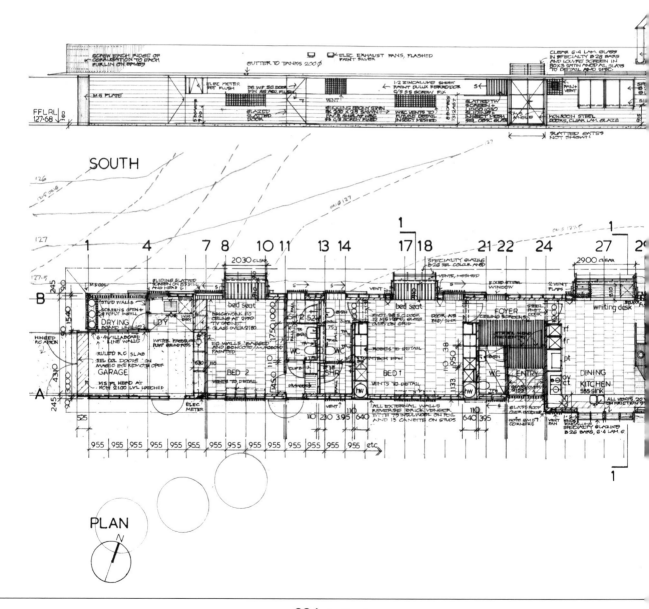

PLAN

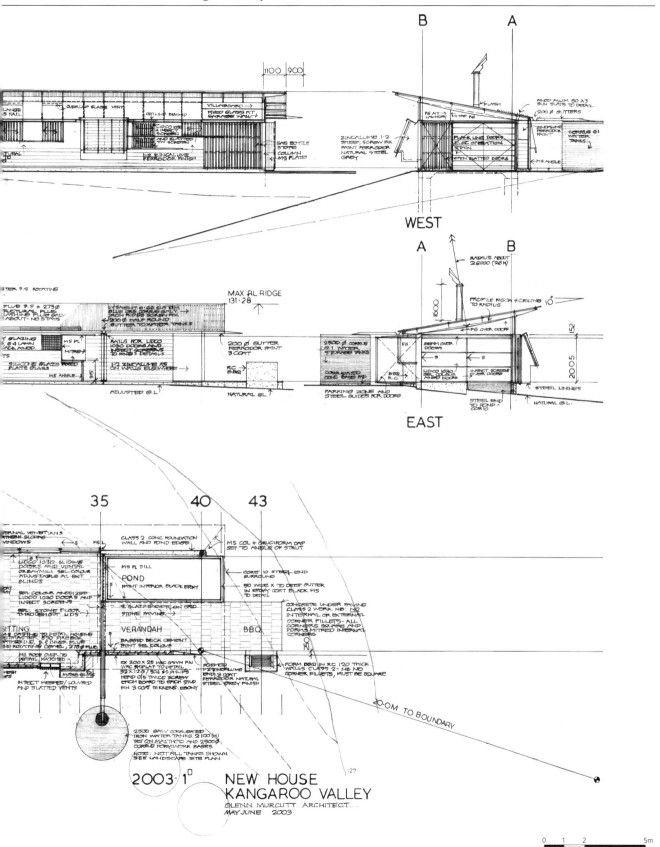

WEST

EAST

2003·1ᴰ　NEW HOUSE
KANGAROO VALLEY
GLENN MURCUTT ARCHITECT
MAY·JUNE　2003

0　1　2　　　5m

リビング断面詳細図。
Detailed section through the living room.

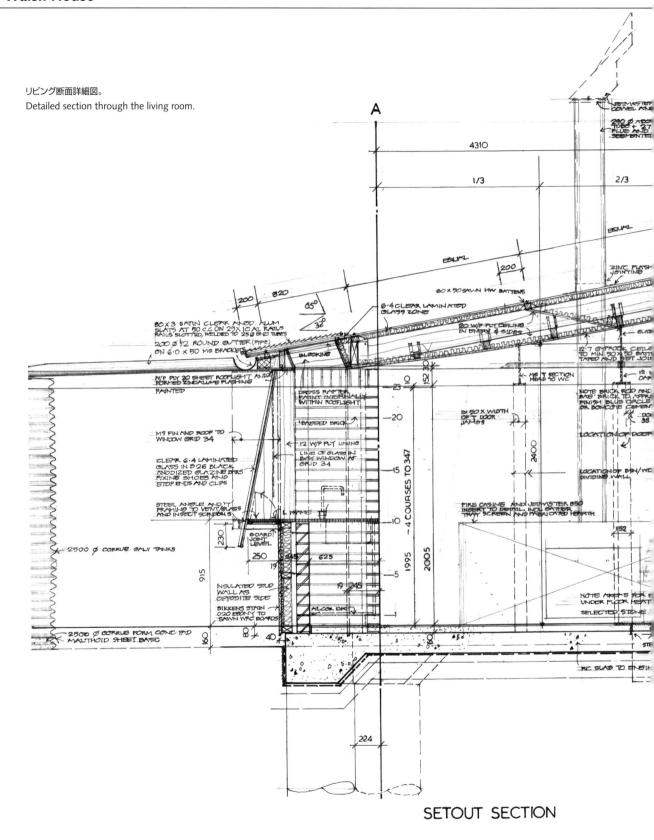

SETOUT SECTION

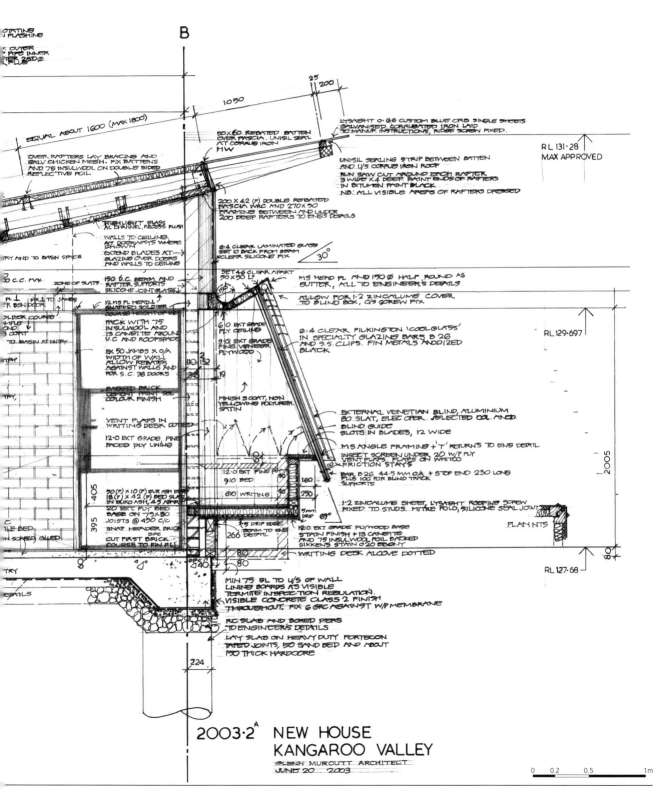

2003·2ᴬ NEW HOUSE
KANGAROO VALLEY
GLENN MURCUTT ARCHITECT
JUNE 20. 2003

0   0.2   0.5   1m

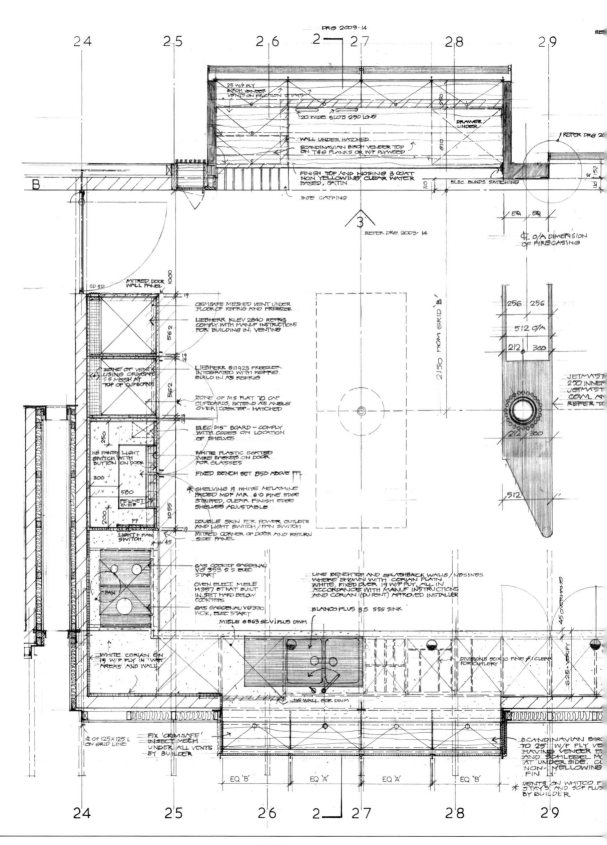

2003·13 B
JOINERY DETAIL SETOUT- KITCHEN/LIVING/WRITING
NEW HOUSE
KANGAROO VALLEY NSW
GLENN MURCUTT ARCHITECT
JANUARY 10, 2005

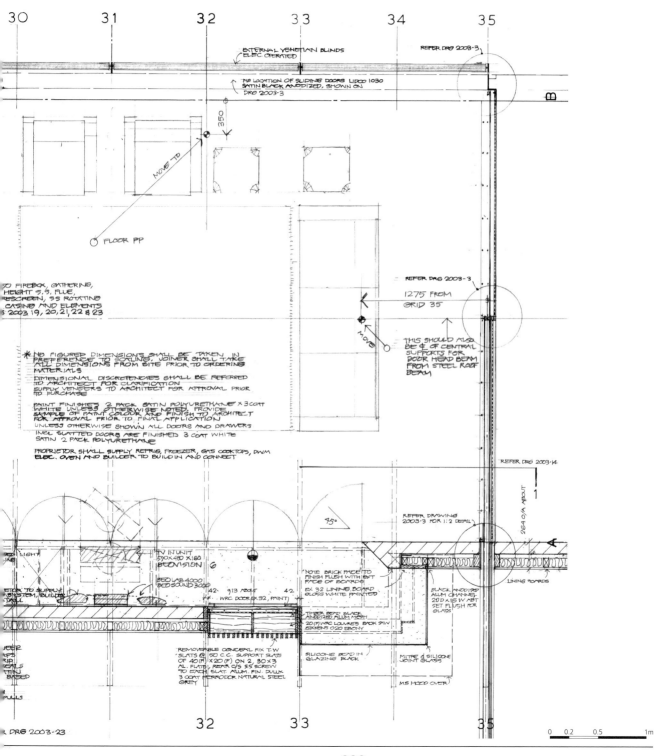

* NO FIGURED DIMENSIONS SHALL BE TAKEN IN
PREFERENCE TO SCALING. JOINER SHALL TAKE
ALL DIMENSIONS FROM SITE PRIOR TO ORDERING
MATERIALS

DIMENSIONAL DISCREPENCIES SHALL BE REFERRED
TO ARCHITECT FOR CLARIFICATION
SUPPLY VENEERS TO ARCHITECT FOR APPROVAL PRIOR
TO PURCHASE

PAINT FINISHES 2 PACK SATIN POLYURETHANE × 3 COAT
WHITE UNLESS OTHERWISE NOTED, PROVIDE
SAMPLE OF PAINT COLOUR AND FINISH TO ARCHITECT
FOR APPROVAL PRIOR TO FINAL APPLICATION
UNLESS OTHERWISE SHOWN ALL DOORS AND DRAWERS
INCL SLATTED DOORS ARE FINISHED 3 COAT WHITE
SATIN 2 PACK POLYURETHANE

PROPRIETOR SHALL SUPPLY FRIDGE, FREEZER, GAS COOKTOPS, DWM
ELEC. OVEN AND BUILDER TO BUILD IN AND CONNECT

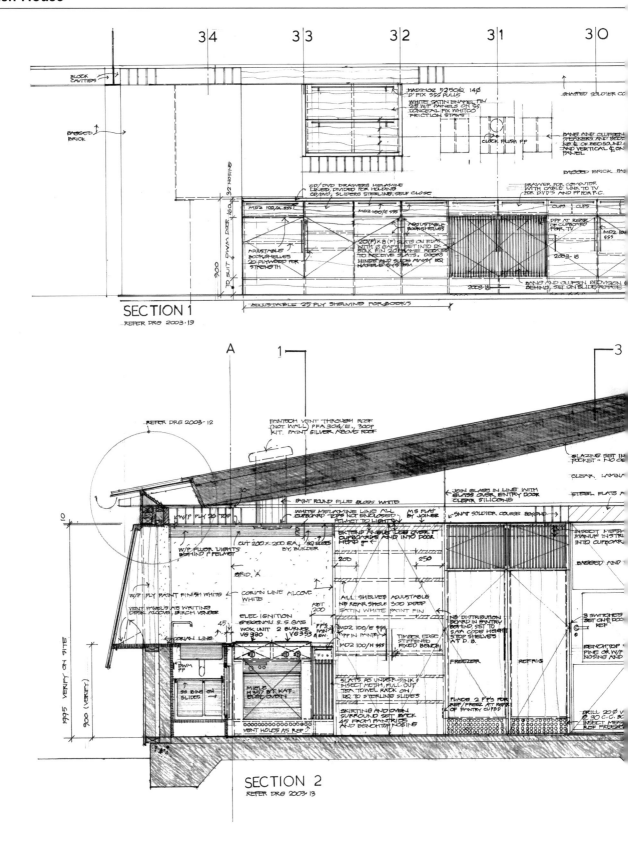

SECTION 1
REFER DRG 2003·13

SECTION 2
REFER DRG 2003·13

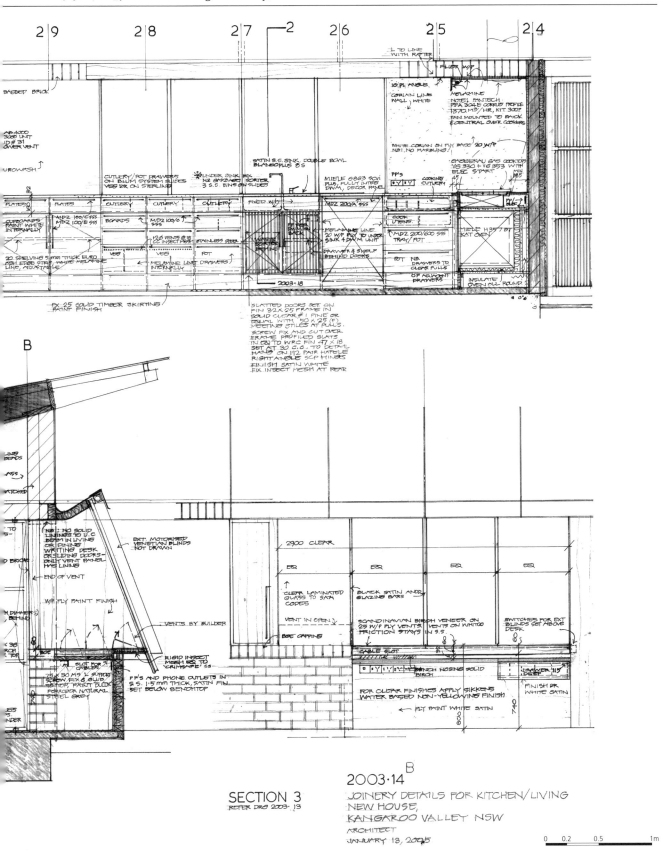

ガラスのない現代建築——
マーカット建築の部分¹的装置としての窓

勢山詔子

TOTOギャラリー・間、グレン・マーカット展（2008年6月12日〜8月9日）は、日本では初の氏の展覧会である。氏の作品は過去著名な日本の建築家の方たちによって紹介されてきたが、その作品を初めて目にする方も多いと思う。マーカット建築の美しさや緻密さ、平面計画の研鑽さに感動しつつ、日本建築のボキャブラリーを認識して親近感をもたれたのではないか。軸組がはっきりとあらわされる構造や、間に納まる建具の表情。さらに、マーカット建築の、建築自体が呼吸するような、自然エネルギーを利用する考え方（煙突効果や重力換気などの自然換気など）は日本の民家にも通じるものがある。しかし、氏の展覧会と作品集の準備のお手伝いをしたこの1年の作業を通じて、風土に沿った建築をつくっている氏は、オーストラリアの固有性に真摯に注目し続けており、結果としての（日本建築との）相似性は気候の1つの共通項にすぎないのだと思い始めた。その固有性とは何か、それがどうマーカット建築の魅力につながっているのだろうかと考えてみた。

1999年に初めてオーストラリアを訪れて、暑い気候にぴったりと合った数々の美しい建築を見た。それらの建物はシンプルだけれど普通の生活をしっかり支えるような哲学をもっていた。マーカットの親しい友達で大学での同僚でもあった、リチャード・レプラスタリエ設計の、ブリスベンに近いメイプルトンの住宅は、スコールに対応するため直径30cmはある雨樋で片流れの屋根を受けている。そしてそれは、窓面を熱い日射しからも守る。熱帯雨林の中にあり、湿気とヘビを避けるために高床である。ベランダへの出入りは引戸だったが、キッチンの窓は、壁の下半分、カウンターの高さにまで下げられて生い茂ったヤシの木に手が届くようであった。アイデアは簡素で実際的だったが、建物は、注意深い設計と施工で建てられていた。

レプラスタリエと同様に、マーカットの建築の美しさは、必要不可欠な要素を読み解くように、彼自身の解釈がデザインに昇華されて生まれる。出世作とな

---

1 「彼の建築が、その気候とランドスケープに関連したサスティナビリティに配慮し始めた。（中略）彼は自然環境に沿った建築をつくることに集中し、ルーバー、換気塔、樋、縦樋、すべての考えうる構造材、トラス、そして深く跳ね出す日射しを遮る庇の使い方などのマクロなところから、建築のつくり方を根本的に変化させている」。ケネス・フランプトン、マーカットヘシドニー大学博士号授与の推薦文、2003年5月

Modern architecture without glass:
the micro[1] elements of Glenn Murcutt's architecture

Shoko Seyama

'Thinking Drawing / Working Drawing,' at TOTO GALLERY・MA, Tokyo, is
the first exhibition of Glenn Murcutt's architecture in Japan (June 12–August 9,
2008). Although some eminent Japanese architects have previously written about
Murcutt's works in Japan's architectural magazines, the European and American
orientation of these publications has limited his exposure, and many Japanese
will see his work for the first time in the exhibition. They may, however, feel some
sense of recognition when they view Murcutt's architecture. While they may be
astonished by the unique beauty of his buildings, by the intensity and precision
of his drawings, and by the absolute sureness of his plans—to which no change is
conceivable—they will find elements which appear somewhat familiar in that they
evoke the traditional architecture of Japan—for example, the clearly expressed
structural frame, and the sliding windows with timber slatted shutters that are set
into the bays. They may also note that Murcutt's shaping of his architecture to
promote natural-ventilation echoes the ways in which old Japanese Minka farm-
buildings were configured to encourage cross-ventilation and to expel heat by
chimney-effect through vents in the tall roof-space—as if the farmhouses breathed
by themselves. During the year that the exhibition and publications were under
preparation I came to understand that while these parallels were interesting, and
reflected some climatic similarities between Japan and Australia, the more important
aspects were the differences. Murcutt's architecture is an Australian architecture,
born of the uniqueness of his country. And, it is his manner of response to this
uniqueness that gives Murcutt's architecture its irresistible beauty.

Visiting Australia for the first time in 1999, we found many fine buildings tailored
precisely, and extremely inventively, in response to the hot climatic context. The
forms of the buildings were simple and un-rhetorical, but they embodied a very
strong philosophy about the creation of architecture as a support for the conduct
of ordinary life. At the time, many leading architects in Japan seemed primarily
concerned with abstract architectural theory, so it was both surprising and inspiring
to find an architecture which conferred such a value on ordinary things. At
Mapleton House, near Brisbane, for example, the architect Richard Leplastrier—
a very close friend and colleague of Glenn Murcutt—elevated the building above
ground to avoid snakes and the damp of the tropical climate, and laid the pitched

---

[1] 'His architecture has become progressively more concerned with the
issue of sustainability in relation to both the climate and the landscape. …
in this genre ringing the syntactical changes at the micro level, in terms
of louvers, vents, gutters, down pipes and every conceivable type of frame,
truss and over-hanging weather-screening canopy.' 'Kenneth Frampton,
Reference to the Candidacy of Glenn Murcutt for the award of the Doctor
of Science (Architecture) by the Senate of the University of Sydney

マグニー邸（ビンジーポイント）
Magney House (Bingie Point)

ったマリー・ショート邸では、すべてのデザイン要素は、機能や気候に対応した。ずらされた2棟配置は、朝と午後の日射しを受ける2種類の居場所をつくり、それぞれが川かダムへの眺めがある。二重屋根のスリットから小屋裏換気がされる。ガラス・ルーバーと日除けのルーバーは、日射しと風量の調整に使われる。オーストラリアでは、このように自然環境の認識がデザインの底辺をなすことが多い。日射が厳しく、降水量がわずかで、国土はとても広い。一歩人里離れた場所では、上水、下水、電気は通っていないことが多く、建築の設備として備えなければいけない。しかしこのような敷地に建つことの多いマーカットの建築は、重装備の建築ではない。唯一豊潤に蓄えられるのは水で、大きな貯水タンクに見てとれる。それは常に彼の繊細な建物と対照的にあっけらかんと置かれる。しかし、例えば、ビンジーポイントにあるマグニー邸について考える時、その美しいかたちを観察する人たちはまだ多くの理由があるように感じる。屋根形状は雨を集水するためとしても、なぜ樋はこんなに大きいのか、なぜダブルルーフなのか？　彼にとっては明白な形態だが、その文化を知らない私たちにはすぐにはわからないものがある。マーカットの答えは彼の設計プロセスが、表現主義的でもあり機能主義的でもあることを示していると言えるだろう。「地方の雨量によってサイズが決まり、直径80cmの縦樋のヘッドは、ユーカリの葉が30cmほどの長さであることから、流れていきやすいように、詰まりをおこさないように」という理由からと説明されたが、その形態には、水の象徴性が明らかである。

その後、ある日本の民家（作田家）の写真を見せていただいた。今は川崎の日本民家園に移築された、房総の漁村にあった分棟形式の民家について調べると、川島宙次氏によれば、分棟形式は「内部空間は一体不可分の間取りでありながら、外観は二棟以上の合体を証拠立てるように、屋根が分かれている形式をいう」[2]。これは、マグニー邸にはじまり、ボイド・センターなどの大きなプロジェクトまでの、主空間と水廻り空間の機能分割を断面形態にあ

[2]『日本の民家　その伝統美』川島宙次、講談社現代新書、1978年、p 21

roof towards a giant, translucent, gutter of almost 30 centimeters diameter which collects rainwater during heavy tropical squalls but also diffuses the brightness of the sun entering the windows below. The wide kitchen window can be lowered, vertically, into the kitchen counter to unite interior and veranda, and to frame views of the tops of the densely growing palm trees, giving a sense that they can almost be touched. The ideas in the building are simple and direct, but are realized with immense care and craft.

In exactly the same way, the poetics of Murcutt's works emerge from his interpretations and inventions in response to pragmatic needs. Every aspect of his 'breakthrough' project—the Marie Short House—can be explained as functionally or climatically effective—the staggered plan gives alternate places of morning and afternoon sun and shade, and different views towards two water bodies; the corrugated-steel roof sheeting was layered to promote roof ventilation; and the glass louvers and external venetian blinds modify sunlight and air-flow. In Australia, such directness of response to natural conditions is the necessary starting point of design. The characteristics of the country are the harshness of the sun, the minimal rainfall, and particularly the vastness of the landscape which means that in many remote locations the usual supplies of water, electricity and drainage are unavailable, and must be provided independently in the architecture. However, Murcutt's works in such locations never appear in any way 'heavily equipped'—with the exception, of course, of the giant water tanks which Murcutt deploys around his delicate buildings, like celebratory markers of the house's remoteness.

The unusual form of Magney House at Bingie Point can leave one wondering about the origins of the design. Clearly, the roof-form was prompted by the essential need to collect rainwater. But, why are the down-pipes so numerous and very large? Murcutt's explanation showed a design-process that can be simultaneously both expressionistic and plainly functionalist. The size, he explained, was due to the heavy rainfall in that district, and the diameter, shape and angle of the almost 80 centimeters diameter conical 'head' was because 30 centimeters was the typical length of a eucalyptus leaf, and this size and angle feeds leaves vertically into the down-pipe so that they do not block the flow of rainwater. But, the form of the

作田家（川崎市立日本民家園所蔵）
Sakuda House (Japan Open-Air Folk House Museum)

マグニー邸（ビンジーポイント）
Magney House (Bingie Point)

らわすマーカットの手法である。しかし、その建築が分棟形式の民家と大きく違う点は、2つの機能をつなげている部分が、実は最も大切な部分で、この乾いた土地の生命線である水を集水していることである。また、分棟形式の民家が閉じられた住宅であるのに対して、マーカットの2つの機能別の空間は性質が互いにまったく違い、主空間は広大なランドスケープへ開かれている。

そしてマグニー邸のダブルルーフは、ランドスケープへの視線を意識させ、日中の光を豊かに混合して室内に落とす役目をもっている。それはまた、実際的な換気を行い、室内の涼しさを保つ。水廻り空間上部の小さいカーブ屋根の南面（北半球の北面にあたるが）に、構造から押し出されるように水平換気窓が設けられた。新鮮空気を供給、キッチンなどからの余剰熱などをそのカーブにそって排出しつつ、大きな北面の窓に平行に配置されて、雨天においても自然換気（クロスベンチレーション）ができる。この「押し出された要素」は、後のマーカット建築の中でさまざまなかたちに発展する。マーカットは「空間を押し出すことによって、さまざまなことが可能になった」と説明していたが、それは風を採り入れ、光を遮蔽もしくは採光する自然の力を利用できるようになったということだろう。これはさらに（ウォルシュ邸ではかなり広げられたが）空間を広く複雑に使うことができるようになったということでもある。

一点興味深いのは、マーカットは「押し出された要素」の窓で、既成品を再解釈したり、地元の工法を改良したりして使っている点である。乾燥がより厳しく暖かいオーストラリアでは、窓はより簡単な機構で、木の窓枠でつくられることが多い。クィーンズランド州やニューサウスウェールズ州の北の方の住宅の窓では、地元工法に現代建築の考え方が見え隠れし、風土にあったものを発展させている。例えば、間に方立てのない「水平連続窓」[3]。ウィトコ・ヒンジを利用するこの縦回転窓は、どこから風が吹いてきても家の中に採り

<hr />

[3] ル・コルビュジエの「近代建築の5原則」の1つの要素

down-pipes is also knowingly, very consciously symbolic.

Discussing a photograph of the historic fisherman's dwelling, Sakuda House, in an old book about 'Minka' buildings, Murcutt points—in agreement with the historian Chuji Kawashima—to it being a 'two-part' building type, composed as a single internal space with two paired roofs. "Internally," writes Kawashima, "the servant/served spaces are inseparable, but from the outside the double-roof acknowledges the two functions."[2] This is the same served-space/servant-space strategy that characterizes many of Murcutt's houses, and also his larger projects such as Boyd Art Centre, in which the two parts are usually made explicit in the section. Murcutt's buildings, though, are very different from the Minka example in two crucial respects—the joint between the two parts of his buildings is in fact the most important part, being the collector—in often parched landscapes—of precious, life-enabling, rainwater. And, while the two parts of the Minka building form an essentially enclosed building-type, the two parts of Murcutt's buildings are distinctly different, with the 'served' part of Murcutt's buildings being typically transparent and open to the vastness of the Australian landscape.

At Magney House, Bingie Point, the double-curvature of the ceiling gives it a sense of weightlessness, emphasizes views out, and reflects daylight differently down to the two linear parts of the house. This ceiling-form also serves to promote and direct air movement between the tall living-room windows and the high-level horizontal windows of the 'servant' section which are angled outwards, beyond the face of the structural frame, to supply fresh air to the kitchen and bathrooms and provide cross-ventilation even on rainy days. This 'extruded element', which Murcutt originated at Magney Bingie, has been subject to continuous evolution through all of his later works. As Murcutt explained, "pushing these elements outwards allowed me to do varieties of things." These devices catch the wind, shade or reflect the sun, and enable him to create buildings animated and activated by the characteristics of nature. They also enable him—very much enlarged at Walsh House—to make the rooms more complex and spacious.

In his development of these 'extruded elements', the availability of unconventional

---

[2] Chuji Kawashima, 'Nihon no Minka, Sono dentobi' (Japanese Minka House and its traditional beauty), Kodansha, 1978, P.21

マーカット＝ルーウィン邸＆スタジオ
Murcutt-Lewin House and Studio

込めるように、好きな角度に固定できる「風を捉える装置」である。壁の位置まで引ききって、壁をなくしてしまうかのような引戸。また、ガラス・ルーバーは、防犯を確保しつつ全開すると100％の開口率で換気できる背の高い開口である。熱い気候ゆえに、（現代建築で見られたガラス壁のような）透明性ではなく、最大限の換気が優先される。それは結果としてガラスのない近代建築と呼べるものになっている。

マーカット設計の都市部における住宅でも、やはり限られた視線と日光へのアクセスと、風をとらえることが検討される。近作のマーカット＝ルーウィン邸では、上階のリビングのガラス窓がその役目を負う。この縦回転窓は、ちょっとした微風もとらえることができて、室内はいつも新鮮な空気で満たされている。ボイド・センターで検討された合板の縦回転扉は、ここで、庭への視線を遮らない枠なしのガラス窓とされた。ミースのバルセロナ・パビリオンを思いおこさせる、建て込んだ都市における光の採り入れ方——光源に平行に並んだ壁に柔らかい朝と夕方の光を反射させ、細長いプロポーションの室内の奥深くまで光を運ぶという——が考えられている。

マーカット＝ルーウィン邸ではさらに、屋根裏から突き出た「風と光を掬う装置」であるルーバー窓がある。構造から飛び出していることから、ビンジーポイントのマグニー邸で始まった「押し出された要素」と言えるが、マグニー邸の曲線屋根の下の傾斜ガラスから光を採り入れて水平窓で換気する試みは、マーカット＝ルーウィン邸で、ルーバーと内倒し窓を使って必要な風や光を採り込む、より現代的なかたちをもつものになった。これらの「押し出された要素」が、マーカットの考え得る限りの答えとして、常に新しいかたちで進化する幅は大きくその速度はとても速い。それは、マーカット建築の、あるいは建築全体の、サスティナビリティをあわせもつ未来の建築の姿を宣言しているかのようである。

off-the-shelf materials and custom skills has been crucial. In its generally more benign, dryer, and warmer climate, windows in Australia may be more simply fabricated than in Japan, and manufacturers have developed an intriguing variety of window types which correspond with the climatic context and, coincidentally, have affinities with the formal ambitions of Modernism.[3] The hinges produced by the 'Whitco' company, for example, enable the glazing of long, continuous horizontal openings, without mullions. Each pane can be opened to work as a 'wind-catcher' at the best angle to direct breezes into the house. Similarly, glass louvers are used to give security and approximately 100% clear open-ness to tall slit apertures. For the maximisation of ventilation in the often extreme heat, the priority of these systems is their openability, rather than their transparency. The result can be called modern architecture without glass.

At the Murcutt-Lewin House, the frameless glass panes of the living room window, although giving a direct view to the garden, might be compared to the openable solid shutters in the dormitory section of the Arthur & Yvonne Boyd Art Centre. These large glass sheets play the same role, openable beyond 90 degrees to catch and re-direct breezes, but have the additional essential role of reflecting the soft morning and evening sun into the house in a manner that recalls Mies' Barcelona Pavilion, where parallel walls were deployed to work as light reflectors, bouncing rays of sunlight from the courtyard deep into the central spaces.

Penetrating through the roof of Murcutt-Lewin House, a series of roof-windows reach up to scoop in light, and to admit breezes. In essence, they are the same 'extruded element', added outside the line of structure, that originated at Magney Bingie Point and which has reappeared, in modified form, and at very different scales, in each of Murcutt's subsequent buildings. The angled glass plane with horizontal vent at Magney has metamorphosed into the louvered wave-form with vertical vent at Murcutt-Lewin. The degree and speed of evolution of this single idea is extreme, being the product of all the knowledge gained by Murcutt to that point, realized in new form. In this, these 'extruded elements' may be seen as hints to the future character of Murcutt's architecture, or as augurs of the future architecture that will emerge from the continuing development of sustainable solutions.

[3] One of Le Corbusier's five points of architecture

グレン・マーカット

Glenn Murcutt

建築として建っているもの、もしくはこれから建てられるようにデザインされたすべての建築は、つくり出されたものでなく、見出されたものだと言える。建築の本質的な主題は、人間であり、その歴史と文化である。空間、光、素材をどうつなげて建てるか。土地への責任。良いデザインとは、これらを理解してその答えを見つけるまで模索を続けることである。建築とは、見出す過程そのものである。　　　グレン・マーカット

Any work of architecture that has been
designed, any work of architecture
that exists or has the potential to exist, was
discovered. It wasn't created. The central
design issues of architecture are: humans and
their history and culture; space; light; how
things are put together; and responsibility
to the land. Good design involves an
understanding of these issues and pursuing
the questions they raise until you make
appropriate discoveries. Architecture is a path
of discovery.　　　Glenn Murcutt

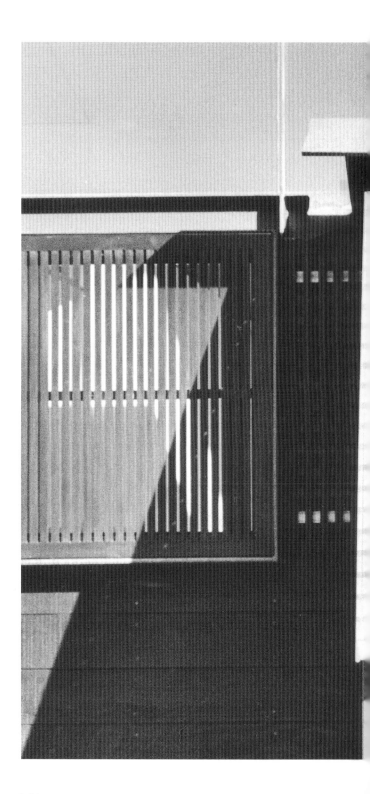

グレン・マーカット

出版物

1985 —— 『鉄の葉っぱ——グレン・マーカット：オーストラリア建築形態の
バイオニア』フィリップ・ドリュー著

1993 —— 『3つの家——ディテールの建築』E・M・ファレリー著

1995 —— 『グレン・マーカット——ワークス ＆ プロジェクツ』
フランシャス・フロモノ著

1999 —— 『大地にやさしく触れる——グレン・マーカットの言葉』
フィリップ・ドリュー著
『グレン・マーカット』
フローラ・ジャルデッロ・ボスティグリョーネ著

2002 —— 『グレン・マーカット——類例のない建築的実践』
ハイグ・ベック ＆ ジャッキー・クーパー著

2003 —— 『グレン・マーカット——ビルディングス＋プロジェクツ
1962-2003』フランシャス・フロモノ著

2006 —— 『グレン・マーカット・アーキテクト』ケネス・フランプトン著

受賞と栄誉

RAIA 州支部建築賞

1973 —— 王立オーストラリア建築家協会（RAIA）／グレイ ＆ マロニー修復
／リノベーション賞

1973-2005 2作品に RAIA ニューサウスウェールズ支部スルマン公共建築賞
6作品に RAIA ニューサウスウェールズ支部ウィルキンソン住宅賞
RAIA 北部準州支部トレーシー公共建築賞
RAIA 北部準州支部バーネット住宅賞

2004 —— RAIA ニューサウスウェールズ支部 25 年賞
（マリー・ショート／グレン・マーカット邸）

RAIA 建築賞

1973-2000 「木造建築」賞
「鉄骨造建築」10年賞
ゼルマン・コーワン賞（ボワリ・カカドゥ・インフォメーション
センター：トロッポ・アーキテクツと協同）
ゼルマン・コーワン賞（アーサー ＆ イヴォンヌ・ボイド・アート
センター：ウェンディ・ルーウィン、レッグ・ラーク・
アーキテクツと協同）
ゼルマン・コーワン公共建築選奨（ケンプシーの博物館）
ロビン・ボイド住宅賞（マグニー邸、ピンジーポイント）
ロビン・ボイド住宅選奨（マグニー邸、パディントン）
アボリジニの住宅に対する審査員特別賞（マリカ＝アルダートン邸）
RAIA25年賞（マリー・ショート／グレン・マーカット邸）

国内の受賞と栄誉

1992 —— RAIA ゴールドメダル

1993 —— RAIA 終身メンバー

1995 —— ニューサウスウェールズ大学 名誉科学博士号

1996 —— オーストラリア勲章

2003 —— シドニー工科大学 名誉博士号

2004 —— シドニー大学 名誉科学博士号

国外の受賞と栄誉

1982 —— ビエンナーレ展（パリ、フランス）

1985 —— イギリス連邦建築家連合（CAA）「場所と文化」建築賞

1991 —— ビエンナーレ展（ヴェネチア、イタリア）

1992 —— アルヴァ・アアルト・メダル

1996 —— ビエンナーレ展（ヴェネチア、イタリア）

1997 —— アメリカ建築家協会（AIA）名誉会員
王立英国建築家協会（RIBA）国際名誉会員

1998 —— ノイトラ財団およびカルフォルニア・ポリテクニックより
リチャード・ノイトラ建築・教育賞

1999 —— 王立オランダ建築家アカデミーより「グリーン・ピン」
国際建築・エコロジー賞

2001 —— ケネス・F・ブラウン・アジア太平洋文化・建築デザイン賞
（アーサー ＆ イヴォンヌ・ボイド・アートセンター：ウェンディ・
ルーウィン、レッグ・ラーク・アーキテクツと協同）
トマス・ジェファーソン建築メダル
王立カナダ建築協会 名誉会員

2002 —— 王立オランダ芸術アカデミー国際賞
フィンランド建築家協会 名誉会員
プリツカー賞

2003 —— ケネス・F・ブラウン・アジア太平洋文化・建築デザイン賞
（マリカ＝アルダートン邸）

2004 —— 王立スコットランド建築家協会 名誉会員

2005 —— 台北建築家協会 名誉メンバー
シンガポール建築家協会 名誉会員

2008 —— アメリカ芸術院 名誉会員

Glenn Murcutt

Biography

1936 ——	Born in London, UK. Parents Australian
1950-1955	Manly Boys High School, Sydney
1956-1961	Diploma of Architecture, Sydney Technical College (UNSW)
1962-1964	Study travel United Kingdom, Europe and Nordic regions
1964-1969	Joined Ancher Mortlock Murray & Woolley Architects, Sydney
1969 ——	Entered private practice
1973 ——	Study travel Mexico, USA, UK and Europe
1984-1985	Study travel Europe and North Africa
1986-1987	Study travel Mexico and USA

Teaching

1970-1979	Design tutor, University of Sydney, Sydney
1985	Visiting professor, University of New South Wales, Sydney
1989-1997	Visiting critic, Master of Architecture, University of Melbourne, Melbourne
1990 ——	Visiting critic, Graduate School of Fine Arts, University of Pennsylvania, USA
1990-1992	Visiting professor, University of Technology, Sydney
1991-1995	Adjunct professor, Graduate School of Fine Arts, University of Pennsylvania, USA
1991 ——	Visiting Distinguished Architect, University of Arizona, Tucson, Arizona, USA
1992 ——	Master Class, PNG University of Technology, Lae, Papua New Guinea
1994 ——	Visiting professor, University of Technology, Helsinki, Finland
1995 ——	Visiting professor, University of Technology, Sydney
1996 ——	Visiting professor, University of Hawaii, Honolulu, USA
1997 ——	O'Neill Ford Chair, University of Texas at Austin, Texas, USA
	Master Class, PNG University of Technology, Lae, Papua New Guinea
1998 ——	Thomas Jefferson Professor, University of Virginia, USA
1999 ——	Visiting professor, School of Architecture, Aarhus, Denmark
	Master Class, Montana State University, Bozeman, USA
	Visiting Fellow, Canberra School of Art, Canberra
2000 ——	Visiting professor, UCLArts, Los Angeles, USA
2001 ——	William Henry Bishop visiting professor, Yale University, USA
	Glenn Murcutt Master Class, University of Newcastle, Australia
2002 ——	Ruth + Norman Moore visiting professor, University of Washington, St. Louis, USA
	International Glenn Murcutt Master Class, University of Newcastle, Australia
	Distinguished J.L. Constant Lecturer, University of Kansas, USA
	Master Class, PNG University of Technology, Lae, Papua New Guinea
	William Henry Bishop visiting professor, Yale University, USA
	Master Class, Cornell University, Ithaca, USA
2003 ——	Eliel Saarinen visiting professor, University of Michigan, Ann Arbor, USA
	Visiting professor, Dublin Institute of Technology, Ireland
	Luis Barragan Visiting Chair, TEC de Monterrey NL Mexico and TEC de Monterrey, Mexico City, Mexico
	International Glenn Murcutt Master Class, University of Newcastle, Australia
2004 ——	Morgenstein visiting professorial chair, Illinois Institute of Technology, Chicago, USA
	Calliston visiting professorial chair, University of Washington, Seattle, USA
	International Glenn Murcutt Master Class, 'Riversdale'/ University of Sydney, Sydney
	Clarkson visiting professorial chair, University of Buffalo, New York, USA
2005 ——	Calliston visiting professorial chair, University of Washington, Seattle, USA
	CriticalMass, University of North Carolina Charlotte, USA
	International Glenn Murcutt Master Class, 'Riversdale'/ University of Sydney, Sydney
	William Henry Bishop visiting professor, Yale University, USA

2006	Visiting professor, School of Architecture University of Ljubljana, Slovenia
	Glenn Murcutt International Master Class, 'Riversdale' West Cambewarra
2006-2008	Adjunct professor, University of New South Wales, Sydney
	Year 3 design professor, University of New South Wales, Sydney
	Calliston visiting professorial chair, University of Washington, Seattle, USA
	CRH professor, School of Architecture, Dublin Institute of Technology, Ireland
2007	Honoris Causa Professor, Universidad de Palermo, Buenos Aires, Argentina

Publications

1985	*Leaves of Iron—Grenn Murcutt: Pioneer of an Australian Architectural Form* by Philip Drew
1993	*Three Houses—Architecture in Detail* by E. M. Farrelly
1995	*Glenn Murcutt—Works and Projects* by Françoise Fromonot
1999	*Touch This Earth Lightly—Glenn Murcutt in His Own Words* by Philip Drew
	Glenn Murcutt by Flora Giardiello Postiglione
2002	*Glenn Murcutt—A Singular Architectural Practice* by Haig Beck and Jackie Cooper
2003	*Glenn Murcutt—Buildings + Projects 1962-2003* by Françoise Fromonot
2006	Glenn Murcutt Architect by Kenneth Frampton

Awards and Honours

RAIA State Chapter Named Architecture Awards

1973	Royal Australian Institute of Architects (RAIA) /Gray and Mulroney Restoration/Renovation Award
1973-2005	Two Sulman Awards for Public Buildings, NSW
	Six Wilkinson Awards for Housing, NSW
	Tracy Award for Public Buildings, Northern Territory
	Burnett Award for Housing, Northern Territory
2004	RAIA NSW Chapter 25 Year Award for the Marie Short/ Glenn Murcutt House, Kempsey, NSW

RAIA National Named Architecture Awards and National Awards

1973-2000	'Timber in Architecture' Award
	'Steel in Architecture,' Award of the Decade
	Sir Zelman Cowan Award for the Bowali Kakadu Visitors Information Centre, in collaboration with Troppo Architects
	Sir Zelman Cowan Award for the Arthur and Yvonne Boyd Art Centre, in collaboration with Wendy Lewin and Reg Lark architects
	Sir Zelman Cowan Commendation for Public Buildings —Museum Kempsey, NSW
	Robin Boyd Awards for Housing—Magney House, Bingie Point
	Robin Boyd Commendation for Housing—Magney House, Paddington, Sydney
	National Jury Special Award for Aboriginal Housing —Marika-Alderton House, Northern Territory
	RAIA National 25 Year Award for the Marie Short/ Glenn Murcutt House, Kempsey, NSW

National Awards and Honors

1992	Royal Australian Institute of Architects Gold Medal
1993	Life Fellow, Royal Australian Institute of Architects
1995	Honorary Doctorate of Science, University of New South Wales, Sydney
1996	Order of Australia (AO)
2003	Honorary Doctorate of Letters, University of Technology, Sydney
2004	Honorary Doctorate of Science, University of Sydney, Sydney

International Awards and Honors

1982	Biennale Exhibition, Paris, France
1985	Commonwealth Association of Architects (CAA) Award for Architecture of its 'Place and Culture'
1991	Biennale Exhibition, Venice, Italy
1992	Alvar Aalto Medal, Helsinki, Finland
1996	Biennale Exhibition, Venice, Italy
1997	Honorary Fellow of the American Institute of Architects
	International Fellow of the Royal Institute of British Architects
1998	Richard Neutra Award for Architecture and Teaching from the Neutra Foundation and CalPoly, Pomona, USA
1999	The 'Green Pin' International Award for Architecture and Ecology from the Royal Danish Academy of Architects
2001	The Kenneth F. Brown Asia Pacific Culture and Architecture Design Award for the Arthur and Yvonne Boyd Art Centre, Riversdale —in collaboration with Wendy Lewin and Reg Lark architects
	Thomas Jefferson Medal for Architecture, USA
	Honorary Fellow of the Royal Architectural Institute of Canada
2002	The Royal Danish Academy of Fine Arts International Award for 'Making a Difference' to the thinking and practice of architecture
	Honorary Fellow ot the Finnish Association of Architects, SAFA
	The Pritzker Architecture Prize
2003	The Kenneth F. Brown Asia Pacific Culture and Architecture Award Honorary Mention for an Aboriginal House, Arnhem Land, Northern Territory
2004	Honorary Fellow , Royal Incorporation of Architects in Scotland
2005	Honorary Member, Taipei Architects Association, Taiwan
	Honorary Fellow, Singapore Institute of Architects, Singapore
2008	Elected, Honorary Member, American Academy of Arts and Letters, USA

クレジット
Credits

写真　Photography
アンソニー・ブローウェル　Anthony Browell
下記以外の全ての写真　Except:
マックス・デュパン　Max Dupain　p.25
グレン・マーカット　Glenn Murcutt　pp.118-119
TOTO 出版　TOTO Shuppan　p.235

図版　Drawings
グレン・マーカット　Glenn Murcutt

特別協力への謝辞
Acknowledgement for special contributions
ウェンディ・ルーウィン　Wendy Lewin
ニューサウスウェールズ州 州立図書館
State Library NSW

図版キャプション　Drawing captions
トム・ヘネガン　Tom Heneghan
Douglas Murcutt House, Fletcher-Page House,
House in the Southern Highlands,
Murcutt-Lewin House & Studio, Walsh House
マリアム・グーシェ & キャサリン・ラッセン
Maryam Gusheh & Catherine Lassen
Marie Short/Glenn Murcutt House, Fredericks/White House,
Magney House (Bingie Point), Magney House (Paddington),
Simpson-Lee House, Marika-Alderton House,
Murcutt Guest Studio, Arthur and Yvonne Boyd Art Centre

和訳　Japanese Translations
勢山詔子　Shoko Seyama

英訳　English Translations
トム・ヘネガン　Tom Heneghan　pp.232-239

アシスタント　Assistants
サーシャ・クロッカー　Sascha Crocker
カーラ・ドハティー　Cara Doherty

お願い　Request to readers:
本書に掲載された住宅は、個人住宅であり非公開です。
マーカット氏は個人事務所として設計活動をされており、
所員やインターンを受け入れておりません。お断りの手紙
を書く時間もなく非礼を詫びることもできませんので、
どうか履歴書などを送らないで下さい。
読者の皆様のご理解をお願い申し上げます。

The houses illustrated in this book are private
residences and are not open to visitors.
Mr. Murcutt reminds readers that he operates his
office as a sole-practitioner and does not employ
staff or interns. He requests you not to send job
applications or CV's as he does not wish to be rude,
but he has no time to reply.
The publisher asks readers to understand and
support Mr. Murcutt's position.

著者プロフィール
Authors' Profiles

マリアム・グーシェ　Maryam Gusheh
ニューサウスウェールズ大学 建築環境学部講師
Lecturer, University of NSW, Faculty of The Built Environment
ニューサウスウェールズ大学卒業。2001年に大学に籍をおくまで建築家として働く。異文化間の建築活動に注目した研究や論文を執筆。ルイス・カーン設計のバングラデシュ国会議事堂についての博士論文がある。
Maryam Gusheh graduated from the University of New South Wales. She worked as a practicing architect prior to joining UNSW in 2001. Her research and publications have focused on cross-cultural architectural practices. Her doctoral dissertation undertakes a close reading of the Parliament Building in Bangladesh, designed by the American Architect Louis Kahn.

トム・ヘネガン　Tom Heneghan
建築家／シドニー大学 建築・デザイン・都市計画学部 建築学部長
Architect / Chair of Architecture, Faculty of Architecture, Design and Planning, University of Sydney
AA スクール卒業後、1990年に東京にアーキテクチャー・ファクトリーを設立するまで同校で教鞭をとった。1994年熊本県草地畜産研究所で日本建築学会賞。2002年福島県あだたらの森キャンプ場で公共建築賞環境賞受賞。
Tom Heneghan graduated from the Architectural Association, London, where he taught until establishing his office 'The Architecture Factory' in Tokyo in 1990. In 1994, he won the Award of the Academy of the Architectural Institute of Japan. In 2002 he was awarded the Japanese Government public building award for ecological building.

キャサリン・ラッセン　Catherine Lassen
建築家／ニューサウスウェールズ大学 建築環境学部講師
Architect / Lecturer, University of NSW, Faculty of The Built Environment
1995年ハーバード大学建築学科修了。2000年シドニーへ移住するまで、レム・クールハース主宰の OMA ロッテルダム事務所とボストン事務所に勤務。2002年事務所設立。2007年シドニー大学における改築プロジェクトで RAIA の建築遺産賞であるグリーンウェイ賞受賞。
Catherine Lassen received her Master of Architecture from Harvard University in 1995. She worked for Rem Koolhaas at OMA in Rotterdam and in Boston Massachusetts before moving to Sydney in 2000. Her office was established in 2002. She was awarded the RAIA Greenway Award for Heritage Architecture for a project she completed at the University of Sydney.

勢山詔子　Shoko Seyama
建築家（一級建築士／王立オーストラリア建築家協会公認建築士）
Architect (Japan/RAIA)
東京芸術大学建築科卒業後、1995年にアーキテクチャー・ファクトリーに参加。2002年にシドニー移住。主なプロジェクトに、北京常青区タウンハウス（ヘネガンと共にプロジェクトアーキテクト）。2006年より180戸の住宅建設が始まっている。
Shoko Seyama graduated from Tokyo National University of Fine Arts, and joined the Architecture Factory in 1995. She moved to Sydney in 2002. Her projects include the Beijing Townhouse project, involving the construction of 180 houses, which she co-designed with Tom Heneghan.

GLENN MURCUTT

Thinking Drawing / Working Drawing

グレン・マーカット：シンキング・ドローイング／ワーキング・ドローイング

2008年6月15日　初版第1刷発行
2023年12月1日　初版第5刷発行

監修協力——グレン・マーカット
著者——マリアム・グーシェ
トム・ヘネガン
キャサリン・ラッセン
勢山詔子
写真——アンソニー・ブローウェル
発行者——渡井 朗
デザイン——太田徹也

プリンティング ディレクション——高柳 昇
印刷・製本——株式会社東京印書館

発行所——TOTO出版（TOTO株式会社）
〒107-0062 東京都港区南青山 1-24-3
TOTO乃木坂ビル 2F
[営業] TEL：03-3402-7138 FAX：03-3402-7187
[編集] TEL：03-3497-1010
URL: https://jp.toto.com/publishing

Printed in Japan　ISBN978-4-88706-294-8